DEBATING
AMERICAN
GOVERNMENT

DEBATING

AMERICAN

GOVERNMENT

Peter Woll
BRANDEIS UNIVERSITY

LITTLE, BROWN AND COMPANY

Boston   Toronto

Library of Congress Cataloging-in-Publication Data
Main entry under title:

Debating American government.

    1. United States—Politics and government—Addresses,
essays, lectures. I. Woll, Peter, 1933–
JK21.D45   1985   320.973   85-19785
ISBN 0-316-95180-3

Library of Congress Catalog Card No. 85-19785

ISBN 0-316-95180-3

9 8 7 6 5 4 3 2 1

DON

Published simultaneously in Canada
by Little, Brown & Company (Canada) Limited

Printed in the United States of America

Photo credits: p. 34—Justice Thurgood Marshall (Courtesy The Supreme Court Historical Society); p. 54—Samuel J. Eldersveld (© Palmer Studio); p. 77—Kevin Phillips (AP/Wide World Photos); p. 98—Archibald Cox, Fred Wertheimer (Courtesy Maxwell Mackenzie); p. 123—Michael J. Malbin (Courtesy American Enterprise Institute); p. 187—Gregg Easterbrook (© 1983 Harlee Little).

For John, Dotte, and with special thanks, David Hoyer

Preface

Designed for the introductory American Government course, this debate reader covers important contemporary political issues and presents them in lively and readable selections to heighten student interest. Joining leading political scientists are conservative and liberal Washington journalists, commentators, pundits, and participants in the political process to give students exciting contrasts as they present their views on government and political institutions.

A profile of Jack Kemp kicks off the book, introducing students to his conservative views on government through a colorful portrayal of the man himself and his political career. A depiction of New York Governor Mario Cuomo follows to make students aware of how a 1980s style liberal copes with the increasingly conservative mood of the country that Jack Kemp has so neatly captured.

Nowhere do views differ more sharply on the proper role of government than in the sphere of affirmative action, taken up in Chapter 2. Supreme Court Justice Thurgood Marshall and Hoover Institute scholar Thomas Sowell take opposing sides.

As the text turns to political processes and institutions that are the subject of contemporary debate and concern, in Chapter 3 Samuel J. Eldersveld and Martin P. Wattenberg present different views on the decline of political parties. Conservative pundit Kevin Phillips and American Enterprise Institute scholar William Schneider discuss the extent of party realignment in the 1980s in Chapter 4.

The role of political action committees (PACs) and campaign finance reform are debated in Chapters 5 and 6. Archibald Cox leads a common cause team that argues PACs are against the public interest, while campaign finance expert Herbert Alexander puts forward the case for PACs. On the subject of regulating campaign finance Elizabeth Drew proposes stricter controls, while Michael J. Malbin suggests that the pluralistic universe of interest groups makes it difficult to regulate them uniformly.

Chapter 7 focuses on the media and the political process, offering the experienced and entertaining hand of Victor Gold in a critical look at the White House press corps, which he argues is far too adversary and superficial. *New Republic* editor Fred Barnes points out that, while the press may be a government adversary, media realignment has brought about equality of representation between liberal and conservative views.

Chapter 8 begins a discussion of important issues concerning the constitutional role and democratic effectiveness of national governmental institutions. Thomas E. Cronin and Robert D. Loevy make a novel proposal to change the presidential nominating process by complementing the party convention system with a national primary. Austin Ranney, on the other hand, warns against too much reliance on direct primaries and suggests that old-fashioned brokered politics may be best for selecting presidential candidates.

What, if anything, is wrong with Congress is the subject of Chapter 9. Gregg Easterbrook propounds the widely held view that the politics of Congress which encourages its decentralization and fragmentation makes the legislature irresponsible. Albert Hunt disagrees, and defends a "messy" Congress.

Whether or not the bureaucracy subverts the constitutional system is the topic of Chapter 10. Neo-liberal Robert Kaus takes the affirmative, and proposes major constitutional changes to deal with what he considers to be excessive administrative discretion. Your editor takes a different tack, suggesting that the bureaucracy fits nicely if not neatly into the constitutional system.

Finally, conservative National Review writer Lino Graglia and federal judge Irving Kaufman offer contrasting viewpoints on whether or not the Supreme Court and the federal judiciary should be curbed because of court usurpation of legislative powers.

Suggestions, guidance, and support for the book have come from many quarters. My editor John Covell's wise counsel, encouragement, and dedication made the text possible. Cynthia Chapin piloted the project through the production maze with skill and great efficiency. Edward (Lee) Cowen and David Strachman did much of the leg work and made excellent suggestions as well. And thanks are due to Barbara Nagy and Lisa Carisella who did the necessary typing.

CONTENTS

DEBATING
AMERICAN
GOVERNMENT

CHAPTER ONE
The Role of Government

Political philosophers, politicians, and citizens concerned with politics have, in free societies, debated the form, character, and policies of government. No political debates in history were more brilliant and important than those of our Founding Fathers, gathered in Philadelphia's Independence Hall in the hot and humid summer of 1787, to shape the destiny of a new nation. They were individuals of extraordinary talent and achievement who could cite chapter and verse from Aristotle, John Locke, Montesquieu, and a wide array of other philosophers to buttress their viewpoints. At the same time, they were practical politicians who drew more upon experience than theory to construct our intricate system of constitutional democracy.

The debates over the Constitution established many themes that were to surface in later political discourse. To support their viewpoints politicians and judges frequently refer to the intentions of the framers of the Constitution. Most often cited by those literate in constitutional history is the brilliant treatise written by Alexander Hamilton and James Madison, *The Federalist,* a series of essays published in New York newspapers in 1787 and 1788 to persuade the citizens of New York and the delegates to their ratifying convention to vote for the Constitution. The extraordinary quality of *The Federalist,* which deftly weaves political analysis and empirical observations together to present a compelling argument for the Constitution, reflects a level of political debate that seldom has been matched.

The fundamental debate over the Constitution itself concerns the role of the national government in relation to the states. The supporters of the Constitution, called the Federalists, who shortly after the ratification of the Constitution became a political party, advocated a strong national government with wide powers. Those concerned with states's rights insofar as they supported the idea of a national government at all, argued for a strict limitation upon its powers. Essentially the constitutional debates concerned how far government should be permitted to go in controlling the lives of citizens, a controversy that continues, as the following selections describing the contrasting views of an important Republican conservative and Democratic leader illustrate.

Is the Best Government the One that Governs Least?

A CONSERVATIVE POPULIST SUPPORTS POPULAR OVER
GOVERNMENTAL POWER

Often mentioned as a leading contender for the 1988 Republican presidential nomination is New York congressman Jack Kemp. The former Buffalo Bill's quarterback was elected to Congress in 1970, and soon made a name for himself on Capitol Hill. At the same time he built an invincible electoral base in his constituency, which regularly elects him with overwhelming majorities. One of the principal congressional sponsors of "supply-side" economics, a school of thought that believes economic prosperity is based upon the stimulation of demand through tax cuts, Kemp was a major influence on President Ronald Reagan's economic program. As chairman of the House Republican Conference, the formal caucus of all House Republicans, Kemp helps to shape his party's program on Capitol Hill while reaching beyond to become a national leader as well. Kemp chaired the Republican platform committee in 1984, giving the party's program a distinctively conservative cast on both economic and social issues. The extent to which Jack Kemp's position may have struck a responsive chord in a broad cross-section of the electorate is the subject of the following selection.

J. KEMP

1

What the Democrats Can Learn from Jack Kemp

JONATHAN ROWE

On an evening in late October, Rep. Jack Kemp arrives with his staff members at the volunteer firehall in Brant, New York, a small rural community east of Buffalo, where he is to speak at a Republican rally. The room is packed with the kind of small-town Republicans who believe in God, country, the highway program, and dairy price supports. At the far end of the community room, on a stage, a swing band in red sports jackets plays jaunty, upbeat favorites. At the other end, pitchers of beer are passed across a somewhat makeshift bar. Down the center are long tables with bowls of pretzels, potato chips, and peanuts, and ."Joe Giambrone for Highway Superintendent" banners line the wall.

Kemp works the room without a hint of self-consciousness, patting backs, engaging in small talk, as though he really enjoys it. ("You've got to be as obnoxious as I am," he once advised New Jersey Senate candidate, Jeff Bell.) After the candidates for state assembly and judge make their pitches, Kemp takes the stage. He is tired; he's been making stops like this all day, and on top of this nonstop campaigning in his own district, he's been flying in and out of town to campaign for Republican candidates around the country. But Kemp has prodigious reserves of energy, and in his blue suit and with his meticulously sculpted hair, he still radiates star presence. In Kemp's first campaign, his handlers had worried that he looked "too kiddish, too pretty" and resorted to the darkroom to bring out slight wrinkles around the eyes on his campaign photographs and errant hairs on his billboards. But now, 14 years later, his stocky, six-foot body is ever so slightly soft,

Reprinted with permission from The Washington Monthly, *January 1985. Copyright by The Washington Monthly Co., 1711 Connecticut Avenue, NW, Washington, DC 20009.*

and his face shows just a hint of respectable jowl—though you still see the pug-nosed, freckle-faced kid who seems to have walked off a Wonder Bread advertisement. This impression is reinforced by his voice, which moves unexpectedly (and hoarsely) through the higher registers. The creases that were once the product of the darkroom are now there, in just the right places, showing the camera discernment, determination, maturity, concern. It is not a Lincolnesque face, like Gary Hart's or Mo Udall's, but essentially boyish and round, more like, well, John Kennedy's in his later years. If our faces took the form of our wishes, then Kemp's would leave little doubt as to what he wishes to become. His travel schedule, which took him to more than 30 states this fall, and his personal PAC, the Campaign for Prosperity, which distributed close to $130,000 to 71 Republican (and one Democrat) House and Senate candidates, point in a similar direction.

But this evening Kemp is on home ground, and he starts off by casting a wide net. "You serve your party best," he says, "by serving your country first." Kemp is almost obsessively aware that Republicans are still a minority party and seems determined to reverse that, reaching out in every speech beyond the precincts of the party as presently defined.

Then he is on to the "elite group of left liberal people who want to run our lives, run our families, spend our money." This is the first time this day that he has descended to demagoguery like this; usually he sticks to the high and inclusive ground of economic policy and growth. But this is a small-town gala and he is throwing them a little meat. "They don't trust people and markets," he continues, the last word strangely out of place, as though spliced in from an economics textbook. Kemp still hasn't figured out how to weave the somewhat obscure theories that underlie his economic message into his stump speeches.

From there he talks at length about how he hasn't forgotten where he's from, how good the people of western New York are. When he travels to other parts of the country to campaign for other Republicans, he says, he does it for the people of his district, so they can have the kind of Congress that they and the country need. Becoming a national figure—and losing touch with the district—has been the road to ruin for more than one House member. Kemp seems just a tad defensive on this point. "There has not been a federal grant program that has been proposed for western New York that has not had my support," he told a League of Women Voters candidate forum a couple of hours before.

Next it's economic issues, and here Kemp's basic message starts to come through. Regarding Social Security, the answer is a strong economy. The steel industry—a sore point in Buffalo—could return to prosperity if we had monetary reform. Kemp is genuinely engrossed by economics and tries doggedly to plough through the subject even in settings like this. When he is tired, as he is tonight, it comes out in cryptic semi-phrases—Phillips curve, revenue feedback, demand-side models, stable currency—as though he's talking in hyphens. At a luncheon speech before the International Longshoremen's Organization earlier in the day, eyes had wandered around the room as he took them through the gold standard and Bretton Woods. But you admire his doggedness, and his sincerity and conviction come through even when the meaning doesn't. Tonight, however, he seems to sense that this isn't what they came to hear, and so he talks about football.

Kemp, of course, quarterbacked the Buffalo Bills to their years of glory in 1964 and 1965, when they won the AFL championship. He is still a local hero, introduced at speeches as "Number Fifteen." In crowds like this it's hard to tell where Jack Kemp the former quarterback leaves off and Jack Kemp the present congressman begins. To this day, Kemp seems to be a sort of life link with the magic world of Sunday afternoons and Monday evenings, a confirmation almost of the worth of that world. When he began his ILO speech by telling them how he always tried to avoid speaking engagements on Monday evenings, the brotherhood was established.

"This is the first time I've ever told this story," he tells the good folks at the Brant firehouse, his voice lowering, taking them into his confidence. "But I just feel this very strongly tonight. When I started out in life I wanted to be a pro football player. It's really all I thought about." Kemp goes on to talk about how he started at Occidental College at five feet, 10 inches, 165 pounds. "One day the coach called me into his office and told me, 'Of all the people on this team, I think you are the only one who can make the pros. I really think you have it, have something inside you, and I want you to work—work just like you were a pro football player.' "

"When I left that office, you know, I would have run through a brick wall for that coach."

Kemp went on to recount the early years he spent kicking around the pros, his final breakthrough, and then he brought the story up to a class reunion he attended last year. "The whole team was there," he recalled. "And you know, it came out that the coach had told every player on the team the same thing—that if they worked hard enough and sacrificed enough, they could make the pros. I was furious, for about a minute. Then I realized that that coach had made every one of us a little bit better, struggle a little bit harder, to reach our potential."

"What is life for if not to inspire us to something better?" Kemp asks, suddenly catching the audience in the coil of energy you feel at a motivational seminar or a good gospel sermon. "There is *no limit* to what the American people can do—to the prosperity we can create, to what we can achieve—if we put *no limits* upon them."

In Washington they try to understand Kemp through econometric models. But Kemp is talking about something else, something at which too many Democrats have come to look down their noses—individual aspiration and hope. "When the president says, 'You ain't seen nothin' yet,' he believes it," he continues, "and folks, I believe it too." It's a warm bath in the America of the president's television ads—"morning again in America"—*Reader's Digest*, Amway, and Reverend Ike.

TAFT DEMOCRATS

Jack Kemp and I came to Washington the same year, he as a Republican congressman, myself as a tax reformer very much on the other side of the street. When I first started to see his speeches in the *Congressional Record*, it seemed like the usual right-wing stuff: feed the rich through tax cuts under the guise of "stimulating the economy," get the government out of the way, and all the flowers will bloom. Kemp did give it more flair than his Republican cohorts—the energy level was higher—but there didn't appear to be much to worry about. The Democrats controlled things and—one assumed—always would.

But then the walls began to crumble. Jimmy Carter didn't hack it; Ronald Reagan, in his presidential campaign, was talking like Kemp, and all of a sudden the so-called Kemp-Roth tax cut bill, which just a few years before had seemed a right-wing backwater idea, just a few steps leftward from the Liberty Lobby, was becoming the law of the land.

But what I remember most vividly from that tumultuous year of 1981 was the way my own party, the Democrats, responded. Or rather, how they had no apparent response. I recall Lane Kirkland, the AFL-CIO president, declaiming in his sonorous monotone that Kemp-Roth—and Reagan economics generally—were a "radical and untried experiment" or words to that effect. Wasn't that what the curmudgeons said about the New Deal? I remember how the Democrats in Congress took to invoking in their cause Henry Kaufman, the sourpuss of the Wall Street bond markets, the man the Republicans used to invoke to throw cold water on the Democrats' own "radical and untried" schemes. I remember the tax bill that Ways and Means Chairman Dan Rostenkowski wrote to counter the president's bill; it was a disgusting special-interest buffet, and Democrats were talking at the time about how they were going to "win" by getting gas producers and kindred groups on their side. I remember thinking, "My God, wouldn't a pure Kemp-Roth bill have been better than this?"

And I remember most vividly, the Democratic campaign just ended, Walter Mondale taking up the Robert Taft banner of balanced budgets and accountancy, while Reagan was playing to the public's desire for a new morning; and in Congress it was Jack Kemp, not the Democrats, who was advocating the view that balanced budgets came second, that what counted was the theme that Jack Kennedy had espoused 24 years earlier—namely, to get the country moving again. And I heard Mondale making his traditional pitches to interest group leaderships, while the Republicans were speaking in metaphors that embraced us as Americans.

Then, just a couple of nights ago, after I had interviewed Kemp for this article, I dropped in on a friend who works for a Democratic congressman. As we walked through the corridors of the Cannon House office building—I realized I was pacing hard, as though trying to work something out of my system—I heard my friend saying something that had flickered across my own mind. This is a man of thoroughly populist instincts who is no friend of concentrated capital and power, yet here he was saying, "I'm starting to wonder why I'm a Democrat."

I am not ready to become a Republican. I still see, through the rhetorical quaaludes of good feelings and growth, the smug patter at the country club, the mink coats, and cars about twice as long as they need to be. I still sense an animating bottom-line impulse of what's-in-it-for-me. But I have to admit that Republicans like Kemp are onto something, at the symbolic level at least and sometimes, I think, at the level of policy. If the Democrats don't grasp this, they are going to become, I fear, what Robert Taft led his own party to become—a permanent minority. To understand what the Republicans are onto, and where it falls short, we could do worse than to look at Jack Kemp.

In case you haven't heard, Kemp has built his political career around a single notion: that by cutting taxes and returning to "sound money," we can unleash the forces of enterprise and production and inspire a resurgence of prosperity in which all will partake. But this is not all Kemp is saying. Where he began as a balance-the-budget conservative who went forth with the desire to foil the spenders (except where Buffalo was concerned), he now castigates his party and the Democrats for "worshipping at the shrine of the balanced budget." While he is not on the front lines of increased social spending, he does not crusade against it: "People don't elect Republicans to repeal the New Deal," he says, putting the whole issue of budget cuts virtually over the horizon of his concerns. Where he once supported a value-added tax (a national sales tax) when Nixon was flirting with it, he now says tersely of Charls Walker, the big-banana corporate lobbyist who supports the idea, "He doesn't think the poor people of this country are paying enough taxes." And probably more than anyone in his party, he is using this message to reach out to blacks, minorities, and blue-collar workers to bring them into the Republican fold. "We Republicans are going to bring our message of hope, opportunity, and economic growth to the northeast and New York state," he told a delegation of New York Democrats, "to cities, to blacks and Hispanics, into labor union hiring halls, to Massachusetts, and even to Georgia. Our plans for a brighter tomorrow exclude no one."

Doggedly advancing these themes, Kemp has achieved a national stature that most senators and even Cabinet members might envy. During the last two weeks of November alone, he appeared on "Face the Nation," "The McLaughlin Report," "This Week with David Brinkley," "Firing Line,"

"Crossfire," "Donahue," "America's Black Interests" (hosted by Julian Bond), and "Adam Smith's Money World." His op-ed pieces appear in major newspapers with regularity.

Partly through Kemp's efforts, the themes have been catching on, at least from a marketing standpoint. A Harris poll for *Business Week* a number of months ago found that by a 51 percent to 39 percent margin, people thought the Republicans would do a better job of stimulating the economy than the Democrats would. "The Democrats have squandered their best issue— economic growth," Harris concluded. "That's the single biggest crisis they face." What's worse, the Democrats have been losing their grip on the symbols with which opportunity and hope are identified. A poll conducted immediately after the election by Vic Fingerhut, a Washington political consultant, found that 73 percent of Democrats and independents who leaned Democratic but voted for Reagan believed that Reagan, not Mondale, was the candidate who was "more in the Democratic tradition of Roosevelt, Truman, and Kennedy in fighting for working people."

'QUITE A PIECE OF HORSEFLESH'

Kemp got his political start in San Diego, where he played for the Chargers before going to Buffalo in 1962 in an unusual waiver foul-up. The editor of the *San Diego Union*, the conservative Copley paper, was Herb Klein, who later became press secretary to Richard Nixon. Klein saw something in Kemp and brought him on to do public relations for the paper. Kemp wrote a weekly column aimed at youth on such subjects as the evils of communism and the beneficence of the profit motive. "In America the quest for profit is inseparably linked to political freedom," Kemp wrote in one column. "The opportunity to strive for economic gain is as much a part of our heritage as our vote and the Bill of Rights." A reporter with the *Los Angeles Times* recalls a meeting between Barry Goldwater and a group of writers and editors at the *Union* offices during Goldwater's 1964 presidential campaign. When the questions became too unfriendly, the reporter recalls, the *Union* general manager gave the ball to Kemp to ask the "proper" ones.

Kemp was also getting involved in politics during these years, working in Nixon's campaign for governor in 1962 and supporting Goldwater for president two years later. In 1967 he worked in the off-season in the administration of California's new governor, Reagan, and a year later, when he was sidelined for the entire season with an injury, he came to Washington to work with the Republican National Committee. That year Kemp also worked with a group called "Athletes for Nixon." He was politically active within pro football as well. He was one of the founders of the AFL players association in 1965 and served as its president from that year until 1970.

The Republican elders in Washington began grooming Kemp. When the Buffalo seat finally opened up, the county Republican chairman called Kemp "the Holy Grail," and the national party regarded his campaign the same way. "He was treated as a 'number one draft choice—a bonus baby,' " writer Pat Ryan recalled in *Sports Illustrated* after the campaign. Consultants and technicians were provided. Herb Klein himself made trips to Buffalo, though the press was not always notified, since identification with Nixon was not entirely a plus in those Vietnam years.

Kemp had everything going for him. Through his football notoriety he had 76 percent name recognition in the district to his opponent's 23 percent. The district, though often touted as "blue collar" and Democratic, in fact consisted of the Buffalo suburbs and had a majority Republican registration. (Kemp's district has since become even more rural and Republican). Until the Johnson landslide of 1964, it had sent to Congress a Republican by the name of John R. Pillion, who is most remembered for opposing statehood for Alaska and Hawaii on the grounds, among other things, that these states would probably send communists to Congress. Moreover, the Democrats were divided; the district's then-current Democratic congressman, Max McCarthy, returned to run an independent campaign after failing to get the nomination for the Senate. Despite these advantages, Kemp almost blew it through his performance in TV debates. On election day, he squeaked by with 96,989 votes to his opponents 90,949.

When Kemp came to Washington, he had unquestionable star quality, at least to the Republicans ("quite a piece of horseflesh," Robert L. Bartley of *The Wall Street Journal* editorial page called him). Towards the end of his first term in Washington, another *Journal* columnist, Alan Otten, called him one of the "clear comers" in the Congress. Kemp did not shy away from such publicity. The *Buffalo Evening News* reported that in his first eight months in office, Kemp issued almost as many press releases as his four western New York House colleagues combined. ("And there's a lot of stuff he's doing that we just don't get to you because we just don't have the capability," a Kemp aide explained.) He was a special favorite of Richard Nixon's: the two had campaigned together for Robert Finch for lieutenant governor in 1966, and Nixon had played an active role in convincing Kemp to run.

For all this, however, Kemp's prominence was confined largely to the Republican party. The House of Representatives is not a place where reputations are made overnight—or, in most cases, made at all. It is hard enough being one of 435 and even worse if you are in the minority, with no committee chairmanships or staff, and no speaker of your own party to help your reelection prospects by pushing a pet bill. Kemp's early years as a congressman did little to distinguish him from the pack. He supported the war in Vietnam (a local peace group gave him the "Bomb of the Year" award), introduced a constitutional amendment to ban busing, and proposed a lid on government spending. His first floor fight was to cut the budget for the National Endowment for the Arts. "The worst thing that I can do as a representative of my district," he said, "is to allow this country's fiscal situation to deteriorate any further." Kemp wanted to cut taxes, but like most conservatives of the time, he saw spending cuts as the key. "I believe," he said, "the Congress must assign the highest priority to provide relief from the overwhelming burden of taxation by tightening the rein of federal spending [and] by reversing the enormous growth in the size and cost of government."

Yet like most congressmen, Kemp was inclined to look more kindly upon such expenditures where his own district was concerned. His first speech on the House floor—March 10, 1971—protested the dropping of Buffalo-to-Chicago service by what was then called "Railpax." (The unfortunate impact upon the nation's overcrowded airports was among his stated concerns.) In his first reelection campaign he proudly took credit for $100 million in water treatment funds for the Great Lakes, $25.3 million for secondary water treatment, and $171 million for a local rapid transit system.

Ninety percent of Kemp's colleagues might have slept soundly upon such achievements, but Kemp was the man *The Wall Street Journal's* Otten had described as having "boundless ambition and a ruthless readiness to put his own needs first; a shrewd instinct for spotting good political openings, and real hustle to follow through and take advantage of them." Not the sort of man to make a career out of sewer grants. During his second term, Watergate hit, and with it the near decimation of his party. Here was a man who was intensely competitive, had spent his entire adult life in pro sports and politics, and who, moreover, was accustomed to calling the plays. Yet he was stuck on defense in a permanent goal line stand against an overwhelming number of liberals.

BACON TO BUFFALO

Kemp sensed a fundamental contradiction in what he was trying to do, a contradiction that his divergent views on spending in general versus spending in his own district merely betokened. Republicans like himself had traditionally come to Washington to prevent government from doing things. They were trying to get the voters excited about a negative—about *less*. The Democrats, by contrast, were promising *more*—more money for education, more protection for consumers and the environment, more job training, more growth—they were even telling the voters that government could borrow the money to do all this. The Democrats were running a discount house while the Republicans were running a store with practically nothing on the shelves. "They had a thesis, the liberal left of the Democratic party had a thesis, which was to spend, finance it with deficits or whatever," Kemp said in a recent interview with *People and Taxes*. "And we had an antithesis which was not to spend. But the synthesis was inexorably shifting toward spending less than they wanted, more than we wanted, and I said, 'Hey, wait a minute, we need a thesis.' "

This bind was especially uncomfortable for a representative from a rustbelt city like Buffalo. Buffalo practically wouldn't exist without government spending, going back to the Erie Canal and on up to the procurement for World War II, which turned the city into what one writer called the "Seattle of the northeast." More recently, with the auto and steel plants closing, Buffalo desperately needed federal assistance, and there was no way a politician of any stripe could avoid this. Kemp has, as mentioned, gone after it with relish. His views on economic policy may impress them on "Meet the Press," but the bacon seems to matter more in Buffalo. Last fall Kemp ran TV ads proudly displaying the city's new half-billion dollar, six-and-a-half-mile rapid rail system with the tagline, "That's what leadership can do."

Kemp was not a hypocrite. "Very early in my political career I realized that the conventional conservative model, political and economic, was not an answer to people who were out of work." The answer, Kemp saw, was growth. But how can you promote growth when you basically don't believe that government should do anything?

KEYNESIAN CONSERVATISM

Well, one thing you can do is cut taxes. Kemp introduced an Accelerated Capital Formation Act that consisted primarily of business tax breaks of the kind Republicans traditionally supported. Like about 99 percent of all congressional bills, it went nowhere. "I came back and realized I hadn't done a very good job of selling my bill, so I changed the name and called it the Jobs Creation Act," Kemp has said. It sounded a bit more like a thesis and attracted more than a hundred cosponsors. This was in the midst of the recession of 1975. Someone had asked then Treasury Secretary William Simon why President Ford wouldn't support a jobs creation act and Simon had replied that it cost too much money. "All of a sudden a light went off in me," Kemp said later. "Gee, if we took a temporary deficit by changing the tax laws to encourage investment and savings and work opportunities, it seemed to me there ought to be some revenue."

Kemp was becoming interested in the work of a Columbia economist by the name of Robert Mundell, who was arguing that Canada actually gained revenue in the early seventies by cutting taxes. Irving Kristol, one of Kemp's mentors, advised him to look into the Kennedy administration, which had pumped up the economy—gotten the country "moving again"—in the early sixties by doing precisely this. Kemp says he asked his staff to draft a tax cut bill as close as possible to the individual rate cuts Kennedy had proposed in 1963 (but which were not passed until after his death). Around this time, he said, he was starting to think that "the key to the economy is not the business entity, it is the individual worker and the individual entrepreneur." He dropped much of the business tax cut from his old bill and introduced an individual cut of 10 percent a year for three straight years. (Walter Heller, who was Kennedy's economic advisor at the time, insists that Kennedy's cut was more generous at the lower income levels. "They keep trying to put the Kennedy mantle on the thing and it doesn't fit," Heller says.)

Now what's the big deal about a tax cut? Haven't politicians been promising them for ages? Yes, but this was a Republican advocating, in effect, deficit financing. If this sounds suspiciously like the New Deal and Keynes, it's because you haven't grasped the whole theory. From the New Deal onward, Democrats had thought of the economy as driven by "demand." The way to "get the economy moving" was to put money into people's hands; in their role as "consumers" they would rush out to the stores, and the resulting purchases would induce investors to build the new factories and buy the new machines. This is called "demand-side" economics. Translated into politics, it meant that those at the lower- and middle-income levels should get the most in tax cuts, since they are the most inclined to spend. Demand-side economics was traditional Democratic economics.

Economists such as Arthur Laffer and Paul Craig Roberts and Jude Wanniski (then of *The Wall Street Journal* editorial staff) had been framing an entirely different view of this problem, looking at people as potential producers rather than as potential consumers. The key fact here was the "marginal" tax rate—the tax you pay on the last dollar you make. Because the income tax is "graduated," you move on through higher tax rates as you make more money. Influenced heavily by supply-siders, Kemp was now arguing that inflation had pushed people into such high tax brackets that they had no more incentive to work or save or produce. Cut taxes, Kemp and these others were saying, and we would unleash a torrent of work effort and investment that would get the country moving again—not because people would have more money to spend, but because they'd have *more reason to produce.*

THE REHABILITATED RICH

It was the next step in the reasoning that turned this economic sunshine into pure surf city. Laffer argued with his famous "Laffer Curve" that such tax cuts could generate so much economic activity that the resulting revenues could make up for those originally lost. The tax cut would pay for itself! The rich would actually pay more taxes than they did before. And furthermore, since there would be extra supply calling forth demand, rather than vice versa, stimulating the economy in this supply-side way would not provoke inflation. The Federal Reserve Board could safely allow more dollars into the economy to finance this supply-side growth. In fact, the supply-siders assumed that the Fed must be willing to do so, which is why they are the most tenacious Volcker-baiters in town.

Are you starting to see the implications? An antithesis—cutting taxes—becomes a thesis—promoting growth. The people get their tax cuts and their spending programs too. Republicans would inherit the mantle of John F. Kennedy (guess what Kemp's middle initial is) and still be free-market conservatives. And now, at last, Republicans would have something besides condolences for minorities and the poor. If a little antithesis could produce a thesis, then wouldn't a bigger antithesis produce even more of one? Kemp adopted the idea of "enterprise zones" for the inner cities, in which even larger tax cuts would be bestowed upon specific depressed areas to attract new businesses there. The Democrats want to give you more welfare; we want to give you less *need* for welfare.

Pretty heady stuff. "Republicans were ripe for this because they were out of power for so long," said Wanniski, who tried first to urge this approach upon the Democrats. Perhaps best of all, here was a tax cut rationale that enabled the rich to stand tall. Under the old Keynesian notion they had no special claim to relief (even less, in fact, since they might save the buck where the poor person would spend it). But under the supply-side notion their claim came first, since they have the greatest proclivity of anyone to invest and hence create supply.

PHANTOM TOLLBOOTHS

There is something about taxes that touches a messianic—or at least obsessive—nerve in the American psyche, and people who study these matters overmuch tend to lapse into a two-factor universe in which there are taxes on the one hand, human behavior on the other, and very little else in-between. If you have ever met a follower of Henry George, the 19-century proponent of the "single tax" on land, then you have some idea what it is like to talk to Kemp on the subject of taxes or anything remotely connected.

Many Democrats would like to believe that Kemp is dumb, but he is anything but. His mental energy seems apiece with his physical, and he has both a genuine passion for ideas and a striking grasp of the intricacies of the tax and monetary theories on which his mind dwells. In private conversation he is more flexible than he is in his speeches and writing; he tends to qualify his views ("I don't mean to sound Pavlovian") and show more self-awareness than I had expected. "I don't know who's more tired of my speech," he said, "my audience or me." He enjoys repartee and is quick with a quip, and our conversation turned into a friendly debate. I enjoyed it.

Still, the House Democrat who says of Kemp, a bit dismissively, that "he has learned how the economic model works and he processes everything through the model" isn't all wrong. Kemp came to reading and ideas relatively late, after he left college, and he's just a little like your sophomore roommate who started reading Freud and thought he had found the key to everything. In his book, *The American Renaissance,* and in his speeches and other writings, Kemp tends to ascribe afflictions far and wide, from industrial decline, inflation, and third world poverty to the erosion of families and communities and even the decline of Broadway, to high marginal tax rates. A sample: "The problem with the auto industry is not that Americans are buying too many Japanese cars. The problem is that Americans cannot buy enough cars of any kind. . . . The answer is to cut tax rates so people can afford to produce, save money, and buy more of everything." Well, sure. But aren't a few other things involved?

No one ever lost votes by asserting that America's problems were due to government's taking too much of our money, and in the late seventies events were making this message even more compelling. The scary inflation was pushing wage earners up into tax brackets that had been designed originally for the rich. This "bracket creep" was especially severe in the middle-income range, where the tax brackets are bunched together like the toll booths on the Connecticut Turnpike. But the Democrats had done very little to assuage this pain. In the beginning of the 1970s, a poll taken by the Advisory Commission on Intergovernmental Relations found the public thought the federal income tax the most fair tax. By the end of the decade people thought it the most *unfair* tax. In California, Howard Jarvis had tapped a well of kindred anger at the way inflation had driven up home prices and hence property tax bills, and now the ground was fertile at the federal level as well.

"We forced the Democrats to become an antithesis party, a party of naysayers, Kemp said, speaking of the way the Democrats lined up against the Kemp-Roth—and later Reagan—cuts. During the last campaign, the Republicans swatted Democratic criticisms like so many flies. "Walter Mondale wants to balance the budget by unbalancing yours" was one of Kemp's favorite lines.

WAITING FOR THE TIDE

Supply-side economics has been good for the economics industry if none other, and you've heard the evidence from the opposition camp: investment still below the levels of the Carter years; personal savings that were supposed to soar under the 1981 tax act, down; real interest rates—and the difference between interest rates and inflation—several times the level at the end of the seventies. Indeed, to the extent Kemp-Roth helped stir a "recovery," it did so mainly through the much-maligned demand side: people had a little more money in their pockets, and they went out and spent it.

But such argumentation isn't exactly inciting the populace into frenzy, as you may have noticed last fall. It helped the Republicans, of course, to have the economic winds blowing at their backs, regardless of the reason. But the supply-side rationale is an attitudinal template as much as it is economics, and to treat it as though it were just the latter is a little like treating a candidate's television advertisements as though they were merely imparting information to a rational voter.

Part of the appeal, as mentioned, is the hearkening to aspiration and hope. The Democrats have become a party of programs, have turned one function of government—social work—into the reason for the whole show. They seem to think that people want most of all to wake up in the morning grateful that Congress has made provision for life's misfortunes, while Kemp and the others have been tapping, on the metaphorical level, the much deeper desire to wake up with a sense of opportunity to improve one's lot. The other politician on the national scene who seems to connect with people in this way is Jesse Jackson, whom Kemp in fact quoted in a speech to the Urban League: "Democracy guarantees opportunity, not success."

Optimism is another side of Kemp. A year after Carter's malaise speech Kemp declared at the Republican convention, "Austerity is not the answer; austerity is the problem. The American people are not the problem. They are the answer." *The American Renaissance* is an assault on the idea of limits; if it had a sound track, it would be the Beach Boys. Kemp is untroubled by questions such as what abundance is for, and whether, even if energy scarcity is a myth, as he asserts, we are necessarily a better country for consuming more of it ourselves.

But perhaps the most powerful aspect of Kemp's appeal is his inclusiveness. Where the Democrats dispense opportunity and justice in little morsels—a program here, a benefit there—Kemp has embraced the encompassing metaphor of the tide that lifts all boats. "While Kemp is talking about growth," said political analyst Alan Baron, "the Democrats are talking about comparable worth—how to pay sales clerks more and sheet metal workers less." Kemp is serious about trying to bring blue-collar workers and blacks into the party, and he has broken from his conservative colleagues by supporting voting rights for the District of Columbia and making Martin Luther King's birthday a national holiday, both emotionally charged issues. While he generally supports the New Right's social agenda, he greatly prefers the high ground of growth to these divisive social issues.

But is the high ground real? And real or not, is it high enough?

Kemp is known on Capitol Hill as essentially a publicist who is not a major player in the daily grind of legislation. On the Appropriations Committee, he does play a significant role in foreign policy, pushing foreign aid bills and opposing the International Monetary Fund's efforts to impose austerity on the third world. But on the issues he cares most about, taxes and monetary policy, Kemp plays mainly from the outside, sitting on neither Ways and Means, which writes the tax laws, nor on Banking, which oversees the Federal Reserve. So situated, he can expostulate all he wants on these subjects without having to make messy choices between, say, realtors yelping in one ear and insurance companies yelping in the other.

Congress needs good issue-raisers, and Kemp is one of the best. But Kemp's outsider role does seem to connect to a larger inclination to use the supply-side growth gospel as a deus ex machina to avoid hard decisions.

In 1982, for example, Kemp opposed the Republican tax bill that raised important revenue, even though the bill focused on corporate loopholes and did little to diminish the supply-side "incentives" in the 1981 bill. "He gets into a leadership position [Kemp is chairman of the House Republican Conference] and then refuses to take responsibility," said a staff member of the Senate Republican leadership, which took the heat on the bill. This year, he continues to contend that we can grow our way out of the deficit, and he avoids discussion of budget cuts. These are the postures of a minority gadfly, not of a congressman who is ready to carry the load.

Kemp is not the sort of politician who tells every interest group what it wants to hear. He opposes protection for the auto and steel industries, even though his free-trade position does not increase his popularity in his district (it helps to have a safe one—he hasn't won less than 70 percent of the vote since his first election). Similarly, he tells business audiences that we shouldn't have corporate subsidies like the Export-Import Bank and the Synfuels Corporation. But running through the core of supply-side thinking is a tendency to pretend that the need for choices does not exist. "The greatest obstacle to opportunity and advancement," Kemp writes in *The American Renaissance*, "is the idea that life is a 'zero sum' game." He elaborated in an interview with *People and Taxes*: "I rejected intuitively the Lester Thurow conceptual framework that this was a battle between savings and consumption, between the suburbs and the city. . . ." It is *good* to strive for a prosperity in which all can share. But some desires must take second place to the common good; it is not possible for everybody to have it all.

The standard liberal critique against Kemp-Roth is that it favored the rich, which it did. After factoring in the Social Security tax increase, you didn't come out ahead under Kemp-Roth unless you made more than $30,000 a year. This might have been tolerable, however, if it truly had been the price for the rising tide that would lift all boats. But that tide never came. The bill did not make choices—it didn't close the loopholes and tax shelters that drain investment away from productive channels. Corporations took their depreciation benefits and engaged in takeover wars or buy-a-tax-break maneuvers. Individual savers simply transferred savings out of passbook accounts into Individual Retirement Accounts. And so on. Kemp assured us that the new lower rates would lure money out of tax shelters. But the tax shelters boomed from $5.5 billion in 1982 to $8.4 billion in 1983. We might just as well have given the money to low- and middle-income people, as Democrats traditionally do. At least the money would have flowed into the productive economy, albeit on the demand side.

Again to Kemp's credit, he has introduced the Kemp-Kasten bill, which would simplify the tax code, and he acknowledges that perhaps such streamlining should have been a part of Kemp-Roth. But even this new bill makes no distinction between, say, stock issues of new enterprises (why tax the gain at all?) and speculation in antiques (why provide any special treatment?).

But there is a more fundamental shortcoming in the supply-side outlook. In the imagination of Kemp and the supply-siders generally, we are all relentless little integers of self-seeking who go forth with pocket calculators and spread sheets reckoning the after-tax consequences of every life decision and acting accordingly. Sometimes, despite his protests, Kemp really does sound Pavlovian: "This is a massive behavioral modification program designed to alter the performance of the economy by changing the behavior of people by altering the rewards."

There is an infectious simplicity to this view, reducing as it does all economic problems to a matter of carrots and sticks. Of course after-tax return counts for something. But lay the blame for the problems of our auto industry on this doorstep? Michael Maccoby, a psychiatrist who has written two books on corporate leadership, pointed out in *People and Taxes* that the chief executive of Volvo, Pehr Gyllenhammer, "makes maybe a fifth of what the G.M. chief executive makes, yet he's working night and day, and he's much more creative." Taxes in Sweden are higher than in the United States. Maccoby also pointed to Edwin Land, who created the Polaroid Corporation and who did not retire a poor man. "He was motivated by the idea of making something work, not by making money." This is not a question of the profit motive not being nice, but of the actual richness and diversity of the aspirations by which we live. Is Kemp really telling us that he held back on the football field because marginal tax rates were higher when he played than in Sid Luckman's day or that he sloughed off as a congressman before the Kemp-Roth tax cuts restored his incentive to do his job the way his constituents expected?

What is true individually is also true collectively. One of the interesting things about the seventies is the number of firms that excelled despite the supposedly debilitating effect of high taxes. "Look at the washing machine industry," says Thomas J. Peters, author of *In Search of Excellence*. "General

Electric had 10,000 people out on the street in Louisville during this past recession. At the same time, Maytag reported record profits and record sales both years. The key is they've got a washing machine that just doesn't break down." Both Maytag and G.E., of course, were operating under the same tax code. "Management is the issue in this country," Peters says, "not [tax] policy." This is not to say, of course, that taxes should be high. It is to say that we cannot solve our economic problems simply by making taxes lower.

What's missing in the supply-side mindset is a curiosity about institutions and the way they actually work. Kemp and the others seem to dwell in a universe of economic abstraction in which supply begets demand (or vice versa) and tax incentives beget work effort, without reference to the institutions and life circumstances in which these activities occur. When Kemp was first getting interested in politics he was absorbed in theory—interested "in the philosophic side," as his mentor, Herb Klein put it. "I had him retain that, but I also wanted him to have a feel for pragmatic politics." Kemp could use a little more feel for pragmatic economics as well. "Why don't they go out and find out what the world's really like before trying to meddle with our whole system?" Maccoby said of the supply-siders generally. The point is not that incentives don't count. It's that other things count too.

But the shortcoming of supply-side thinking is not just economic. Or rather, people like Kemp allow their thinking to become too exclusively economic in the narrow economist's sense of the word. To a degree, the supply-side vision is a healthy corrective, but alone it is not an adequate metaphor for our national life. There is not, for example, the idea of community and service.

Kemp cranks the idea of national service, for example, through his supply-side model and comes out with the need for more *incentives* in the form of higher pay for a volunteer peacetime army. "I didn't want my sons and daughters getting drafted in peacetime when they reached age 18," Kemp told me. But is there no difference between national service and signing on as an IBM management trainee?

The problem here is a reluctance to *expect* anything of anyone. I asked Kemp whether he thought workers and managers needed to moderate their wage demands—whether political leaders needed to encourage this—for the good of the economy. The congressman launched into a discussion of how steelworkers in New York state pay over 40 percent tax. Fair enough; taxes do count for something at the bargaining table. But President Kennedy felt impelled to ask the steelworkers for moderation when taxes were lower than Kemp-Roth makes them today. There isn't always a painless mechanical solution. Sometimes people just have to reach down and give something up. What are leaders for?

HALF-WAY POPULISTS

Kemp and his cohorts in the House call themselves "New Populists," and this is one of the plus sides to their message. They speak from the standpoint of individuals rather than institutions, entrepreneurs rather than corporations; they want power to reside in the grass roots rather than at the center. More than anyone in Congress, Kemp has challenged the tight money policies of the Federal Reserve Board, and tight money was an overriding Populist concern.

But there is a crucial element of Populism that the New Populists tend to overlook. Partly it's the concern for justice. The Populists of history were incensed, for example, that their tax dollars were used to subsidize tax-exempt railroads (the ones that were gouging them) and would not have looked with favor at the 1981 tax bill, which granted a good many of the largest corporations in this country a similar privileged status. But more, the Populism of history was a social movement as well as an economic movement; not social in the Mondalean sense, in which "we are a generous people" seems to mean, primarily, that we are happy to pay taxes so civil servants can do good works for us. Rather, social in life practice. "In things essential, unity; and in all things, charity" was the motto of a Farmers' Alliance lodge in Texas; and the Populist movement itself was rich in projects to organize lending libraries, chautauquas, relief for the elderly and indigent, and the like. Even in the economic realm, these were not isolated integers of self-advancement assaulting the world like so many Horatio Algers. They organized cooperatives to purchase seeds and supplies and to market their grain so they could stand strong together. "We are emerging from a period of intense individualism, supreme selfishness, and ungodly greed to a period of cooperative effort," said a Kansas Allianceman in a statement that would give one reason for cheer if it appeared in a newspaper today.

Kemp makes an occasional reference to community in his book and speeches. But it is somehow not quite in the focal center of his vision. He makes an important contribution when he speaks for enterprise, initiative, aspiration, and hope. These are all things to which the Democrats must speak. But individual striving is only half the equation. There is also a concern for the team. "That word 'selflessness' as opposed to 'selfishness,' " as Vince Lombardi once put it, "is what I try to teach."

DEBATE FOCUS

Is the Best Government the One that Governs Least?

A PRACTICAL LIBERAL STRESSES THE IMPORTANCE OF GOVERNMENT
BUT DOES NOT VIEW IT AS A CURE-ALL

New York Governor Mario Cuomo's keynote address to the Democratic National Convention in 1984 brought the delegates to their feet in loud and appreciative applause. It was a stunning performance, one that immediately gave Cuomo national recognition and made him potentially a leading contender for the 1988 Democratic presidential nomination.

Media-hype had thrust Cuomo to the forefront of the national political scene, and promised to keep him there. His convention speech seemed to make him a New Deal descendent, squarely in the liberal camp. Conservatives mocked Cuomo for being out of step with the times, which they believed were moving to the right, reflected in Ronald Reagan's overwhelming victory.

Cuomo's political career, however, suggested that the New York governor, far from being a liberal ideologue, was a pragmatic politician fully capable of adapting his positions to accommodate political realities. His 1982 campaign for governor against the millionaire businessman Louis Lehrman at a time when "Reaganomics" was widely accepted, forced Cuomo to present his own plan for cutting taxes and reducing the size of government. Lehrman's vigorous campaign, which effectively used media saturation to reach the electorate, called for implementing Reagan's tax and expenditure cutting programs at the state and local levels. Cuomo knew that he could not simply repeat liberal litanies and win against an apparent rising conservative tide. His slim 51–48 percent victory over Lehrman was the result of support in New York City, where voters backed him by a 2 to 1 margin.

In the *Diaries of Mario M. Cuomo* the New York governor has summed up his political philosophy. "I agree," he wrote, "that government should allow the strong, the wealthy, the so-called producers to stay strong, and even encourage them to grow stronger. But I also believe that there are two major groups that deserve more of government's attention than they are receiving at the moment. The first consists of those who work for a living, . . . the so-called middle class. The second group is made up of those who want to be in the first but haven't been able to make it: those who want to work but can't because they're too old or too frail or because there just isn't a job for them."* Cuomo believes that political societies should be viewed as "families," in which the

Diaries of Mario M. Cuomo (New York: Random House, 1984), pp. 6–7.

20

members recognize "the indispensable importance of sharing benefits and burdens, the notion of communal strength and of obligation to the whole."†

Examined in the following selection is Mario Cuomo's political philosophy and approach to politics, which offers a contrast to the conservatism of Jack Kemp, but not as sharp a difference as many people believe.

†*Ibid., p. 7.*

M. CUOMO

2

Meet Mario
The Moderate

FRED BARNES

Remember Mario Cuomo, the last full-throated liberal, the politician who electrified the Democratic convention last July with his keynote speech defending traditional liberal principles? As other leading Democrats were trimming their sails and as even Walter Mondale, in his acceptance speech, talked about "our mistakes" and promised "no laundry lists that raid our treasury," the governor of New York shot to national celebrity with a passionate attack on social inequality under President Reagan and an unabashed plea for activist government. Remember him?

Well, forget that Mario Cuomo. Meet Mario Cuomo the moderate. Or as he prefers to label himself, the "progressive pragmatist." This is the image that Cuomo and his advisers are now burnishing for him. Cuomo has complained intermittently for years about being unfairly labeled a "liberal" (though he was not heard to complain about the adulation he garnered from traditional liberals with his keynote address). Now he is adamant. And it is as if talking points had been distributed to all of Cuomo's advisers and confidants, instructing them to promote the same line: Mario is not now, and never has been, a liberal. "He's in the middle ideologically, and that's where he's comfortable," insisted a close associate. "His heart is on the left, but his wallet's on the right." Even Cuomo's arch-rival, New York City mayor Ed Koch, says, "Cuomo is fundamentally a centrist." Koch says that in trying to change his image, Cuomo is "doing what any intelligent, mainstream, rational Democrat will always do." Cuomo, characteristically, denies that there is anything new. "I haven't changed a single idea I've had," he says.

Some of Cuomo's admirers argue that the Cuomo of the keynote address was an aberration. "He did what he had to do to get Mondale elected," says Alan Chartock, an Albany political scientist who interviews Cuomo on a weekly radio show. "He was a good soldier. He moved to the left for the election and now he's moved back to where he was before." This is implausible, since Cuomo's speech was more progressive than anything Mondale said during the whole campaign. But if Cuomo can capitalize on the renown that speech brought him, while disowning its message, he may be perfectly positioned for the 1988 Democratic nomination: less liberal than Senator Edward Kennedy, more personable than Senator Gary Hart, better known than Senator Joseph Biden, and so on. "Cuomo's genius is that he is fast on his feet," says David M. Smick, a Republican party strategist who advises both Representative Jack F. Kemp and Lewis Lehrman, Cuomo's opponent in 1982 for governor. "Just when you thought he was little more than the eloquent twin brother of Walter Mondale, he is showing an ability to transcend ideology without losing credibility."

In fact, he's stronger than ever. When Iowa Democrats held their off-year caucuses in February, they voted overwhelmingly to invite Cuomo to address their annual Jefferson-Jackson dinner. The vote of over 1,000 Democrats was: Cuomo, 73 percent; Hart, 15; Kennedy, 8. When administrative assistants in the House of Representatives voted in March on who would be the Democratic nominee in 1988, Cuomo won again: Cuomo, 39 percent; Hart, 25; Kennedy, 17. When several hundred political operatives gathered in Boston recently, they picked Cuomo as their favorite for the nomination. These are just straws in the wind, of course. But a national poll taken in January for David Garth, the political consultant and Cuomo adviser, found that Cuomo is a major factor in 1988 calculations. The presidential preference result: Kennedy, 30 percent; Hart, 27; Cuomo, 18. "To be 12 points behind Teddy Kennedy with 40 percent of the people not knowing who you are is a tremendous showing," Garth says with some justice.

In 1983 and 1984 Cuomo and his strategists did nothing to discourage press stories that described him as the nation's most attractive and well-spoken liberal, a compelling new force in the Democratic Party. "How could we?" says a Cuomo associate. "Those pieces were all praising Cuomo to the hilt. Should we have quibbled over a label?" Now Cuomo is quibbling. "I never allow [reporters] to get into a label game," he says. "I always say, 'What is a liberal? What is a conservative?' " Cuomo says he does not want to be judged by "a keynote speech, an inaugural address, a cover of *The New York Times*," naming three of the building blocks of his current celebrity. The inaugural address, like the keynote speech, was regarded as fervently liberal, and the 1982 *New York Times Magazine* profile linked Cuomo to what it called "the old liberalism."

"I'm a governor," Cuomo says. "The way to judge me is by the budget. You campaign in poetry. You govern in prose." Ed Koch agrees: "The eloquent phrases are important, but they are simply part of his persona, not his total persona. His actions as governor have been mainstream America."

The new budget Cuomo unveiled in January calls for an income tax reduction of $2.1 billion over three years. "Why?" he asked. "To increase incentives, to make us more competitive. We're balancing the budget while we're doing it. We're not developing a $220 billion mortgage," a dig at President Reagan's deficit. At the same time Cuomo proposes to increase state spending by eight percent, including a $3.5 billion housing program and a ten percent boost in the basic welfare grant. In an interview for this article Cuomo cited the tax cut but didn't mention the spending increase.

Cuomo was irritated when *The New York Times* described his State of the State speech this year as an attempt to "revive the spirit of the New Deal." That speech did contain some pretty Reaganesque language. Cuomo touted his tax cut as "a clear signal to the business community of our commitment to economic growth." And he added that, "as important as the tax cut is, it's not enough. There is an equal need for financial reform, for an even greater commitment to fiscal prudence, to living within our means."

The day after the election last November, Cuomo mocked the absurd notion that anyone should consider him a traditional liberal. On Alan Chartock's radio show he remarked, "One of the senators, I forgot which one, is supposed to have said, 'We have read all of Governor Cuomo's speeches and they are New Deal.' I laughed. What are you when you reduce public employees by 9,000? What are you when you say need should be the criterion [for welfare benefits]? What are you when you come out for a tax cut? What are you when you refuse to raise the basic taxes? What are you when you spend more on your defense budget, which we call corrections, than any governor in history?"

In my interview Cuomo cited a precedent for combining radical rhetoric with more moderate policies. "Look at the difference between President Reagan's campaign poetry and President Reagan's governing prose. He used to talk like a radical rightist and then he governs like a moderate." Not everyone will find this description accurate or—accurate or not—worthy of emulation. But that is Cuomo's model. For those "interested in labeling my policies," he says, "simply go back to all my speeches since 1974. They have a boring consistency to them. My record is there to be seen. I've described myself as a progressive pragmatist for years."

To make it easy for reporters, Cuomo recently distributed a collection of his speeches and writings over the last ten years. As a result, he said, "reporters in Albany have stopped with this liberal stuff. They finally surrendered." This evidence largely supports Cuomo's claim. It shows him to be a dedicated centrist, a compromiser. It reveals his disdain for militantly left-wing Democrats, whom he calls a "new kind of Democrat" and blames for alienating middle-class voters. And it shows his willingness to take up issues like crime that some liberals are wary of, declaring that "the mugger has become the midnight mayor of the metropolis, the streets his jurisdiction, and the subways his private limousine."

The Cuomo collection features passages from his published diary of 1972, when he was mediator of a tense dispute between New York City officials pressing to locate a low-income housing project in Forest Hills, Queens, and angry residents opposed to the project. Not only did he zing George McGovern, then the Democratic presidential nominee, but he also attacked "liberals" in contemptuous language that would do a certified neoconservative proud. "Today a number of 'liberal' organizations released a statement condemning the mayor for having adopted the compromise proposal," he wrote. "Like so many other 'liberal' pronunciamentos, this one appeared to be primitively absolutist."

Running unsuccessfully for lieutenant governor in 1974, Cuomo gave a speech chastising left-liberal elements in the Democratic Party for inflexibility and elitism. Liberals, Cuomo said, had driven away a "major segment of our constituency," the middle-class worker. "For some reason he felt alienated by a new Democratic Party which he thought neither understood nor related to him. He was made to feel voiceless, powerless, and frustrated. So he became a Republican or a Conservative." Democrats should "serve the poor without crushing the middle class," Cuomo said.

The most conservative-sounding rhetoric in Cuomo's little booklet is in his speeches on crime. In 1977, when he lost to Koch in the mayor's race, he said, "These are good times for the mugger, the rapist, the burglar, the murderer, the kidnapper, the tax evader, the Medicaid and Medicare rip-off artist, the nursing home manipulator, the heroin and cocaine wholesaler and retailer." He advocated hiring more police. "The mugger that is arrested is back on the street before the police officer. The person mugged might not be back on the street for a long time, if ever." In 1981, as lieutenant governor, Cuomo declared that New Yorkers live in near-terror and "only an adventurer dares walk in the park at night. Homeowners have so many locks on their doors that the principal problem has become finding a way out of the house should, God forbid, a fire occur."

Cuomo got his left-liberal image largely because of his 1982 race for the governorship against Koch, his convention keynote address, and another speech last year at Notre Dame University in which he challenged the right of Catholics to impose their anti-abortion views on the nation. In 1982 Cuomo became the vehicle for the anti-Koch forces—left-wing activists, labor, blacks, the Liberal Party. They adopted him as their own, but it was Cuomo's strength upstate, which is more conservative and where mayors of New York City are never popular, that allowed him to defeat Koch. Then in the fall campaign against Republican Lewis Lehrman he adopted the conventional liberal rhetoric used by Democrats in economic hard times.

As for the keynote address, Cuomo describes it now as an upbeat answer to Reagan's "philosophy of lower expectations." He asks rhetorically, "Was it giveaway programs?" Perhaps not. But the speech did use the seldom-heard language of class warfare in criticizing Reagan; it endorsed the nuclear freeze; and it condemned the government of El Salvador. That was precisely what made it so noteworthy.

Cuomo's record as governor is not one Republicans will be able to portray as dangerously left-wing. In 1983, against the wishes of liberal Democrats in the state legislature, Cuomo refused to raise income, corporate, or sales taxes to balance the budget. Instead, he raised some nuisance taxes, pared some social programs, and laid off state workers. Cuomo boasts about how he stood up to the interest groups, as other Democratic governors have not. "The progressives so-called, the NYPIRG [New York Public Interest Research Group], the student groups, the education lobby, the environmentalists all say you got to raise taxes the way Dick Celeste did [in Ohio], the way Bob Graham did [in Florida], the way Jim Blanchard did [in Michigan]. I said we can't raise our taxes any more. . . . The best thing you can do in government is give people a chance to earn their own bread. Better than welfare. Better than anything you can do. The closest thing to a panacea." In judging Cuomo's two years as governor, Miriam Pawel of *Newsday* reported that Cuomo had "alienated many of those who considered themselves his natural constituents. Today some of the most complimentary things being said about Cuomo are coming from traditionally conservative constituencies like the law enforcement community and the business council."

Cuomo may have stumbled recently by getting out front as a vehement opponent of the Treasury plan for federal tax reform. The day after the plan was announced, Cuomo declared that it would "pulverize" the middle class by ending the deductibility of state and local taxes. Cuomo's position has led to an entertaining squabble with Representative Jack Kemp. Cuomo snapped at Kemp for not joining his protest that the plan would hurt New York. Kemp responded by calling him "Governor Status Como" and accusing him of trying to preserve high income tax rates. "I'd prefer to be 'Status Cuomo' to 'Backtrack Jack,'" Cuomo said, arguing that Kemp would "take us to 1913," when state and local taxes were made deductible. Cuomo's position may help him get reelected governor next year, but it puts him on the wrong side of a popular national issue. Lately Cuomo has been emphasizing that he doesn't oppose tax reform generally, just the particular parts he doesn't like. Of course that's what all opponents of tax reform say.

Cuomo is evasive and noncommittal when asked about foreign policy issues. Some of his advisers are urging him to keep away from foreign policy now, especially from any positions that would identify him with what one Cuomo associate calls "the McGovern-Carter foreign policy." Cuomo "realizes he has a clean slate on foreign policy," the associate said. "Why ruin it? Think how he would surprise people [in 1988]. He could come out and say, 'Sure, I'm liberal on domestic issues, but look how conservative I am on foreign policy.' "

On the other hand, it's hard to know why Cuomo is going to all this trouble to adjust his national image, since he insists that he is not running for president. He has turned down dozens of speaking requests around the country, including the one to address the Iowa dinner. "I'd answer the question the way I have 100 times," he told me. "It really is a matter of whether you are going to run for governor or for president. You can't do both. . . . The present setup doesn't allow it." While others are feverishly pursuing the presidency, he will run for reelection as governor in 1986. "To think that you can take that on, that in the middle of it they [the Democratic contenders] will stumble and the world will turn to the east and say, 'Maybe there's a governor somewhere with bags under his eyes who fits exactly what we want' . . ." The thought apparently was too farfetched for him to complete the sentence.

Cuomo first uttered his disclaimer in an interview with *The New York Times* last September. It was not an airtight statement. "He's not saying he absolutely, unequivocally will not run," says Meyer S. Frucher, the president of the Battery Park City Authority and a Cuomo pal. Advisers now wince when he is asked publicly about his position on a presidential race, much as Reagan aides cringe when he sails into uncharted territory at a press conference. "Cuomo says it a little differently every time," says one adviser. When badgered by columnists Rowland Evans and Robert Novak on their CNN television show last December, Cuomo ran into trouble. Did he mean he definitely wouldn't be a presidential candidate? "Oh, no, I didn't say that at all," he said.

"I thought you did," said Evans.

"Oh, no, no, no," Cuomo said.

Is a presidential bid "in the realm of the possible?" asked Novak.

"No, well, you know, if you say run, no, the answer is no," Cuomo answered. "It's possible that I will be elected president of Citicorp. It's possible I'll be president of Miami University. It's possible I'll finally make it to centerfield for the Pittsburgh Pirates. I mean possible, probable, the most probable thing is I'm going to run for governor in 1986. Beyond that, who knows?"

Some of his advisers think they know. They say Cuomo is pursuing what might be called a reverse-Mondale strategy. Mondale spent four years doing nothing but run for president. Cuomo's strategy would be this: win a smashing reelection victory next year, sit out presidential politics in 1987 as a Cuomo ground swell mounts, noisily defy a few traditional Democratic pressure groups, and then jump into the race around the time of the early primaries.

"If he wins with a strong victory in 1986, he'll be national news," says David Garth. "You can start [running for president] very late," meaning as late as early 1988. "If Cuomo wanted to put together a national network, he could do it in a month," says another adviser. "He wouldn't have to do anything at all in 1987. He has flexibility. Who's likely to catch on? Probably nobody. If someone does, Cuomo won't be a spoiler. But if nobody does and he's still high in the polls, he can get in." Frucher says Hart and Kennedy have had their serious shots at the nomination, and Democrats will be looking for a new face in 1988. "I don't think they are going to be looking for Joe Biden or Dale Bumpers. They want someone who can distinguish the Democratic Party from the Republican Party. Cuomo does that better than anyone."

Nobody in Washington thinks that Cuomo's ambitions are limited to being governor of New York. "Cuomo says he's not running for president," went a joke passed around Washington recently. "The next thing you know, he'll be claiming he's not Italian."

CHAPTER TWO

Civil Liberties
and Civil Rights

For Americans, the Bill of Rights symbolizes justice in all of its diverse forms. Guaranteed by the First Amendment are the fundamental freedoms of speech, press, association, and the right to petition government for a redress of grievances, all of which are so important to the preservation of political liberty and democracy. Protected also is religious freedom, sustaining the spiritual liberty that is an outstanding characteristic of a free society.

INCORPORATION AND EXTENSION OF THE BILL OF RIGHTS

The premier part of the Bill of Rights is the First Amendment, recognized by the Supreme Court, which as early as 1925, in *Gitlow* v. *New York,* held the freedoms of speech and press to be so fundamental that they were to be incorporated into the "liberty" protected by the due process clause of the Fourteenth Amendment against state invasion. Although the First Amendment freedoms were the first to be "nationalized," the Court under Chief Justice Earl Warren in the 1960s finally recognized that most of the other provisions of the Bill of Rights were sufficiently fundamental to be extended to the states under the due process clause of the Fourteenth Amendment. Aside from the First Amendment, the incorporated rights protected those accused of crime, including the Fourth Amendment protection against unreasonable search and seizure; the Fifth Amendment safeguard against double jeopardy and self-incrimination; the Sixth Amendment provisions for speedy and public trials by impartial juries of the state and district where the crime was committed, and the right to counsel and other procedural protections; and the Eighth Amendment proscription of cruel and unusual punishment.

THE EQUAL PROTECTION OF THE LAWS

Using the Fourteenth Amendment due process clause to apply the Bill of Rights to the states was often controversial, opposed by dissenting Supreme Court justices and advocates of states' rights alike, as an unwarranted national invasion of state power. But another part of the Fourteenth Amendment caused far more political controversy—the equal protection clause, which prohibited a state from denying to any person within its jurisdiction the equal protection of the laws. The Court held, in *Brown* v. *Board of Education* (1954), that the legally segregated school systems which existed in southern and border states and the District of Columbia were intrinsically unequal, denying equal protection of the laws to the segregated black students. The Court applied the equal protection clause of the Fourteenth Amendment to support its ruling concerning the states, and in the case involving the District of Columbia, *Bolling* v. *Sharpe* (1954), held that equal protection standards governed national action under the Fifth Amendment due process clause. Congress, which ruled the nation's capital, no less than the states had to uphold equal protection.

The equal protection revolution started slowly, as the Supreme Court allowed the implementation of its *Brown* decision to be delayed pending federal district courts' determinations that local school systems were ready for the change. Directed to proceed with "all deliberate speed," the lower courts nevertheless acted cautiously in applying the potentially politically inflammatory *Brown* decree. Desegregation came to the South slowly, but, spurred by the Civil Rights movement of the 1960s, most southern schools were fully desegregated by the late 1960s. Desegregation was helped also by federal court decisions that required the bussing of school children if necessary to achieve integration in formerly segregated districts.

EXPANSION OF EQUAL PROTECTION

As school desegregation was finally being achieved, the federal courts began in earnest to extend equal protection standards to new groups and policy arenas. The *Brown* decision had overturned de jure segregation. The initial bussing decisions applied only to school districts with a history of legal discrimination. As the civil rights movement gathered strength in the 1960s its effects were widely felt. Not only blacks but other minorities began to demand equal rights and opportunities. Feminism gathered strength and women began to raise the consciousness of society about gender discrimination, which the Equal Rights Amendment was designed to eliminate.

PASSAGE OF THE CIVIL RIGHTS ACT OF 1964

Responding to civil rights protests and his own abhorrence of discrimination, President Lyndon B. Johnson, after his overwhelming 1964 electoral victory, successfully led the fight for the passage of the 1964 Civil Rights Act, which provided in Title VI:

> No person in the United States shall, on the ground of race, color, or national origin, be excluded from participation in, be denied the benefits of, or be subjected to discrimination under any program or activity receiving federal financial assistance.

Title VII of the law governed equal employment opportunity and banned discrimination on the grounds of race, color, religion, sex, or national origin. Title VII did not provide for a federal funds cutoff remedy, but for enforcement of its provisions by the Equal Employment Opportunity Commission, which investigates charges of discrimination, attempts informal settlement, and works with other agencies to secure enforcement, including referral of cases to the Attorney General for legal action.

ENFORCEMENT OF THE CIVIL RIGHTS ACT THROUGH AFFIRMATIVE ACTION

To enforce Titles VI and VII, President Johnson added a new twist to the law when he issued his famous 1965 executive order that required recipients of federal funds, which included employers and educational institutions of all kinds, that had a history of discrimination, to install affirmative action programs that would give preferential treatment to minorities and women in hiring, job advancement, and student admissions. The purpose of affirmative action is to remedy the effects of past discrimination. This discrimination placed disadvantaged groups in an unfair competitive position. Proponents of affirmative action believe that remedial action is necessary to give equal opportunity to minorities and women, even if it means "reverse discrimination," which in effect discriminates against white males who have never been denied equal opportunity on the basis of their race or sex.

Affirmative action programs became highly controversial. Johnson's executive order went beyond the intent of Congress, a claim strongly made on the basis of a close reading of the law. Congress neither explicitly authorized affirmative action nor did it provide for a cutoff of funds under Title VII, which the executive order authorizes. On a more general and philosophical level, affirmative action programs may be viewed as discriminatory, establishing racial quotas or special treatment of minorities and women that deny equal access to opportunities on the basis of merit. Also questioned is the necessity of special treatment. In response, proponents of affirmative action argue that truly equal opportunity requires, at least for a time, the preferential treatment of groups that society has dealt with unfairly.

DEBATE FOCUS

Affirmative Action—Equal Opportunity or Reverse Discrimination?

A SUPREME COURT JUSTICE SUPPORTS AFFIRMATIVE ACTION

"MARSHALL NAMED FOR HIGH COURT, ITS FIRST NEGRO," blared the *New York Times* headline after President Lyndon B. Johnson's historic decision to nominate Thurgood Marshall to the Supreme Court in 1967 to fill the vacancy left by the retiring Tom Clark.* The son of a Pullman porter and the grandson of a slave, Marshall had a distinguished legal career at the time Johnson chose him. Born in 1908, he graduated cum laude from Lincoln University in 1930, and received his degree from Howard University Law School in 1933 at the height of the Great Depression.

Marshall began his legal career with the National Association for the Advancement of Colored People (NAACP), becoming the head of its Legal Defense and Education Fund in 1940. He spearheaded the national efforts of the NAACP to protect the civil rights of blacks, culminating in the 1954 *Brown* case, where Marshall was counsel for the black plaintiffs. His reasoned and empassioned arguments before the Supreme Court helped to lay the foundation for its momentous decision.

President John F. Kennedy appointed Marshall to the United States Court of Appeals for the Second Circuit, where he served from 1961 to 1965 when Lyndon B. Johnson chose him to be the United States Solicitor General. Marshall argued and won the government's case before the Supreme Court supporting the 1965 Voting Rights Act, against a challenge that it was unconstitutional.

Although Marshall was strongly opposed by all but one of the Democratic senators from the deep South, spearheaded by Democrat-turned-Republican Strom Thurmond of South Carolina, he easily won confirmation by a vote of 69 to 11 on August 31, 1967.† A month after the Senate confirmation, President Johnson, in a gesture recognizing the importance of the occasion, personally went to the Supreme Court to witness Marshall's swearing-in ceremony.

Marshall predictably took his strong liberal views, especially on civil rights issues, to the Supreme Court, where he has consistently sided with justices supporting judicial activism and a strong governmental role in the protection of individual rights. A forceful advocate of affirmative action, Marshall argues

*For the events surrounding the nomination, see Henry J. Abraham, *Justices and Presidents* (New York: Oxford University Press, 1974), pp. 266–269.

†Southern Democrats voting for Marshall were William J. Fulbright of Arkansas, Albert Gore of Tennessee, and William Spong, Jr., of Virginia. Republican Howard Baker, Jr., of Tennessee also supported Marshall, as did both Texas senators, Democrat Ralph Yarborough and conservative Republican John Tower.

in the following selection that past discrimination against blacks requires remedial government action, including "benign" discrimination *in favor* of blacks. His views are drawn from his opinion in *University of California Regents* v. *Bakke* (1978), which involved a challenge to the University of California, Davis Medical School affirmative action program under which a number of seats for the incoming class were reserved for blacks and other minorities. Bakke, a white male applicant, had been denied admission, and claimed that his Medical Board scores and other academic qualifications were higher than many who had been admitted under the affirmative action plan, resulting in discrimination against him in violation of the equal protection clause of the Fourteenth Amendment. Marshall joined the Court's majority opinion holding that racial qualifications could be taken into account in admissions programs; however, he wanted the Court to go further by upholding the racial quota system of the Davis Medical School. But Justice Louis Powell, who had joined Marshall and four of his colleagues to form a majority that supported taking into account race in admitting students, swung his vote on racial quotas to the conservative side to form a majority stating quotas were discriminatory in violation of the Fourteenth Amendment and the 1964 Civil Rights Act.

3

T. MARSHALL

The Need for Affirmative Action (from University of California Regents v. Bakke)*

JUSTICE THURGOOD MARSHALL

I agree with the judgment of the Court [in the Bakke case] only insofar as it permits a university to consider the race of an applicant in making admissions decisions. I do not agree [with the Court's majority] that petitioner's admissions program [which establishes a *quota* in the first year class for racial minorities] violates the Constitution. For it must be remembered that, during most of the past 200 years, the Constitution as interpreted by this Court did not prohibit the most ingenious and pervasive forms of discrimination against the Negro. Now, when a State acts to remedy the effects of that legacy of discrimination, I cannot believe that this same Constitution stands as a barrier.

I

A. Three hundred and fifty years ago, the Negro was dragged to this country in chains to be sold into slavery. Uprooted from his homeland and thrust into bondage for forced labor, the slave was deprived of all legal rights. It was unlawful to teach him to read; he could be sold away from his family and friends at the whim of his master; and killing or maiming him was

*Concurring opinion by Thurgood Marshall in University of California *Regents* v. *Bakke*, 438 U.S.265, 387 (1978).

not a crime. The system of slavery brutalized and dehumanized both master and slave.[1]

The denial of human rights was etched into the American Colonies' first attempts at establishing self-government. When the colonists determined to seek their independence from England, they drafted a unique document cataloguing their grievances against the King and proclaiming as "self-evident" that "all men are created equal" and are endowed "with certain unalienable Rights," including those to "Life, Liberty and the pursuit of Happiness." The self-evident truths and the unalienable rights were intended, however, to apply only to white men. An earlier draft of the Declaration of Independence, submitted by Thomas Jefferson to the Continental Congress, had included among the charges against the King that

> "[h]e has waged cruel war against human nature itself, violating its most sacred rights of life and liberty in the persons of a distant people who never offended him, captivating and carrying them into slavery in another hemisphere, or to incur miserable death in their transportation thither."

The Southern delegation insisted that the charge be deleted; the colonists themselves were implicated in the slave trade, and inclusion of this claim might have made it more difficult to justify the continuation of slavery once the ties to England were severed. Thus, even as the colonists embarked on a course to secure their own freedom and equality, they ensured perpetuation of the system that deprived a whole race of those rights.

The implicit protection of slavery embodied in the Declaration of Independence was made explicit in the Constitution, which treated a slave as being equivalent to three-fifths of a person for purposes of apportioning representatives and taxes among the States. Art. I, § 2. The Constitution also contained a clause ensuring that the "Migration or Importation" of slaves into the existing States would be legal until at least 1808, Art. I, § 9, and a fugitive slave clause requiring that when a slave escaped to another State, he must be returned on the claim of the master, Art. IV, § 2. In their declaration of the principles that were to provide the cornerstone of the new Nation, therefore, the Framers made it plain that "we the people," for whose protection the Constitution was designed, did not include those whose skins were the wrong color. . . .

The individual States likewise established the machinery to protect the system of slavery through the promulgation of the Slave Codes, which were designed primarily to defend the property interest of the owner in his slave. The position of the Negro slave as mere property was confirmed by this Court in *Dred Scott* v. *Sandford*, 19 How. 393 (1857), holding that the Missouri Compromise—which prohibited slavery in the portion of the Louisiana

---

[1]The history recounted here is perhaps too well known to require documentation. But I must acknowledge the authorities on which I rely in retelling it. J. Franklin, From Slavery to Freedom (4th ed. 1974) (hereinafter Franklin); R. Kluger, Simple Justice (1975) (hereinafter Kluger); C. Woodward, The Strange Career of Jim Crow (3d ed. 1974) (hereinafter Woodward).

Purchase Territory north of Missouri—was unconstitutional because it deprived slave owners of their property without due process. The Court declared that under the Constitution a slave was property, and "[t]he right to traffic in it, like an ordinary article of merchandise and property, was guaranteed to the citizens of the United States . . . ." *Id.*, at 451. The Court further concluded that Negroes were not intended to be included as citizens under the Constitution but were "regarded as beings of an inferior order . . . altogether unfit to associate with the white race, either in social or political relations; and so far inferior, that they had no rights which the white man was bound to respect . . . ." *Id.*, at 407.

B. The status of the Negro as property was officially erased by his emancipation at the end of the Civil War. But the long-awaited emancipation, while freeing the Negro from slavery, did not bring him citizenship or equality in any meaningful way. . . . Despite the passage of the Thirteenth, Fourteenth, and Fifteenth Amendments, the Negro was systematically denied the rights those Amendments were supposed to secure. The combined actions and inactions of the State and Federal Governments maintained Negroes in a position of legal inferiority for another century after the Civil War.

The Southern States took the first steps to re-enslave the Negroes. Immediately following the end of the Civil War, many of the provisional legislatures passed Black Codes, similar to the Slave Codes, which, among other things, limited the rights of Negroes to own or rent property and permitted imprisonment for breach of employment contracts. Over the next several decades, the South managed to disenfranchise the Negroes in spite of the Fifteenth Amendment by various techniques, including poll taxes, deliberately complicated balloting processes, property and literacy qualifications, and finally the white primary.

Congress responded to the legal disabilities being imposed in the Southern States by passing the Reconstruction Acts and the Civil Rights Acts. Congress also responded to the needs of the Negroes at the end of the Civil War by establishing the Bureau of Refugees, Freedmen, and Abandoned Lands, better known as the Freedmen's Bureau, to supply food, hospitals, land, and education to the newly freed slaves. Thus, for a time it seemed as if the Negro might be protected from the continued denial of his civil rights and might be relieved of the disabilities that prevented him from taking his place as a free and equal citizen.

That time, however, was short-lived. Reconstruction came to a close, and, with the assistance of the Court, the Negro was rapidly stripped of his new civil rights. . . .

The Court's ultimate blow to the Civil War Amendments and to the equality of Negroes came in *Plessy* v. *Ferguson*, (1896), . . . upholding a Louisiana law that required railway companies to provide "equal but separate" accommodations for whites and Negroes. . . . Ignoring totally the realities of the positions of the two races, the Court remarked:

> "We consider the underlying fallacy of the plaintiff's argument to consist in the assumption that the enforced separation of the two races stamps the colored race with a badge of inferiority. If this be so, it is not by reason of anything found in the act, but solely because the colored race chooses to put that construction upon it."

Mr. Justice Harlan's dissenting opinion recognized the bankruptcy of the Court's reasoning. He noted that the "real meaning" of the legislation was "that colored citizens are so inferior and degraded that they cannot be allowed to sit in public coaches occupied by white citizens.". . . He expressed his fear that if like laws were enacted in other States, "the effect would be in the highest degree mischievous." . . . Although slavery would have disappeared, the States would retain the power "to interfere with the full enjoyment of the blessings of freedom; to regulate civil rights, common to all citizens, upon the basis of race; and to place in a condition of legal inferiority a large body of American citizens. . . ."

The fears of Mr. Justice Harlan were soon to be realized. In the wake of *Plessy*, many States expanded their Jim Crow laws, which had up until that time been limited primarily to passenger trains and schools. The segregation of the races was extended to residential areas, parks, hospitals, theaters, waiting rooms, and bathrooms. There were even statutes and ordinances which authorized separate phone booths for Negroes and whites, which required that textbooks used by children of one race be kept separate from those used by the other, and which required that Negro and white prostitutes be kept in separate districts. . . .

Nor were the laws restricting the rights of Negroes limited solely to the Southern States. In many of the Northern States, the Negro was denied the right to vote, prevented from serving on juries, and excluded from theaters, restaurants, hotels, and inns. Under President Wilson, the Federal government began to require segregation in government buildings; desks of Negro employees were curtained off; separate bathrooms and separate tables in the cafeterias were provided; and even the galleries of the Congress were segregated. When his segregationist policies were attacked, President Wilson responded that segregation was " 'not humiliating but a benefit' " and that he was " 'rendering [the Negroes] more safe in their possession of office and less likely to be discriminated against.' "

The enforced segregation of the races continued into the middle of the 20th century. In both World Wars, Negroes were for the most part confined to separate military units; it was not until 1948 that an end to segregation in the military was ordered by President Truman. And the history of the exclusion of Negro children from white public schools is too well known and recent to require repeating here. That Negroes were deliberately excluded from public graduate and professional schools—and thereby denied the opportunity to become doctors, lawyers, engineers, and the like—is also well established. It is of course true that some of the Jim Crow laws (which the decisions of this Court had helped to foster) were struck down by this Court in a series of decisions leading up to *Brown* v. *Board of Education* (1954). . . . Those decisions, however, did not automatically end segregation, nor did they move Negroes from a position of legal inferiority to one of equality. The legacy of years of slavery and of years of second-class citizenship in the wake of emancipation could not be so easily eliminated.

II

The position of the Negro today in America is the tragic but inevitable consequence of centuries of unequal treatment. Measured by any benchmark of comfort or achievement, meaningful equality remains a distant dream for the Negro.

A Negro child today has a life expectancy which is shorter by more than five years than that of a white child. The Negro child's mother is over three times more likely to die of complications in childbirth, and the infant mortality rate for Negroes is nearly twice that for whites. The median income of the Negro family is only 60% that of the median of a white family, and the percentage of Negroes who live in families with incomes below the poverty line is nearly four times greater than that of whites.

When the Negro child reaches working age, he finds that America offers him significantly less than it offers his white counterpart. For Negro adults, the unemployment rate is twice that of whites, and the unemployment rate for Negro teenagers is nearly three times that of white teenagers. A Negro male who completes four years of college can expect a median annual income of merely $110 more than a white male who has only a high school diploma. Although Negroes represent 11.5% of the population, they are only 1.2% of the lawyers and judges, 2% of the physicians, 2.3% of the dentists, 1.1% of the engineers and 2.6% of the college and university professors.

The relationship between these figures and the history of unequal treatment afforded to the Negro cannot be denied. At every point from birth to death the impact of the past is reflected in the still disfavored position of the Negro.

In light of the sorry history of discrimination and its devastating impact on the lives of Negroes, bringing the Negro into the mainstream of American life should be a state interest of the highest order. To fail to do so is to ensure that America will forever remain a divided society.

III

I do not believe that the Fourteenth Amendment requires us to accept that fate. Neither its history nor our past cases lend any support to the conclusion that a university may not remedy the cumulative effects of society's discrimination by giving consideration to race in an effort to increase the number and percentage of Negro doctors.

As has been demonstrated in our joint opinion, this Court's past cases establish the constitutionality of race-conscious remedial measures. Beginning with the school desegregation cases, we recognized that even absent a judicial or legislative finding of constitutional violation, a school board constitutionally could consider the race of students in making school-assignment decisions. . . .

Nothing in those cases suggests that a university cannot similarly act to remedy past discrimination. . . .

IV

While I applaud the judgment of the Court that a university may consider race in its admissions process, it is more than a little ironic that, after several hundred years of class-based discrimination against Negroes, the Court is unwilling to hold that a class-based remedy for that discrimination is permissible. In declining to so hold, today's judgment ignores the fact that for several hundred years Negroes have been discriminated against, not as individuals, but rather solely because of the color of their skins. It is unnecessary in 20th-century America to have individual Negroes demonstrate that they have been victims of racial discrimination; the racism of our society has been so pervasive that none, regardless of wealth or position, has managed to escape its impact. The experience of Negroes in America has been different in kind, not just in degree, from that of other ethnic groups. It is not merely the history of slavery alone but also that a whole people were marked as inferior by the law. And that mark has endured. The dream of America as the great melting pot has not been realized for the Negro; because of his skin color he never even made it into the pot.

These differences in the experience of the Negro make it difficult for me to accept that Negroes cannot be afforded greater protection under the Fourteenth Amendment where it is necessary to remedy the effects of past discrimination. . . .

It is because of legacy of unequal treatment that we now must permit the institutions of this society to give consideration to race in making decisions about who will hold the positions of influence, affluence, and prestige in America. For far too long, the doors to those positions have been shut to Negroes. If we are ever to become a fully integrated society, one in which the color of a person's skin will not determine the opportunities available to him or her, we must be willing to take steps to open those doors. I do not believe that anyone can truly look into America's past and still find that a remedy for the effects of that past is impermissible. . . .

Affirmative Action—Equal Opportunity or Reverse Discrimination?

A BLACK CONSERVATIVE SCHOLAR ARGUES AGAINST
AFFIRMATIVE ACTION

Hoover Institute scholar Thomas Sowell has written extensively and controversially about ethnic America. As a conservative black who argues that affirmative action is not desirable nor necessary to give black Americans equal opportunity, he stands outside of the mainstream of black politics. Blacks and liberals alike attack him as a traitor to what they feel should be his cause. But Sowell sticks to his position that the facts do not warrant affirmative action, a provocative argument he takes in the following selection.

T. SOWELL

4

The Degeneration of Racial Controversy

THOMAS SOWELL

There was a time, back in the heady days of the civil rights movement, when people expected to "solve" the racial "problem"—almost as if life were an academic exercise, with answers in the back of the book. Twenty years and many disappointments later, the question is whether we can even discuss the subject rationally.

The poisonous atmosphere surrounding any attempt to debate issues involving race and ethnicity is demonstrated in many ways. In addition to the usual *ad hominem* attacks and overheated rhetoric, there has also developed a fundamental disregard for the truth, which has become widespread not only among some journalists, but is even beginning to creep into scholarly publications. Not since the days of Senator Joe McCarthy has the drive to discredit so overridden every other consideration. Lies out of whole cloth are not uncommon and straw men dot the landscape.

SAMPLE STRAW MEN

After a decade of research, writing, and lecturing in opposition to the theory of genetic racial inferiority, including several articles and chapters of books devoted solely to that subject, I have been depicted as a *supporter*

Excerpts abridged from pp. 124-129, 131, 133, and 135 of "The Degeneration of Racial Controversy" from Civil Rights: Rhetoric or Reality? *by Thomas Sowell. Copyright © 1984 by Thomas Sowell. By permission of William Morrow & Company.*

of genetic racial inferiority theories by Lem Tucker on the nationwide *CBS Morning News* and by a professor of economics in the "scholarly" *Journal of Ethnic Studies.*

In a passage so phrased that a reader could easily think that it was a direct quote from me, syndicated columnist Carl Rowan expressed what was supposedly my position on my own career:

> I did this all on my own, with hard work, so I don't want government to give any lazy bastard anything.

What I actually wrote about my career was:

> It would be premature at best and presumptuous at worst to attempt to draw sweeping or definitive conclusions from my personal experiences. It would be especially unwarranted to draw Horatio Alger conclusions, that perseverance and/or ability "win out" despite obstacles. The fact is, I was losing in every way until my life was changed by the Korean War, the draft, and the G.I. Bill—none of which I can take credit for. I have no false modesty about having seized the opportunity and worked to make it pay off, but there is no way to avoid the fact that there first had to be an opportunity to seize.

The Rowan version was echoed by CBS correspondent Lem Tucker, who told millions of viewers of the *CBS Morning News* that my position was "that he alone, almost without bootstraps, pulled himself out of the ghetto through Harvard and the University of Chicago." . . .

The name of the game is showing that one's opponent is "simplistic." How it is done obviously does not matter. . . .

An almost comic example of the genesis of straw men grew out of reactions to a pair of articles of mine in the *Washington Post.* I argued that some blacks from the old elite, which denigrated and discriminated against other blacks, were now exhibiting the extreme reactions typical of reformed sinners by being blacker-than-thou. Among the examples was Patricia Roberts Harris, once a member of a sorority which refused to admit darker-skinned college girls. The uproar that followed mention of this fact—too widely known to be denied—produced the straw man that I was criticizing Mrs. Harris for being light-skinned! Mrs. Harris herself said that I was using "South African apartheid concepts of racial gradations." Roger Wilkins said in *The Nation* that I was denouncing black leaders for "having light skins," while St. Clair Drake accused me of "an almost paranoid preoccupation with a nonexistent 'light skin elite.' " Other individuals and publications have echoed the same theme. Not one of them has given any inkling that I had criticized *behavior*, not complexion. . . .

Straw men need to be examined not only in themselves, but also as indicators of what positions are too weak to defend in any other way. Many of these positions involve discrimination and policies for dealing with it.

"REPRESENTATION" AND DISCRIMINATION

For at least twenty years, the media, politicians, the courts and intellectuals have been using numerical "representation" data to infer racial, sex, and other discrimination. The issue here is not whether any discrimination exists. The issue is whether what is used as evidence is in fact evidence. In a legal sense, the question is whether it distinguishes between the innocent and the guilty. In a larger social sense, the question is whether it clarifies or obscures the causes of very real and sometimes very large economic differences between groups.

One of many reasons why various racial and ethnic groups are not equally represented in all occupations and institutions is that they differ greatly in their average age . . . Those who put together straw men try to turn this into an argument that age differences alone explain virtually all racial and ethnic differences, to the complete exclusion of discrimination.

. . . [T]he U.S. Commission on Civil Rights, in a November 1982 report, depicted me as claiming that group differences result from differences in age and education and are "not a result of anything else." But it is the Civil Rights Commission that has had a single, all-purpose explanation of intergroup differences—discrimination. It is precisely in opposition to this automatic inference of discrimination that such factors as age—and numerous other variables—are mentioned.

In comparing people with the "same" education, to show what income differences remain as the effects of discrimination, the U.S. Commission on Civil Rights resolutely ignores vast *qualitative* differences in education that exist at every level. Black and Hispanic youngsters do not take as much mathematics in school, nor score nearly as high on standardized mathematics tests as white or Asian youngsters. Similarly, black and Hispanic Ph.D.'s specialize in a vastly different mix of subjects from those in which white or Asian Ph.D.'s specialize, the former concentrating in subjects that do not require mathematics and do not pay as much. To call group differences in income between people with the "same" education, in a purely quantitative sense, "discrimination" is to play games with words. . . .

THE CASE OF THE VANISHING ASIANS

Two of the recurring themes in the literature on race and ethnicity are (1) the enormous impact of past discrimination on current incomes, and (2) the great difference between white ethnic groups, who can eventually blend into the American society, and groups marked by indelible color differences, who cannot. I have been repeatedly accused of ignoring this latter difference. But I have in fact discussed this difference in every book

I have written on ethnicity—and have repeatedly found empirically that there is less there than meets the eye.

Asians disappear mysteriously from the discussions of those who make the white-nonwhite difference economically crucial. So do West Indian blacks.

A massive study by the U.S. Civil Rights Commission was typical of this approach—and of the vanishing Asians. Their 1982 report inundated the public and the media with statistical differences ("disparities" and "inequities") in the employment and income patterns of blacks, Hispanics, and women. Against this backdrop, they unfurled the usual explanations of racism and sexism. But not one speck of data on Asians appeared in this voluminous compilation—even though the explanations being offered would apply to Asians, as well as to other physically distinct minorities.

Near the end of the report, Asians were mentioned in passing, but still without any economic data. The Civil Rights Commission acknowledged that there were "discriminatory immigration laws" against Asians in the past, but was strangely reticent about acknowledging any of the other massive discriminations—not to mention violence and deaths—that they suffered. The final word of the Commission's brief discussion of Asians:

> In the relatively small number of occupations in which Asians were allowed to participate they were able to attain a moderate level of economic success.

In short, Asians are *confined* to such occupations as mathematicians, scientists, and engineers! By a rare coincidence, they seem to be confined to precisely the same kinds of occupations in other countries. This form of racism seems particularly odd, since the net result is that Asians, including Pacific islanders, now average ten percent higher incomes than whites, according to the 1980 Census. If this is only "moderate" success, whites must be failures.

BOOTSTRAPS AND BLAME

One of the recurring themes in attempts to discredit critics of the welfare state is that they would leave the disadvantaged to lift themselves by their own bootstraps. "Bootstraps" is one of the classic straw man words of our time—a word used *only* to describe someone *else's* philosophy. No one has advocated it but everyone is sure that someone else has. It is symptomatic of a broader misconception that automatically translates statements of causation into statements of advice to the disadvantaged or moral statements of "blame" for the "victim."

Various publications have referred to the advice supposedly offered to the disadvantaged in [my book] *Ethnic America* —but none could ever quote any of it. There is a reason: There is no such advice there. Partly that is because so many decisions have been taken out of people's hands by the government.

Nevertheless, I am depicted as saying that blacks should be following the path of the Jews—or the Irish, the Chinese, or others, according to taste. Yet this would be strange advice indeed after my pointing out repeatedly how many of the options of former times have been destroyed by government policy. Walter Williams' book, *The State Against Blacks*, is built precisely around that theme. Yet he too is often accused of offering the same advice.

The confusion between analysis and advice has become enshrined in media thinking. One of many clever journalistic devices is to ask: "But what would you say to the welfare mother, the unemployed black teenager, the disadvantaged Hispanic?" One may as well ask a medical researcher: "But what would you say to the mother whose child is dying of leukemia?" The purpose of cause-and-effect analysis is not to offer advice or consolation to people in impossible situations, but to attempt to reduce the occurrence of such situations.

Whatever advice I have offered on public policy has almost invariably been directed toward policy makers. This advice has ranged from deregulation to education vouchers to repeal of minimum wage laws to tougher crime control. Little of this real advice has ever been quoted, certainly not nearly as much as the fictitious advice.

"Blaming the victim" is another of the mindless clichés of our time. Blame is as irrelevant as bootstraps. No one can be blamed if he did not bring the same skills from Mexico as someone else brought from Germany, or if his school or home did not teach him what people need to know in order to function in a modern technological society. But neither can employers be blamed if people who have more of the required skills are more in demand and others "under-represented." In scientific and technical occupations, for example, Hispanics are under-represented relative to Germans *in Hispanic countries.* Nor is this peculiar. Most of the members of the St. Petersburg Academy of Sciences under the czars were of German ancestry. Chinese students are heavily concentrated in technical fields, from Malaysia to Australia to the United States. People are not magically homogenized by crossing a national border. If anyone should be blamed, it is those who argue as if they are.

THE IRRELEVANCE OF EVIDENCE

Many who argue most vehemently about race and ethnicity make no distinction whatever between (1) conclusions that follow logically as corollaries from their general vision of society and (2) conclusions for which there is empirical evidence. Indeed, concrete evidence against their conclusions may be countered by *ad hoc* explanations, whose only support is their consonance with the prevailing vision.

Those who support affirmative action, for example, are faced with the embarrassing fact that the economic rise of minorities has slowed noticeably as the "equal opportunity" policies of the 1960s metamorphosed into affirmative action quotas in the early 1970s. An *ad hoc* explanation offered by [sociologist] Christopher Jencks is that "the gains during the 1960s were in 'easy' areas, where resistance was minimal." He adds: "Achieving comparable gains during the 1970s was bound to require stronger pressures on employers." Not a speck of evidence was offered for any aspect of this explanation.

In reality, the historical data show that (1) the economic rise of minorities *preceded* passage of the Civil Rights Act of 1964 by many years, (2) the existing upward trend was *not* accelerated, either by that Act or by quotas that became generally mandatory in 1971, and (3) during the era of affirmative action, such disadvantaged blacks as young males with little experience or education, and members of female-headed households, actually *retrogressed* relative to whites of the same description, while more advantaged blacks rose both absolutely and relative to their white counterparts. In short, although affirmative action invokes the name of the disadvantaged, these are precisely the people who have fallen further behind under its auspices.

Attempts to blame general conditions in the economy or racism among employers run into the hard fact that both advantaged and disadvantaged progress are measured during the same years in the same economy, and one is just as black as the other, especially to racist employers.

These are not mere curious facts. They illustrate effects which elementary economic principles would predict. As the government makes it more dangerous to fire, demote, or even fail to promote, members of minority groups, this tends to increase the demand for the more demonstrably able among them and reduce the demand for the average or below average, or those with too little experience to provide a reassuring track record. But for the true believers in affirmative action, both analysis and evidence are irrelevant.

As in so many other areas of social policy, what matters most politically is not the logic or the facts but the vision—in this case a vision of an incorrigibly corrupt society, whose only saving grace is the presence of a few wise and noble souls, like themselves. Hamlet warned: "Lay not that flattering unction to your soul." But the laying of flattering unction to one's soul has become a major industry, extending far beyond race.

Nor is this a recent development. Back in the late 1960s, Professor Charles L. Black wrote in the *Harvard Law Review* that allowing housing decisions to be made by the marketplace meant "abandoning the Negro to the slum-ghetto that 'private enterprise' has made ready for him." Despite the apparent certitude and air of moral condescension characteristic of those with the civil rights vision, Professor Black advanced no evidence whatever for this conclusion.

In reality, most northern big cities had far less residential segregation of blacks in the late nineteenth century than today, even though (1) there were no "fair housing" laws or policies then, (2) racially restrictive covenants were perfectly legal, (3) blacks had no political power, (4) the federal government took little or no interest in blacks after the Compromise of 1877 [ending federal occupation of the South and returning political control to the whites], and (5) the courts were at best indifferent to blacks during the era from the *Dred Scott* decision of 1857 through *Plessy* v. *Ferguson* in 1896.

In short, all the supposed "prerequisites" for ending rigid ghettoization did not exist—but neither did rigid ghettoization. What changed— dramatically and suddenly—in the early twentieth century were not "perceptions" but realities. The great migrations from the South flooded the northern cities with blacks far less acculturated than those already there—a point made bitterly in the black newspapers of the times and still expressed years later by the "old settlers" in the black community. Rigid segregation in housing developed in this era, in response to this reality. Where the influx from the South occurred earlier—as in Washington, D.C.—the change in racial residential patterns occurred earlier. Where the influx from the South occurred much later—as in San Francisco—the change in racial residential patterns also occurred much later.

"Private enterprise," the supposed villain of the piece, existed both in the early era of wide dispersion of blacks among whites and in the later era of rigid segregation. The striking down of racially restrictive covenants by the Supreme Court in 1948 made no dramatic difference in residential housing patterns. Nor has the rise of government housing projects, free of the taint of private enterprise. As in so many other areas, those with the civil rights vision have made that vision a substitute for evidence.

Nowhere is evidence more irrelevant than when making assertions about the motives of opponents. For example, Professor William Julius Wilson's book, *The Declining Significance of Race*, was explained away in this fashion:

> By writing a book of this nature, Wilson seems bent on being accepted or begging to get into the white academic world because this is what you have to do when you're not in. You're on the periphery . . .

The facts? Wilson is chairman of the department of sociology at the University of Chicago—the top ranked sociology department in the nation. How he could get any more "in" is hard to imagine. A distinguished economist named Joseph A. Schumpeter once pointed out that the only person's motivation we really know is our own—and that what we project onto others provides, at best, clues to our own motives. The man who made this charge against Wilson is a professor of education in an undistinguished university. The charge has, however, been repeated in the media.

A common charge against me is that my own career is due to the very affirmative action I criticize. In all the places where this charge has been repeated, not one bit of evidence has yet been offered. It so happens that I have not achieved anything in my career that was not achieved by other blacks before me—and therefore long before affirmative action.

My graduation from Harvard came more than 80 years after the first black student graduated from Harvard. When I received a Ph.D. from the University of Chicago, it was from an institution that had already produced a disproportionate share of all the black Ph.D.'s in the history of the United States. E. Franklin Frazier was working on his doctorate at Chicago before I was born.

St. Clair Drake asserts that my appointment at Cornell University was "due to black militant pressure"—but without evidence or any apparent sense of need for evidence. When I was offered an appointment at Cornell in December 1964, there weren't enough black students there to pressure anybody to do anything. Blacks were so rare at Cornell that when my wife and I encountered another black couple at a campus restaurant, we all four stopped dead in our tracks, and then burst out laughing.

But even at Cornell, I was not the first black professor of economics. Nor was I the first black economist in the Labor Department or at AT&T, among other places. In all these places I was doing what other blacks had already done—before affirmative action.

The unsupported assertion that my career is due to affirmative action is sometimes accompanied by the unsupported assertion that writing about race has made my career. But in reality I had tenure at U.C.L.A. more than a year before numerical "goals and timetables" were mandated—and before ever publishing a single article or book on race. I had published books on economics and articles in economics journals—as had Abram L. Harris, a black economist a generation before me, who was a full professor at the University of Chicago when I was a graduate student there.

There is no reason why critics should have known such personal trivia. But there is also no reason why they should make sweeping assertions without knowing what they are talking about.

THE CURRENT CLIMATE

The strong feelings and contending visions that surround issues of race and ethnicity are not enough to explain the current intellectual intolerance and reckless disregard for truth. There have always been strong feelings and contending visions. Yet when W.E.B. Du Bois wrote a highly critical review of a book by his arch rival, Booker T. Washington, he nevertheless referred to Washington's "very evident sincerity of purpose" and acknowledged that he "commands not simply the applause of those who believe in his theories, but the respect of those who do not." We have come a long way since then, but not all of it has been progress.

In the early years of the civil rights movement, there was not only an optimism about the future but a confidence that the facts and rational thinking were on the side of civil rights advocates. *Evidence was an ally.* Chief Justice Earl Warren's portentous reference to "modern authority" in *Brown* v. *Board of Education* symbolized the role of "social science."

One of the many painful contrasts between that era and today is that evidence is increasingly evaded by those who speak in the name of civil rights. Whether it is low test scores or high crime rates, the first order of business is to dismiss the evidence and discredit those who bring it. Even good news—successful minority schools or the rise of a black middle class—is denounced when it does not fit the preconceived vision. Unvarnished facts are today more likely to arouse suspicion and hostility than any joyous anticipation of more ammunition for the good fight.

There are reasons for this. Despite much racial progress, there have also been some very fundamental disappointments. Ghettos persist, and in many ways are becoming worse for those trapped in them. School integration has largely been thwarted by the demographic facts of "white flight." But even where it has occurred, it has produced neither the educational nor the social miracles once expected. Job barriers have come down but black teenage unemployment has soared to several times what it was 30 years ago. Many white allies in the early struggles for civil rights have become critics of the later phases, such as affirmative action and busing. A small but growing number of black critics has also appeared.

How and why this all happened is a long and complicated story. In essence, however, two things have happened: (1) the battle for civil rights was won, decisively, two decades ago, and (2) the succeeding years have painfully revealed that blatant denials of civil rights were not the universal explanation of social or racial problems. Intellectual and institutional inertia persists in calling racial and ethnic political issues "civil rights" issues and often designing strategy, policies and rhetoric as if they were. Andrew Young perhaps best epitomized this tendency when he said:

> We struggled in the 50s to integrate the schools and the buses. We struggled in the 60s to integrate the lunch counters and the ballot boxes. And we've got to struggle in the 80s to integrate the money.

But the mindset and agenda of the past are no longer working. Like the blind men who each felt only one part of the elephant, many minority leaders mistake that for the whole elephant. Those who point out that other parts are quite different, and that the whole elephant is quite different, are seen as contradicting a tangible reality which has been seized upon and held fast for years. For many, "discrimination" and "racism" are not partial truths but whole truths, not just things to oppose but explanations to cling to, like a security blanket. Evidence that undermines the status of these old enemies also undermines the comforting vision that has grown up around them.

People do not change their vision of the world the way they change clothes or replace old light bulbs. But change they must if they mean to survive. No individual (or group) is going to capture all of reality in his vision. If the only reaction to other visions—or uncomfortable evidence—is blind mudslinging, then the limitations that are common to all human beings become, for them, ideological prisons.

CHAPTER THREE
The Functions of Political Parties

Democratic politics, once it encompasses more than town meetings and small groups in which people can participate directly in decision making, has traditionally involved political parties. They are the organizations, composed of a wide array of political players, leaders through followers, that supply candidates for elected offices and influence patronage appointments. Within legislative bodies political parties choose leaders and make committee assignments. The majority party controls the seats of power, such as the Speaker of the House of Representatives, the majority leaders on both sides of Capitol Hill, and committee chairmanships. Party affiliations within government make a real difference in the allocation of power.

PARTIES AND POPULAR PARTICIPATION IN GOVERNMENT

In democratic theory and practice, parties serve a broader purpose than merely providing rewards to their members in the form of offices and other positions of power. Parties are supposed to bridge the gap between people and governments by developing programs and offering the electorate a meaningful choice, which requires the majority party to carry out its promises. Parties also should help to aggregate interests while maintaining competition among the diverse political strands of a pluralistic society.

PARTIES AND ELECTORAL CHOICE

A two-party system optimizes meaningful democratic choice by facilitating majority rule. Voters confronted with only two parties will return one to government as the majority, enabling the victorious party to control the government and enact its programs. To achieve this goal, however, elected officials must be disciplined in support of their parties.

Political parties have existed from the earliest days of the Republic and have strengthened the democratic process. It is difficult to imagine politics without them. Political parties have given the electorate choice among candidates and programs, and have been important instruments of political change. They have helped to sharpen debate over what direction the country should take, and in office they have facilitated the legislative process and often helped to bridge the gap between executives and legislatures created by the separation of powers at both national and state levels of government.

PARTIES AS FACTIONS

While parties have been vital and necessary components of the political process, anti-party rhetoric has been part of our political tradition since James Madison attacked faction, by which he meant parties or interest groups, in the famous tenth paper of *The Federalist*. Factions are inevitably opposed to the national interest, wrote Madison, and although they should be tolerated they must be controlled and their potential power reduced as far as possible. In *Federalist 10* he observed that the federal and representative form of government would dilute the political effects of faction by containing their power within the states and filtering their demands and power in national politics. Madison and the Founding Fathers also recognized that the separation of powers between the elected branches of government—the President and Congress—would make majority party rule difficult if not impossible. The constitutional environment, then, was hostile to party government although not to the formation of parties themselves, a freedom of association protected by the First Amendment.

THE DECENTRALIZED PARTY SYSTEM

Political pluralism, as well as the Constitution, has caused a more loosely organized and undisciplined party system than hoped for in democratic theory. National parties are understandably broad confederations of largely autonomous state and local party interests, not tightly knit and disciplined organizations ruled from the top.

Even the multitude of state and local parties does not complete the picture of political decentralization that undermines a meaningful concept, let alone practice, of party government. An important and relatively new diffusive political force is the media, which, with the aid of a growing corps of political consultants, enables candidates to circumvent traditional organizational politics by making direct appeals for electoral support.

The apparent disarray and diversity of party politics has made charges of the "decline" of political parties seem to be more a truism than a point for debate. The following selections reveal that while parties may not be uppermost in the minds of the electorate, they continue to perform important political functions.

DEBATE FOCUS

Have Political Parties Become Meaningless?

A LEADING POLITICAL SCIENTIST ARGUES THAT PARTIES REMAIN VITAL
COMPONENTS OF DEMOCRACY

Samuel Eldersveld discusses the meaning of party decline in the following
selection, arguing that parties continue to be important on many political levels.
He suggests that the decline of parties may be more a matter of image than
reality.

S. J. ELDERSVELD

5

Party Decline: Fact or Fiction?

SAMUEL J. ELDERSVELD

Political parties are complex institutions and processes, and as such they are difficult to understand and evaluate. There are several different yardsticks by which parties could be evaluated: whether they are democratic structures in which rank-and-file supporters can participate effectively; whether they produce competent leaders who deserve public support; whether they propose (and adopt) policies which meet the needs of our society; whether they are coherent and responsible organizations; and whether they communicate in such a way with the public that citizens feel confident about parties and their performance in our political system. These concerns about parties as "linkage structures" have been a major focus of this study of parties. Controversies abound today over these questions, and the complex issues they pose. An attempt shall be made here to present some concluding observations about the state of our parties today. . . .

There have always been serious criticism of, and attacks on, the American party system. At the level of government the role of parties has been seen as anarchic, fragmented, leaderless, and undisciplined. In leadership selection it has often been criticized as too decentralized in control, or undemocratic, or both. In the way parties conduct campaigns they have regularly been characterized as nonrational, uncoordinated, improvisational, unsystematic. As organizations they are viewed, aside from the big city machines (which are denounced as too efficient oligarchies), as loose aggregations of factional subgroups, ideologically at odds and minimally active. All these criticisms have been heard for years, and yet the United

From Political Parties in American Society *by Samuel J. Eldersveld.* © *1982 by Basic Books, Inc., Publishers. Reprinted by permission of the publisher.*

States party system has been far from dysfunctional. To many citizens this party system has remained through all these trying years, years of serious threats, as a meaningful set of social and political groups to which they can relate and be loyal. They have remained important linkage and mobilizational structures, performing critical functions. In the last analysis, the great policy decisions are those that parties, and the leaders produced by parties, have had a major role in—whether it was the Emancipation Proclamation, the anti-trust legislation, the New Deal legislation, the civil rights acts, energy legislation, or any other piece of significant legislation. The *parties*— not the Chamber of Commerce, not the UAW, not the American Legion, not the American Medical Association—usually are the *prime movers* in the adoption of such landmark laws *and* are usually held responsible for such actions.

Nevertheless, despite the recognition of their contributions of the past, parties and party systems change. The United States party system has been changing also, so much, as a matter of fact, that serious question is now raised as to the suitability, centrality, indeed the viability of the system. Students of parties see two major developments in recent years: demobilization (decline in involvement) and dealignment (decline in party identification). And they argue from this that the parties have been losing their "relevance," their critical capacity in responding to social needs and problems. Thus their support by the American public and their ability to maintain the loyalty of citizens in this party system is in decline. Today, many scholars do not see parties as great actors on the American scene. Rather, they see the decomposition, dismantling, and atrophying of parties. It may be, however, that what is occurring is a metamorphosis in the forms of party organization, not a decline. Our parties may be as active and relevant, but in new ways. This question of the changes in parties is the subject of this final evaluation.

THE MEANING OF PARTY "DECLINE"

Parties in all systems undergo "change"—in organizational nature, in types of leadership, in policy direction, in electoral strength, in social group support, and in competitive relationships to other parties. But in the United States the basic concern is over the decline in the *role* and *significance* of parties in the system. Two major foci of concern relate to our conceptions of "parties in the electorate" and "parties as organizational systems." Thus, one kind of change which observers of the American parties are primarily preoccupied with is the alleged decline in *the public's support relationship* to the party system. This can be variously specified as: (1) a decline in the strength and extent of partisan loyalty and commitment; (2) a decline in interest in elections and voting; and (3) a decline in a feeling that parties are important for policy decisions, and for governing generally.

Linked to these meanings of the decline of parties are the views of scholars that parties have declined as *organizational systems*. Again, there are several ways of operationalizing this concern, and the emphasis can be on the decline in (1) the existence and amount of organization; (2) the power of leaders and agencies in the organization; (3) the capacity and competence (particularly in the professional skills) of the party organizational leadership; (4) the activity of the organization; and (5) the importance of the organization in performing its key functions (such as nominations, campaigns, policy deliberation, decision making)—in comparison to the role of interest groups, mass media, candidate-centered committees or specialists in propaganda.

In essence, the decline conceived of often is in the institutional nature of parties—that the parties as organizational apparatuses have atrophied. The writings of many scholars referred to earlier can be cited to document these observations—among them, [political scientists Walter] Burnham, [James] Wilson, and [Jeane] Kirkpatrick. Thus, Wilson in 1973 argued that parties, as organizations, "have become if anything weaker rather than stronger—parties are more important as labels than as organizations." And to Jeane Kirkpatrick, 1976 provided "fresh evidence of the parties' decreasing capacity to represent voters, mount campaigns, elicit resources, and recruit leaders who were devoted to the institution," and one of her central theses is that the decisions to reform the parties have been responsible for "hastening party deinstitutionalization."

Here is the convergence of two streams of concern or alarm—the alleged decline in the public's support for and interest in parties, and the decline of the party organizations as active and effective entities. Both of these streams emphasize the declining "relevance" of parties for the system, for the society, for the solution to our problems as important instrumentalities for political action, and, in the final analysis, for the lives of Americans as they are affected by government.

It is important to distinguish here between *what is alleged, what is perceived,* and *what is reality.* Scholars may assert that there is no organization, *but* that may be an inference not supported by reality. Or scholars may assert that the public is disillusioned with parties because parties have no important policy role, *but* to support such an argument two types of evidence are important: Is that in fact the public's perception? Is it factually correct that parties have no policy role? In analyzing party decline, then, both *perceptions* and *performance* must be examined. It may very well be argued that what is perceived is more important than what is reality, since attitudes of disillusionment by the public (and by scholars) reflect perceptions. But if there is a divergence between perception and reality, we have only begun to understand the problem and we then need a careful analysis of why. The analytical context for the discussion is suggested by [Table 1].

Many scholars assume that the situation of Box D in the table obtains, and if it does, parties may well be responsible for negative attitudes. But this must yet be demonstrated. If, on the other hand, the conditions of Box C exist, then there is a conflict between perceptions and actual performance. This too needs to be demonstrated and the factors responsible for the disjunction identified. Box A suggests the conditions which many assume to have existed in the past when we had higher turnout, less independence, and so forth. But actually we may have had Box B conditions all along— to secure evidence on this historically is very difficult. In any event, when the "decline" in our parties is discussed it is necessary (1) to document the change in the level of party organizational performance; (2) to document the change in the content of public perceptions of parties; (3) to document the extent to which the decline in one is related to the decline in the other; and (4) if the two do not co-vary, to explore explanations for the decline in public affect for parties which may not be linked to party organizational effort. This is a major research task, and the evidence now available and relevant to that task will be presented here. But by no means is all the information needed to enlighten definitively and correctly all aspects of this phenomenon of party decline yet at hand. It is a puzzle which can only partially be pieced together at this point.

A FIRST MAJOR QUESTION: HAS PARTY ORGANIZATION ACTIVISM DECLINED AT THE LOCAL LEVEL?

The familiar refrain in commentaries on American parties these days is that the rise of the direct primary and of new campaign technology has meant the loss of control by the party organization, as presumably it existed in the past, over nominations, campaign strategies, candidates, issues, resources, elected leadership, *and* that this has meant "the decline of local

[TABLE 1] EVALUATIONS OF PARTIES: FOUR BASIC TYPES

Perceptions of Party Performance and Relevance	Party Organizational Preference	
	High	Low
Positive	A Healthy condition if it ever existed	B Very possibly what may have been true in the past
Negative	C Basic conflict	D Party role in system negative or neutral

TABLE [2] PERCENTAGE OF UNITED STATES PUBLIC REPORTING CONTACTS BY LOCAL PARTY ACTIVISTS

Party	1952	1956	1972	1976
Democrat	6	11	19	17
Republican	7	11	13	13
	13	22	32	30
	13	22	32	30

Source: Michael Wolfe, "Personal Contact Campaigning in Presidential Electiions" (A paper presented at the Annual Meeting of the Midwest Political Science Association, Chicago, April 1979), p. 11a.

party activism" . . . But what is the evidence of the decline in local party activism? None of the scholars making these general assertions have demonstrated that this is the case. In fact, there is evidence to suggest that the opposite may be true. Wolfe's careful analysis of the Center for Political Studies' data from 1952 on indicates that the proportion of the American public who have been contacted by party campaign workers in recent years is much greater than previously (see [T]able [2]). Whereas in 1952 only 12 percent of the public report contacts, by 1976 it was close to 30 percent; in 1980 it was 24 percent.

What is interesting to note is the extension of such local party contact efforts in all parts of the country, to blacks, as well as whites, and to lower

TABLE [3] EXTENSION OF PARTY ACTIVISM EFFORTS GEOGRAPHICALLY, RACIALLY, AND BY EDUCATIONAL LEVEL (AS A PERCENTAGE)

| Category | Contacted by Party Canvassers Each Year | | | | Increase |
	1952	1956	1972	1976	1952–76
Regions					
South	9	15	18	21	+ 12
Border	9	16	25	20	+ 11
Mountain and Far West	20	18	40	36	+ 16
Northeast	15	17.5	19	30	+ 15
Mid-Atlantic	12	15	26	28	+ 16
Midwest	12	20	40.5	32.5	+ 20.5
Race					
Whites	12	16	28	27	+ 15
Blacks	6	12	18	18	+ 12
Educational Level					
Completed college	15	22	33	35	+ 20
High school	13	22	29	27	+ 14
Less than high school	10	13	19	16	+ 6

Source: Michael Wolfe, "Personal Contact Campaigning in Presidential Elections" (A paper presented at the Annual Meeting of the Midwest Political Science Association, Chicago, April 1979), pp. 8a, 6a, 16a. Based on University of Michigan SRC/CPS data.

TABLE [4] CHARACTERISTICS OF PERSONS CONTACTED BY THE PARTIES AND CANDIDATES, 1980 (AS A PERCENTAGE)

Respondents	Total for Group	Contacted by			
		Republicans	Democrats	Both Parties	Other
Contacted in campaign	24.4	36.4	33.5	21.6	8.4
Ideology					
Liberal	31	23	46	23	
Moderate	25	39	31	22	
Conservative	26	41	22	28	
Party identification					
Strong Democrat	30	20	55	18	
Weak Democrat	21	36	34	18	
Independent Democrat	21	35	27	27	
Independent	23	42	20	29	
Independent Republican	21	42	36	23	
Weak Republican	27	44	24	24	
Strong Republican	30	53	24	18	
Age					
Young (18–29)	17	44	30	11	
Older	25	33	33	28	
Old	30	33	39	24	
Oldest (65 and over)	29	41	32	17	
Educational Level					
Grade school	17	21	50	14	
High school	22	37	37	16	
College	29	39	26	28	

Source: University of Michigan CPS/NES, 1980.

educational groups, as well as to the college educated (see [T]able [3]). True, those with low socioeconomic status are not as frequently the targets of campaign activists as are those of higher status, but there is some evidence of expansionism in contacts, particularly for blacks and those with a middle (high school) educational status.

In this connection it is instructive to look at the results of the 1980 national surveys which also asked all those in the sample if they had been contacted in the campaign. Although there was a slight decline in the overall percentage (to 24.4 percent), the characteristics of those who were contacted are revealing (see [T]able [4]). The Republican effort was slightly greater in 1980, particularly among conservatives (41 percent), young persons (44 percent) as well as the oldest citizens (41 percent) and , of course, among Republican identifiers. The Democrats seemed to spend more canvassing effort among liberals (46 percent), those with a lower educational status (50 percent) and, of course, among Democratic identifiers (55 percent). What is significant also, however, is that both parties appealed to all groups, including each other's partisans. One-fifth to one-fourth of strong partisans were called on by the opposite party. The same phenomenon holds true for other categories of voters. In the light of the election results perhaps the overall net advantage to the Republicans lies in their greater effort with Independents. They seemed to have contacted about 10 percent more of them than the Democrats did. And since 85 percent of those contacted said they voted (an exaggerated report, but nonetheless the proportion was still high), this extra Republican effort may have been relevant to Republican success.

A great many questions can be asked of these data, including who the canvasser was (whether a party organization person or not), what the content of the contact was, and whether these recalls of contact are at all reliable. Obviously, many more adult citizens are being contacted now by party and campaign personnel than ever before. Although there is a continuous socioeconomic bias in these efforts, such contacts are reaching out to a larger proportion of blacks and less well-educated people than ever before, and this seems to be going on throughout the country. There has always been much organizational slack in the performance of the key tasks by the local party organization, except in certain big city machines, but there is really no convincing evidence that recently the local party is less active or less efficient than formerly. In fact, the data on Detroit and Los Angeles, comparing local party activity of 1980 with 1956, suggests no decline, as does the Wolfe analysis above.

A SUBSIDIARY QUESTION: ARE THE LOCAL PARTY ACTIVISTS LESS LIKELY TO BE COMPETENT WORKERS THAN PREVIOUSLY?

Although it may be true that local parties are as active as previously, it is contended that the party activist today is different in two respects—he, or she, is more ideological and less pragmatic, and also less professional (and more amateur). This type of argument uses data particularly about the delegates to the national conventions, relying heavily on the 1972 delegate studies, a year which certainly on the Democratic side was perhaps somewhat abnormal. The Democratic National Convention in 1972 certainly did see what Jeane Kirkpatrick has called "new breed" of activists—more youth, more black, more women, and presumably more amateur and ideological. But, as Kirkpatrick herself has stated, the 1976 Democratic convention had more delegates with "prior party experience, more who had held party and public office, fewer who were indifferent to winning. . . ." Yet she is still concerned about the presence of activists in both parties who are not loyal to the party, who are candidate-oriented, who have limited professional competence, and who are unrepresentative in social and economic status in relationship to the parties' rank and file. [Washington Post columnist] David Broder is similarly concerned, citing figures that governors and congressmen are represented much less at recent Democratic conventions. But in 1980 this trend presumably was altered with the adoption of the new rule that 10 percent of the delegate seats in a state are set aside for elected party leaders.

The American parties have always been wide open structures. They have always had ideologues (a minority) and pragmatists, amateurs and professionals, those intermittently involved and those making a career out of party organizational work. To argue that our parties have changed radically, have declined, because there are today many more nonprofessional, nonpragmatic ideologues than formerly is not substantiated by any trend data available.

ANOTHER SUBSIDIARY QUESTION: IS PARTY ORGANIZATION AT THE LOCAL LEVEL LESS IMPORTANT TODAY?

The point has been made by several writers that the local party organization is less critical today for our parties and for political campaigns, that state and national parties operate independently, that candidates depend less on the local organization, and that the mass media have replaced the local doorbell ringer as the major source of information about politics and the major stimulus to voting. As has been seen in the previous analysis of the research on the media, there can be no question but that since 1952 television particularly is relied on heavily by voters. But this has not meant a decline in the proportion of Americans exposed to the efforts of the local party organization. As for the extent to which candidates rely on the party organization in their districts, the evidence reviewed earlier by no means suggests that the new specialists in campaign technology have over time replaced the local organizations–for registration drives, for money, for mobilization of campaign personnel, for "getting out the vote." Scholars of Congress are inclined to emphasize the congressman's relationship to his constituency, and this includes his district party organization, through which he often rose to the top, whose views about politics he shares, and which could run an opposition candidate against him if that organization feels ignored. Again, the evidence on this point is not by any means overwhelming, and the importance of the local organization apparently varies greatly from state to state and from community to community. But to dismiss the local organization as superseded by the mass media or scorned by the candidate-centered campaign or ignored by the incumbent congressman (or state legislator), *particularly as something which has happened recently*, is not supported by the available data.

A SECOND MAJOR QUESTION: HAS PARTY ORGANIZATION AT THE STATE AND NATIONAL LEVELS BECOME WEAKER?

Have state and national party organizations declined in power and influence in the role they play in campaigns, leadership recruitment, and policy decisions? Contradictory arguments are advanced. One argument is that there is a nationalization trend and that state parties are losing out. But it is also maintained that the parties have lost control over nominations and campaigns to public relations agencies, professional consultants, and candidate organizations.

The evidence that state and national party organizations have lost power is not conclusive. Thus, the Democratic National Committee has expanded its control over the selection of delegates to the national convention both through the Compliance Review Commission, to which state organizations must submit descriptions of the process they use in selecting delegates, and in 1980, by informing the states that delegates selected in open primaries, not confined to declared Democrats, will not be acceptable at the national convention. The assertion of these two powers alone had meant a modest centralization tendency in American parties. True, those who would have "europeanized" our parties at the Kansas City mini-convention of 1974 by giving the national committee much more authority (over party policy, for example) were defeated. But the natonal committees have never been centers of party power, and thus recent developments represent, if anything, a slight increment in national committee power, rather than a decline.

As to the question of the decline in the role of the state and national organizations over nominations and campaigns, there is probably no question that some attrition has occurred. In 1980, and for the Democrats in 1976, the national convention did not make the final decision on the presidential nomination. The primaries selected over 70 percent of the delegates, and Reagan and Carter won the majority of the delegates needed for nomination long before the conventions met. This does depreciate the role of state organizations at the national convention—then and now. But, the national convention may still be important in nominations in the future. In the meantime it remains a major plenary body of party decision making—on the platform and on the rules and permanent organization of the party—as well as being a major forum for consensus building and party unity.

As for the role of the national parties in the campaigns for president and vice-president, the national organization was often only peripherally involved and rarely central in the planning and executing of campaign strategy. This role depended on the pleasure of the presidential candidate. Certainly Carter, Nixon, Johnson, Kennedy, to name only a few, did not place the national committee in the center of the campaign operation. It is true that the Federal Election Campaign acts since 1971, by providing public funds for presidential campaigns, most of which are given to the candidate, not to the committee, may appear to have weakened the role of the national committee. Yet, the Republican national organization under Chairman William Brock is credited with a major role in the 1980 presidential victory. Brock worked to renovate state and local organizations, organized training sessions on campaign techniques, the use of the media, and the use of surveys of public opinion, and actually ran a "campaign management college." Above all, large sums of money were collected and funneled through the national organization to United States senatorial, congressional, and state legislature candidates.

A major study of state party organizations recently has concluded that since 1960 the budgets of state organizations have more than tripled and their staffs have increased greatly. The authors conclude, "If state parties were in the undeveloped state ascribed to them by political scientists in the 1950s and early 1960s, they have since developed into relatively strong and durable organizations."

In short, to argue that party organization at the state and national levels has been decisively weakened in recent years is difficult to substantiate, and such claims assume strong parties in the past. In reality this country has always had a decentralized and stratarchical party organizational system, and some would argue that that is the strength of our parties. It has forced parties to be responsible to local interests, to adapt to local differences, to force upper-level party structures to be truly consultative of lower-level structures and to maintain, thus, a minimum of rapport in a very heterogeneous system. If anything, the national committee has more power today, and the party caucus in Congress is asserting its authority more than it has for many years. The decline in our parties, therefore, is difficult to demonstrate, empirically or in terms of a historical perspective.

THIRD BASIC QUESTION: HAS THERE BEEN A DECLINE IN THE PUBLIC'S AFFECT FOR, AND CONFIDENCE IN, THE PARTIES?

This may turn out to be the critical question in the party decline controversy. For, in the last analysis, it is *the* test of the viability of any particular party and of any particular party system. If there is a continuous decline in the public's positive evaluation of parties, rooted in disaffection over party capability and performance, then withdrawal of public support will occur which is meaningful and difficult to reverse, a concern about which empirical evidence is available.

There are several components of this concern which are separable. First, to what extent is there a change in the extent to which the public *thinks*

TABLE [5] MEASURES OF THE PUBLIC'S INTEREST AND CONFIDENCE IN PARTIES (AS A PERCENTAGE)

Interest	1952	1956	1960	1964	1968	1972	1976	1980
Use of "party" in evaluating candidates (all citizens)	46	41	41	34	40	24		
Use of "party" in evaluating candidates (identifiers)	52	46	47	37	44	27		
Positive evaluation of own or both parties	74	72	74	64	59	49	49	50
Feel parties "help a good deal in making the government pay attention" to the public				41	36	26	17	28
Do not mention one or the other of the parties as doing the best job on a problem the respondent considers most important (that is, the percentage who are neutral or indifferent)			38	34	48	51	54	50

Sources: Norman H. Nie, Sidney Verba and John R. Petrocik, The Changing American Voter *(Cambridge: Harvard University Press, 1976), pp. 56, 58, 171; Jack Dennis, "Trends in Public Support for the American Party System," in Jeff Fischel, ed.,* Parties and Elections in Anti-Party Age *(Bloomington: Indiana University Press, 1978), p. 10; Martin Wattenberg, "The Decline of Political Partisanship in America: Negativity or Neutrality?"* American Political Science Review *(December 1981); all data based on University of Michigan CPS/SRC/NES.*

in "party content" terms at all? If "party" is less salient to people, something they spontaneously talk and think about less frequently, that in itself is a significant development. The little data available on this matter indicates that, indeed, such seems to be the case today (see [T]able [5]). Surveys show a decline in the 1970s in the public's inclination to evaluate candidates in "party" terms, a finding that holds true for party identifiers also. Second, when people do think of parties, they are less positive in their general evaluations of them than previously—a steady decline since the 1960 election, when 71 percent were positive, to 49 percent by 1976. Third, this does not necessarily mean an increase in negative evaluations but seems to be associated with more neutrality in the way people view parties. When people are asked, "Which party can do the best job in dealing with the most important problem(s), as you perceive those problems?" more citizens are inclined to say, "the parties are about the same," or "no party" or "neither party." And this is perhaps the most significant development of all—that close to 50 percent of the public today has great difficulty in identifying one or the other of the parties as best capable of solving our problems. In 1960 the proportion was 38 percent. These are the people who seem more inclined to stay home on election day.

The decline in the relevance of parties for the solution of problems may well be the nub of the matter. The general decline in affect for parties may be the result of a change in the image of the role of parties—from positive to neutral—in the policy process. It is not so troublesome that large proportions of the public over the years do not perceive clear-cut differences between the parties. That has been going on for years—the United States studies in the 1950s revealed that less than 20 percent of strong identifiers saw important differences between the parties on issues. Rather, what is new and significant is the declining relevance in public cognitions of parties combined with an increased neutralism and indifference to parties. This in turn may be linked (although scholars differ on this) to a decline in the correlation of partisanship to the vote—a drop after 1952 from .50 to .14 in 1976. To understand why that has occurred would lead to a closer understanding of the meaning of the decline of parties.

The "puzzle" as it has emerged thus far is: Compared to most other countries, the United States is unsurpassed in level of political activity and in amount of party identification, but far down in rank in voting turnout (54 percent in the presidential election of 1980, compared to 75 percent or more in most European countries and also Japan). Further, political activity is not declining in the United States, nor is party effort declining on the basis of the reports from the respondents in surveys since 1952. The parties are contacting a larger proportion of the citizens. At the same time our politics seem more competitive than before (closer elections in many parts of the country, including the South). There is more issue awareness and ideological involvement with politics recently which, at least in the interpretations of some scholars analyzing these data, indicates citizens are linking their issue positions to the vote more than they did before. In all of this, however, the image of parties has been declining, is less positive; parties are seen as less relevant to problem solving. Thus, the "puzzle" (see [Table 6]).

[TABLE 6] RELATIONSHIP OF PARTY DECLINE TO PARTY INVOLVEMENT

A. A decline in positive evaluations of parties, particularly as problem solvers *Plus* B. Decreasing voting turnout	*At the same time there is*	1. Much party activity 2. Still relatively high party identification 3. No decline in *personal* political activity 4. More issue politics

This poses the "why" question in a particular theoretical context. It suggests that the way *the image* of political parties is communicated recently, as having relevance for today's issues and problems, is changing, and this in turn may be partly responsible for nonvoting. Further, it suggests that all this is going on *because of, or despite,* the activities of political party organizational personnel and activists. It also suggests that the type of politics which interests people these days and with which parties and their activists must be engaged is different—special issue and special interest politics. Above all, it suggests that there should be a careful examination of *what is being communicated to the public about parties* and *by whom.* What is being communicated by party workers, by party organization leaders, by candidates for office, by incumbents in office, by television, by newspapers and other mass media, by opinion leaders, by interest group leaders? If the image of parties is declining despite a relatively consistent level of organizational contact work and political activity, then it is not the inactivity which is at fault, but *the message.*

Much more research needs to be done on the question of why, before there can be any definitive answers. A configuration of forces seems to be at work which can be summarized in the following terms.

Party canvassing and contact efforts may today emphasize the party less frequently and less effectively than in the past. . . .

A second point to keep in mind is that the way party leaders and candidates think about parties and talk about parties in their appeals to the public may be a major factor in the public's image of parties. If the leadership plays down parties, if candidates de-emphasize their party affiliation or seek to maintain aloofness from the party organization, then indeed the public's rejection of parties will be encouraged. . . .

The third approach to explaining the decline in the public's positive images about parties is to lay the blame on the mass media, including not only television but also radio, newspapers, and other printed media. There has been some research on the role of the media in campaigns. The extent of the research directly related to the question of the impact of media content on the voter's images of political parties is much less, however. Some recent studies are more pertinent and do indeed suggest that the mass media role may be significant.

Much of the public is highly exposed to television and newspapers during campaigns as the only real source of political information, ideas, and images. Television has, since the 1960s, gradually become the major source, replacing newspapers, for certain types of voters, particularly those in the lower economic brackets. Both television and newspapers are extensively utilized and thus must be primary sources of political awareness. Certain scholars, such as [political scientist] Michael Robinson, have argued that persons relying on television have a lower sense of political efficacy than those relying on newspapers, radio, or magazines for their political information.

Implicit in [other] research is the clear implication that public feelings toward institutions are influenced by what the media communicate. Parties as key institutions are often treated poorly by the media. The criticism of our politics by the media appears clearly linked to cynicism, and this in turn may well exact its toll on the public's view of parties. Because of negative stories about parties and the cumulative impact of negative reporting a frame of reference emerges in terms of which the citizen judges what the party organizations and party leaders do, and this affects the nature of his identification with and belief in the party system.

[CONCLUSION]

If there is a weakness in our [party] system today, it is not that we have too much organizational control and leadership, but too little. There are obviously other reforms which should be sought—in Congress, party leadership, presidential nominations, state party organization, campaign techniques, and finance. But in all of this our major principles and objectives should be kept firmly in mind. Primarily we seek to make our parties more basic and useful instruments for the popular control of government, for the solution of social problems, and for the achievement of system integration. They have been functionally central for the achievement of these purposes in the past. Despite their defects they continue today to be major instruments for democratic government in this nation. With necessary reforms we can make them even more central to the governmental process and to the lives of American citizens. Eighty years ago Lord James Bryce, after studying our party system, said "In America the great moving forces are the parties. The government counts for less than in Europe, the parties count for more. . . ." If our citizens and their leaders wish it, American parties will still be the "great moving forces" of our system.

Have Political Parties Become Meaningless?

A CONTEMPORARY POLITICAL SCHOLAR SEEKS IMPROVEMENT IN THE
PUBLIC IMAGE OF PARTIES

Parties are, perhaps, doing their job far better than critics of the party system are willing to admit. The preceding selection pointed out that high levels of political activity and party identification characterize American politics, although voting turnout is low. Moreover, there is a high degree of issue awareness and ideological involvement; nevertheless, the public does not seem to view parties as being politically important.

In the following selection Martin Wattenberg addresses the question of party images, concluding that effective political partisanship and electoral competition require greater public understanding and appreciation of the role parties play.

6

M. P. WATTENBERG

Decline of American Political Parties

MARTIN P. WATTENBERG

In his last book, *The Responsible Electorate*, V. O. Key outlined a basic theory of political behavior that came frequently to mind as I wrote this book. According to Key, "The voice of the people is but an echo chamber. The output of an echochamber bears an inevitable and invariable relation to the input. As candidates and parties clamor for attention and vie for popular support, the people's verdict can be no more than a selective reflection from among the alternatives and outlooks presented to them." The explanation for party decline in the electorate that [I argue] squares nicely with Key's echo chamber analogy.

The public did not decide all of a sudden that parties were bankrupt political institutions and mandate their decline. Rather, voters reacted gradually over the last quarter of a century to the way in which politics was presented to them. Political parties themselves became less institutionally relevant and the public adjusted their views of them accordingly. As party leaders have come to act more and more on their own initiative and to communicate with voters directly through the media, the public has increasingly come to see the crucial short-term domestic and foreign issues only in terms of the candidates. It is candidates rather than parties that are now viewed as being responsible for solving, or failing to solve, our current political problems. Therefore, the parties are receiving much less credit or blame for political outcomes than they did several decades ago. Despite the decay in public confidence in American political institutions in recent years,

69

people have not turned sharply negative toward the parties. Instead they have come to see political parties as less relevant to what goes on in the everyday world of politics, and hence have become far more neutral toward them.

If the answer to the phenomenon of party decline in the electorate can in fact be found in the real world of elite political maneuvering, one might question why it is necessary to analyze mass survey data. My reply would be that although public opinion acts something like an echo chamber, without survey data one can never be sure just *what* people are reacting to. After all, there have been major political catastrophies (Vietnam, Watergate, economic recessions) for both parties in recent years, which could quite reasonably have led many voters to become negative toward both. Yet the change in the public's attitudes about the parties has been shaped not so much by specific political events as by how the events have been handled by leaders and presented by the media.

In order to reinvigorate political partisanship in the future, then, the public must be convinced that political parties perform a useful function in the American political process. The challenge that the parties face is not merely to espouse programs with popular appeal, but also to demonstrate that they play a crucial political role—from the recruitment of leaders to the implementation of policies. If the echo chamber analogy is correct, then it is reasonable to assume that if leaders begin once again to act as partisans and be presented by the media as such, the decline of partisanship in the electorate can potentially be reversed.

The need for such a revitalization is hardly a new theme. Over thirty years ago a committee of distinguished political scientists concluded that our party system was functioning poorly in sustaining well-considered programs and mobilizing public support for them. Numerous recommendations were compiled, all of which the scholars believed would facilitate a more responsible and effective party system—one that would be accountable to the public and able to deal with the problems of modern government.

These suggestions became an instant source of controversy and were justifiably criticized for their unrealistic call for more disciplined, programmatic, and ideologically distinctive parties in a political culture in which interests are too diverse to be expressed in the centralized fashion outlined in the recommendations. Despite this critical flaw, however, what remains the central problem of the American party system was illuminated—namely, the relevance of political parties in solving governmental problems: "The party in power has a responsibility, broadly defined, for the general management of the government, for its manner of getting results achieved, for the consequences of inaction as well as action, for the intended and unintended outcome of its conduct of public affairs, for all that it plans to do, for all that it might have foreseen, for the leadership it provides, for the acts of all its agents, and for what it says as well as for what it does." The sense of these scholars in 1950 that the parties were not adequately meeting their responsibilities led them to send out an alarm that a serious problem existed; the fact that parties are now even less capable of meeting these responsibilities is reflected in the survey data results presented in this book.

The skeptic might examine the long history of concern with the future of American political parties and conclude that some have cried wolf at least once too often. After all, over three decades later the two parties still remain intact in the world's oldest surviving party system. There seems to be no danger that the parties will suddenly vanish from the scene and leave catastrophic political and social chaos in their wake. The "party" is far from over, as Samuel Eldersveld has recently concluded.

But although parties have not disintegrated they have clearly declined in relevance, and the consequences have been significant. In 1950 the scholars foresaw several dangers if no action was taken to make the party system more responsible. Their warnings seem eerily prophetic over three decades later; their fears have turned into our present-day realities. Indeed, examining what they saw as the dangers of a weakened party system illuminates some of our current problems.

A major fear was that if the parties could not develop comprehensive programs that could be successfully implemented, voter frustration might set in motion more extreme tendencies of both the left and the right, leading to a deep political cleavage "to which neither our political institutions nor our civic habits are adapted." This fear has been at least partially realized in the turmoil of the 1960s and the development of strident single-issue groups. Parties once channeled political conflict and kept policy differences within reasonable bounds. One result of the decline of partisanship is that we now have a system that is capable of expressing a wide diversity of viewpoints but is rather poor at aggregating them. With parties increasingly less able to resolve these conflicts, the tone of American politics is becoming more negative and bitter, and policy compromises are much harder to come by.

A second possible consequence mentioned was the danger of overextending the presidency. As the only branch of government capable of leadership direction and unity of action, the presidency is the logical institution to expect the unmet responsibilities of the parties to fall upon. The problem with placing such expectations on the President that "either his party becomes a flock of sheep or the party falls apart. In effect this concept of the presidency disposes of the party system by making the President reach directly for the support of a majority of votes. It favors a President who exploits skillfully the arts of demagoguery, who uses the whole country as his political backyard, and who does not mind turning into the embodiment of personal government."

A generation before them these political scientists speculated, such a prospect would have been dismissed as "fantastic." Today it is part of the modern presidency. Major policy proposals are presented to the public first and foremost as *presidential* programs. The economic program of the current administration, for example, is widely referred to not as Republican economics but as "Reaganomics." Of course it is members of the press rather than the president who have pinned this label on the program. However, . . . such press concentration on the president and presidential candidates has increasingly become the norm. It is no wonder that within such a political context the American public has become increasingly indifferent to the parties.

In 1950 just such a prospect was foreseen if party accountability were not restored. That the public might "turn its back upon the two parties" was a real possibility, and was in fact already beginning to occur: "Present conditions are a great incentive for the voters to dispose of the parties as intermediaries between themselves and the government. In a way, a sizeable body of the electorate has shifted from hopeful interest in the parties to the opposite attitude. This mass of voters sees itself as the President's or his opponent's direct electoral support." Over three decades later this statement is now even more true.

Partisanship once provided the American electorate with a sense of continuity and stability. With its decline many citizens have been set adrift without an anchor in a political world full of strong eddies and currents. As a result, some no longer vote; others are swept first one way then another by the currents, causing the much talked-about rise of political volatility. Throughout the 1980 campaign political commentators frequently remarked on the high degree of changeability in voter preferences. One pointed indication of this volatility is the large percentage of voters who waited until very near the end of the campaign before they decided how to vote. In *The American Voter*, Campbell and his colleagues noted that most voters in 1952 and 1956 had made up their minds by the time of the nominating conventions, indicating "that the psychological forces guiding behavior arise before the campaign opens." In 1980, however, half of the voters interviewed stated that they had made their decisions during the campaign, and an unprecedented 9 percent waited until election day to make up their minds (only 2 percent did so in each of the Eisenhower-Stevenson contests).

What was most striking about the last-minute decision-making in the 1980 campaign was the suddenness with which a virtually even race turned into a landslide victory for Ronald Reagan. As might be expected, given their lack of partisan direction, those who were neutral toward both parties on the like/dislike questions accounted for a large proportion (47.8 percent) of the undecided voters in the CPS [University of Michigan Center for Political Studies] preelection survey. Furthermore, they, much more than any other group of undecided voters, were swayed toward Reagan—casting an astounding 70.3 percent of their votes for him compared to 18.9 percent for Carter and 11.8 for Anderson. This is not to say that these voters alone accounted for the last-minute shift, but clearly it does indicate their great potential for volatile political behavior.

In conclusion, party coalitions in the United States have undergone a series of processes of decay over the last three decades, increasing the possibilities of *both* short-term and long-term change in the near future. With the weakening of the public's images of the parties, it is no wonder that volatility has become the new catchword of American politics. As the long-term forces that serve to anchor electoral behavior decline, the potential increases for large oscillations in the vote because of short-term issue and candidate factors. Furthermore, given that there is less of what V. O. Key called a "standing decision" for people to return to, there is also an increased potential for the translation of short-term forces into long-term ones. Such a process, however, will require that the issues and candidates responsible for the short-term changes become firmly linked with public images of the parties. When and if that happens, a new era of American electoral politics will have begun.

CHAPTER FOUR

Political Parties and Elections

Ronald Reagan's 1980 victory and his overwhelming 1984 vote margin over Democratic opponent Walter Mondale sent political scientists and pundits scurrying to find out if Reagan's success reflected a long-term realignment of the electorate from the Democrats and New Deal-Great Society liberalism to Republican conservatism.

TYPES OF ELECTIONS

CRITICAL ELECTIONS

The late political scientist V. O. Key, Jr., described realigning elections as "critical."* Elections have a profound impact upon the political system, bringing about through party shifts long-term changes in elected executives and legislative bodies. Critical realignment began to occur from the Republicans to the Democrats in the 1920s, culminating in the election of Franklin D. Roosevelt in 1932. That election began a long era of Democratic control of the presidency, Congress, and of state governments.

DEVIATING AND REINSTATING ELECTIONS

At the national level, Dwight D. Eisenhower's 1952 victory temporarily interrupted Democratic dominance, but his "deviating" election did not change the fact that a majority of the electorate identified with the Democrats. Voters chose Eisenhower more for personal reasons than party considerations. This was reflected in continued Democratic control of Congress after the first two years of the Eisenhower administration and in the large number of Democratic governors and state legislatures. When the highly popular Eisenhower left office, Democratic voters, who remained in the majority, sent John F. Kennedy to the White House in the reinstating election of 1960 that returned control of the Presidency to the majority party.

*V. O. Key, Jr., "A Theory of Critical Elections," Journal of Politics, Vol. 17, No. 1 (February 1955).

POLITICAL CHANGE AND SHIFTING PARTY ALIGNMENTS

Profound political changes began to occur in the 1960s, as the civil rights, women's, youth, and anti-war movements created a potentially explosive political mixture. Even before the 1960s political pot began to boil, the presidential contest of 1964 reflected party polarization as Arizona conservative Republican Senator Barry Goldwater challenged incumbent Lyndon B. Johnson, whose Great Society had taken New Deal programs to their liberal pinnacle. Johnson won a stunning victory, but was soon to see his popularity vanish as the Vietnam War stirred nationwide protests.

DEMOCRATIC PARTY DISARRAY

As the political turmoil mounted in Johnson's second term, traditional party alignments appeared to be on the threshold of change. By the time Johnson stepped down in 1968, throwing his weight behind his vice president, Hubert Humphrey, the great liberal who was tarnished with Johnson's unpopular Vietnam War, the Democrats were in disarray. The Democrat's 1968 Chicago convention was a debacle, controlled by traditional party bosses and leaders, causing women, minorities, and youth to charge that they were unfairly being excluded. Mostly young anti-war protestors marched in the streets outside the convention hall as the delegates met in Mayor Richard J. Daley's city to nominate Humphrey. The cries of exclusion had their intended effect—the convention established a reform commission to make the rules for the selection of delegates more democratic. The commission, chaired by Senator George McGovern of South Dakota, successfully pushed for the grass-roots choice of delegates, which appropriately helped McGovern himself become the party's nominee in 1972.

REPUBLICAN RESURGENCE

The Democrats remained in a majority among the electorate in 1968, but the party lost to Richard M. Nixon in part because of disaffections because of war. Nixon had won the nomination of his party by shifting to the right to fend off Ronald Reagan's challenge, after isolating Republican liberal Nelson Rockefeller's bid for the nomination from the left. The Republican platform of 1968 was far more moderate than it had been in 1964 and than it was to become in the 1980s. Nixon defeated Humphrey by less than one percent of the popular vote, although he won an overwhelming electoral vote majority. Nixon was undoubtedly hurt by the third party candidacy of Alabama Governor George C. Wallace, who garnered 13.5 percent of the popular vote, drawn mostly from the "silent majority" of conservatives that Nixon had hoped to tap.

The seeds of political change were sown in the 1960s. After the transition period of the 1970s, in which the Watergate scandal severely hurt the Republican party and possibly deflected the electoral shift that was taking place toward it, Ronald Reagan's sweeping victories in 1980 and 1984 suggested that a conservative electoral realignment was back on the track.

Has There Been a Party Realignment in the 1980s?

A POLITICAL PUNDIT BELIEVES AN EMERGING REPUBLICAN MAJORITY
MAY BE SHORTCIRCUITED BY FRAGMENTATION OF THE PARTY SYSTEM

The author of the following selection, an adviser to the Republican presidential campaign in 1968 and the author of *The Emerging Republican Majority,* (1972) concluded in the 1980s that party organizational and procedural changes coupled with media politics had short-circuited the conservative realignment that should have occurred. In his view *supra* party coalitions and third-party candidacies may characterize the future more than traditional two-party politics. Nevertheless, he argues that should Reaganomics succeed, the Republican party may be able to overcome intra-party squabbles and decentralizing forces to forge a long-term electoral realignment.

K. PHILLIPS

7

The Party System: Realignment or De-Alignment?

KEVIN PHILLIPS

> You're looking at the most massive shift of party identification that has occurred in the past twenty five years . . . a rolling realignment.
>
> *Reagan pollster Richard Wirthlin (July 1981)*

The ongoing, low-key debate over party realignment—and over the vitality of the current American party system—took on new dimensions in the spring of 1981, within months after President Reagan's inauguration. Even Republicans admitted that the 1980 election itself had not yielded a classic political realignment. However, as polls showed a narrowing gap between Democratic and Republican identification among voters, the President's own pollster, Richard Wirthlin, opined that for the first time in our history our politics might be experiencing a period of "creeping realignment." Some analysts agreed; more did not. Survey results, as usual, could be read both ways. Nevertheless, in the guise of a controversy over numbers and cycles, another important issue surfaced, namely: If a political system could not realign in the face of the upheavals and pressures of the 1960s and 1970s, what was the electorate really up to?

Hitherto, realignments have usually taken the form of a "big bang," a watershed election (like the one in 1932) in which the newly ascendant party swept to a massive victory up and down the ballot. The 1980 election was hardly one of those, not with the Democrats continuing to hold majorities of governorships and in the U.S. House and the state legislatures. That left three alternative interpretations: (1) continued, undisrupted New Deal coalition/Democratic Party majority status; (2) creeping realignment of the Republicans into majority status; and (3) de-alignment—the decomposition of the party system with new minor parties springing up as the old ones prove incapable of maintaining or reassembling national majorities. This last scenario, alas, is what might be expected to flow from the other erosions—economic, institutional and psychological—that I have described.

I have never understood the thinking of those who, even in the late 1970s, espoused the first thesis. The New Deal coalition is dead, having given out audible noises of disintegration since the 1960s. The average Democratic share of the total vote in the last four presidential elections was just 43 percent, down from an average 49 percent in 1948–64, and an average 57 percent in 1932–44. Whole Roosevelt-era constituencies are milling at the partisan exits, while the principal credos of yesteryear's cohesion, the New Deal and Keynesian economics, are in substantial disrepute. Even if the Democratic Party pulls itself back together during the 1980s, the way it does that is unlikely to involve a further extension of the New Deal philosophy of coalition.[1] Scarcely anyone believes in more New Deal except a few aging Washington lawyers and employees of the Brookings Institution.

The theory of "creeping realignment" is somewhat more plausible. For more than a decade, our political system has been stumbling toward what in a bygone era would have been realignment—a new partisan majority. And since it has not come in a big bang, thanks to Watergate and the growth of ticket-splitting, some suggest it is creeping into existence. There was an element of "creep" back in 1972. Few polls were monitoring party trends on a week-to-week basis from August to November 1972, but those that were found some intriguing shifts. . . . Pennsylvania pollster Albert Sindlinger, a close consultant to the White House, turned up a strong trend favoring the Republicans between August and mid-October, strong enough for the gap between the parties in voter self-identification to narrow to only a few percentage points. Then, in late October, as the Watergate scandal strongly suggested White House guilt, that shift ebbed and broke. Turnout intentions also plummeted. The Republicans may have lost a big-bang opportunity in 1972 or lost a potential for creeping alignment in 1973. No one will ever know.

[1]Some interpretations of the 1982 elections can be expected to suggest a resurgence of the New Deal coalition. For thirty years, Republican Administrations have been undercut in midterm elections—1954, 1958, 1970 and 1974—by recessions and unemployment. But the subsequent presidential elections, in which Democratic weaknesses resurfaced, produced two GOP landslides (1956 and 1972) and two hair's-breadth Democratic victories (1960 and 1976). The definitive proof of the collapse of the (1932–48) New Deal presidential-level coalition lies in the 1968–80 sequence of *presidential* election results—a massive reversal of old patterns.

As for the creeping realignment of 1981, the question was less about its magnitude than about its permanence. Not all polls agreed, of course, but most did show a GOP gain, with Democratic self-identification among voters dropping some 10 points into the 30–40 percent range, while Republican self-identification climbed 5 points into the 25–30 percent range. Skeptics made two rebuttals: first, creeping realignment can't occur, or at least never has yet—it's big bang or nothing; second, the great volatility of voter political self-identification, not just in 1980–81 but over the previous decade, militates against another firmly rooted realignment of the type that occurred in the period from 1860 to 1932. Instead, our current volatility suggests a process of *de-alignment.* Under that thesis, party decomposition continues in one way or another, though that broad trend does not gainsay short-term party gains.

Definitive answers must await the outcome of the elections of 1982 and 1984. Nevertheless, early evidence seems to favor the de-alignment thesis.[2] Polling data show great volatility. All too often, Gallup shows one thing and NBC News another. That degree of variation suggests not erratic survey planners but an erratic electorate.

That the Republicans chose in 1981 to hitch their wagons to a supply-side economic-policy star presents the big reason to be skeptical about any thesis of realignment. Bold promises of an economic renaissance helped elicit an enthusiastic early response from the electorate, but long-range success will be necessary to secure a full and extended commitment. Meanwhile, the European experience of past "price inflations" and our own experience of the present one gives conservatives little to be optimistic about. Because the United States has never before experienced severe peacetime inflation, its politics have never before seen realignment while its economy was in the midst of a period of inflation. Moreover, it can be said that in Canada and Europe the conservative regimes elected since the 1970s have shown little success straightening out national economic difficulties their election rhetoric had blamed on previous left or liberal governments. The prime examples here include Canada, Britain, Holland, Sweden and Israel. Indeed, the principal reason for the ebb and reversal during 1981 and 1982 of the West's post-1975 "trend to the right" is the number of conservative governments unable to cope with stagflation. Conversely, the fall of France's center-right coalition in the spring 1981 elections underscored the extent to which voters were still ready to turn against conservative governments on issues of participation and income maldistribution—issues that some analysts on the right had proclaimed dead. Though Europe's *previous* price revolutions antedated the era of democratic elections, it still seems relevant to note that the later years of the Second Price Revolution (1550–1620) and

---

[2]A September 11, 1981 *Christian Science Monitor* poll of American Political Science Association members found an 85–15 ratio indicating that *de-alignment* rather than *realignment* was under way.

the Third Price Revolution (1770–1820) were characterized by sheer political volatility. Ministers, parliaments and even rulers fell as they proved unable to deal with the pressure and turbulence induced by inflation. Contemporary politicians could encounter the same.

So whether we "creep" toward realignment or "de-align" depends on whether the new Republican economics can deliver a healthier economy. How much time is available for making good is not clear, but certainly by 1984. Absent success, the 1980s are likely to be a time of ongoing de-alignment in which the major parties prove unable to rally a new institutional majority while minor parties achieve increased success. Such a period would probably see considerable instability, as one might expect, given the debilitating legacies of the last two decades.

In *Mediacracy: American Parties and Politics in the Communications Age* (1975), I suggested that traditional realignment might be slipping beyond the realm of the possible, expecially after Watergate confirmed the massive agenda-setting capacity of the news media. Political parties no longer serve the function of mobilizing and communicating to the electorate—a function they arose to serve, or at least took modern form to serve, back in the second quarter of the nineteenth century. Putting it a bit differently, the contemporary form of the political party is a creature of the Industrial Revolution and the rise of mass enfranchisement. Until the 1830s or so, they were unnecessary, and as of the last quarter of the twentieth century, one must again ask how necessary they are. The advances of information-age technology may soon lead to a "wired electorate," reducing the role of the traditional party still further. In such a climate, how can the dynamics of old-style, deep, long-lasting party realignment occur? One can argue by this logic that realignment is now simply impossible: no traditional parties, no realignment.

At this point some speculation is useful and perhaps even essential. If we *are* in a period of de-alignment nurtured by inflation, by a partial revolution in popular and elite ideologies and by the change wrought by electronic communications, what does the future hold? I would lay out four trends and developments, listed roughly in the order of how confident I am about their taking place.

Short Political Cycles

The New Deal Democratic era (1932–1968) may not go down as the last of our party cycles, but the odds are very good that it *will* be the last of the long 28–36-year cycles. Politics in a communications age can turn on a dime—or at least on the perception of the major media. Advanced information technology seems to speed up the evolution of political ideas and movements, as well as quickly consuming those who manage or merchandise them. The ideas of eight or ten years ago are far more remote to the political decision makers of 1982 than ideas of a similar vintage were to decision makers of 1882. The last two decades may have seen a transition. The years between 1968 and 1980, when political realignment was due but did not occur, can be considered an electoral "no man's land," featuring the first of a series of short regimes: a backlash, law-and-order Nixon-Wallace cycle from 1968 to 1972, followed by a period of national mortification from 1974 to 1980; then, since 1980, a nationalist time of "back to old values." More likely than not, we'll now begin to see regimes lasting from four to eight years, transient hegemonies having but shallow roots in fluid party situations.

A Multiplicity of Parties

The United States is the last major Western nation with a two-party system, to say nothing of a system based on two parties that happened to have received their economic, geographic and social definition one hundred and twenty-odd years ago. Other political-institutional arrangements—in Canada, Britain and Germany, for example—allow third-party entry much more easily and possess substantial third parties. However, new-party entry into American presidential elections, although difficult, is by no means impossible. Post-Watergate election reforms now provide federal funding in the presidential election for any party or candidate managing to get at least 5 percent of the national vote in the one four years earlier. Thus, with 7 percent of the vote, John Anderson's 1980 independent candidacy qualified for 1984 return funding, and Anderson has given strong early indications of running again and turning his independent movement into a new center party of sorts. The Libertarian Party, which has run candidates in the last three presidential elections, drew 1 percent in 1980 and is determined to institutionalize itself not only at the national level but in most states. Some observers give the Libertarians a chance of electing a governor in Alaska and possibly elsewhere. Even leaders of the anticorporate Citizens Party, which drew only one quarter of 1 percent in 1980, with envionmental-ist Barry Commoner as its presidential candidate, feel that the times support its institutionalization. In 1981, several magazine articles discussed Citizens Party success in local races from Burlington, Vermont, to Santa Monica, California.

[Table 1] profiles the principal Anderson, Libertarian and Citizens party support centers. Most European countries have minor parties with a centrist cast, as well as "Green" (environmentalist) parties, and it may well be that the American minor parties of 1980 will be able to stake out similar turf and roles. Here again, a lot depends on the new Republican economics.

[TABLE 1] TOP SPLINTER PARTY STATES, 1980
(In Percentage of Total Vote for President)

Top 10 Anderson States		Top Ten Libertarian Party States		Top Ten Citizens Party States	
Massachusetts	15.18%	Alaska	11.79%	Oregon	1.15%
Vermont	14.52	Montana	2.70	Vermont	1.09
Rhode Island	14.21	Wyoming	2.55	D.C.	1.05
New Hampshire	12.54	Oregon	2.19	Maine	0.84
Connecticut	12.22	Colorado	2.17	Virginia	0.75
Colorado	11.03	Arizona	2.15	California	0.71
Washington	10.62	Idaho	1.93	Washington	0.54
Hawaii	10.56	Nevada	1.76	Hawaii	0.51
Maine	10.20	California	1.74	New Mexico	0.48
Oregon	9.53	Washington	1.68	Colorado	0.47

Note: Overall, it's fair to say that the 1980 splinter-party vote was heavily concentrated in states—and especially in communities within those states—with heavy ratios of what could be called post-industrial, Third Wave, post-bourgeois or "Green" voters. The pre-eminence of New England, Colorado and the Pacific states—with their disproportionate numbers of universities, environmentalists, resort areas and high-tech concentrations—is the key. In New England, the splinter parties together pulled almost 15% of the vote, likewise in Colorado. Alaska was a bit higher because of its Libertarian strength. Splinter-party strength hit 13% in Washington and Oregon, 12% in Hawaii and 11% in California. It's notable that these concentrations include most of the states futurists usually look to as U.S. trend setters. Also, it's useful to bear in mind that in the United States, the growth and characteristics of splinter parties has usually signaled a major upcoming force in national politics.

Plebiscitary Parties and Presidencies

One of the more intriguing—and so far least understood—phenomena in Republicanism and New Right populist conservatism is the extent to which advanced communications technology is being used by both to pursue an increasingly plebiscitary politics. By this I mean five particular new practices and biases: First, we can see growing emphasis on the presidency as a vehicle to get the attention of the public and mobilize the electorate, especially since Ronald Reagan as "The Great Communicator" is uniquely able to use television to marshal national opinion; second, we can see unprecedented mobilization of grassroots communications and voter support to pressure senators, congressmen and interest groups to embrace a particular issue; third, we can note mushrooming and massive use of direct mail for issue agitation and fund raising; fourth, we can see a growing philosophic embrace of plebiscitary mechanisms. In 1979 and 1980, conservative presidential candidates from John Connally to Philip Crane endorsed national plebiscites on the Panama Canal treaties and a balanced budget, while the Republican governors and/or parties in New Jersey, Texas, Minnesota and elsewhere plunked for state-level adoption of a national initiative-and-referendum plebiscitary devices. Meanwhile, Congressman Jack Kemp and his "tax revolt" allies have called for adoption of a national initiative-and-referendum mechanism; and fifth, we can see GOP strategists making specific use of initiative and referendum as an ideological and institutional tool. Republicans in states like California have begun to use tax-cut, anticrime and antibusing referenda as a device to mobilize political opinion. The GOP has also begun to use the initiative mechanism as a targeted political weapon—in states like Massachusetts, Ohio, Oklahoma and California—to try to undercut Democratic legislatures by changing their organizational rules and by putting their redistricting plans on the ballot for public scrutiny and rejection.

I think that this trend is enormously important. Moreover, there is nothing conservative about it in the traditional sense, and New Right populist conservatives are among the strongest proponents of the plebiscitary approach. Plebiscitary politics undercuts the role of party, putting increased emphasis on technology, the mood of the public and short-term issue-based coalitions. Such developments are entirely compatible with either a populist reinvigoration of atrophying institutions *or* a trend to Caesarism.

Supraparty Coalitions

As it became apparent during the late 1970s that the opportunity for party realignment was slim, conservatives—especially New Right populist conservatives—took the lead pushing supraparty coalitions based on shared philosophy. In a number of Southern states, the coalitions were neither unusual nor especially innovative—Republicans and conservative Democrats simply agreed to vote together against moderate and liberal Democrats to organize at least one legislative house in Texas, Louisiana and Florida. In New Mexico and New Hampshire, by contrast, the successful philosophic coalition enlisted conservatives of both parties to vote against liberals of both parties. Meanwhile, the New Right-linked Free Congress Foundation has staged several conferences around the country with an eye to getting a supraparty coalition to organize the House of Representatives. Intriguingly, similar arrangements of coalition were necessary to organize the House in the midst of the *last* major breakup of our party system. In 1855 a group of Whigs, Republicans and Free Soil Democrats voted to elect Nathaniel P. Banks Speaker. That sort of thing could happen again in the 1980s. The Reagan Administraton successfully attracted conservative Democrats into issue-coalitions on tax and budget legislation; meanwhile, House Ways and Means Committee chariman Daniel Rostenkowski spoke openly in mid-1981 about the possibility of conservative Democrats going into coalition with Republicans to organize the House in 1983. Which has a certain institutional logic. If de-alignment is to be the hallmark of party politics of the 1980s, then coalition may succeed yesteryear's mode of electoral realignment.

Whether we de-align or realign is the key question. My own sense is that both parties have been and still are in a process of long-term erosion. As of 1981, the Democrats elicited the loyalty of only 30–40 percent of Americans, down from roughly 50 percent in the mid 1960s and the years after Watergate and Nixon's resignation. The Republicans, with 25–30 percent, were back up to 1968–72 levels, but well below their Eisenhower-era percentages. The most enduring phenomenon of the years since the war in Vietnam and Watergate has been the rise in the ranks of *independents.*

Admittedly, a strong economic rebound in the 1980s could overmatch the forces of de-alignment and create something resembling a traditional Republican realignment. And if the Republicans avoid erosion, that automatically eases pressure on the Democrats. The threat to the two-party system, the most plausible spur to accelerated de-alignment, is a 1981–84 failure of *Republican* economic policy in the wake of the 1977–80 failure of *Democratic* economic policy. Coming on top of all the political and social stresses of the last two decades, such double failure would create great strains—and new-party pressures.

The disintegration of the old Democratic coalition during the last two decades is now widely accepted. Failure now by Republicans in economic policy making could provoke a similar unraveling on their side of the aisle. The Sun Belt, fundamentalist-tilted forces of the New Right, and the GOP's lingering New England/Great Lakes/Pacific Northwestern social progressives are as hostile and incompatible as the McGovern/New Class and George Wallace Democrats were in the late 1960s and 1970s. Without the optimism of the early days of Reaganomics and a Republican realignment, their cohesion may not last the decade. In my view, the 1980 John Anderson constituency, though just 7 percent of the electroate, is fascinating, possibly foreshadowing a new center party not unlike the Social Democratic/Liberal grouping taking shape in Britain and the Free Democrats in West Germany. Heavily based in university towns, affluent resorts, moderate Yankee GOP strongholds, affluent suburbs and the new high-tech industrial areas, Anderson's is the first major American political splinter effort since the GOP in the 1850s to draw on a predominantly middle-to-high income, socioeconomic "cutting edge" electorate. . . . The usual appeal of a splinter party has been to alienated, less affluent peripheries. Should Reaganomics not pan out, the Administration would be obliged to intensify its appeal to populist lower-middle-income conservatives with provocative social and foreign-policy themes. Whereupon the Anderson electorate could mushroom into an important 1984 independent political grouping. Moreover, if Vice President Bush should succeed to the presidency or win the Republican nomination in 1984, the New Right could bolt. *Both* ideological wings of the GOP are loose.

[TABLE 2] LIBERAL AND MODERATE REPUBLICAN TRENDS, 1976–80
Two-Candidate Preferences of Voters, 1976–80
(CBS News/New York *Times* Poll)

	1976 % GOP	% Dem.	1980 % GOP	% Dem.
Liberal Republicans	83	17	72	28
Moderate Republicans	89	11	86	14
Conservative Republicans	94	6	94	6
Conservative Democrats	35	65	44	56

Source: New York Times, *November 8, 1980*

The major intraparty problem facing Reagan Republicanism, of course, can be found among the party's old Yankee and Northeastern establishment moderates. The problem visibility, though quite obvious in 1980 election returns, was hidden in early 1981 as party moderates rallied around the Administrations's tax and budget proposals. But that support was necessarily short-lived because Reagan Administration socioeconomic incompatibility with the old liberal GOP strongholds was inevitable. According to the Gallup poll, Reagan drew only 86 percent of the national Republican vote in 1981, the lowest of any party nominee since Barry Goldwater, who took only 80 percent. As [Table 2] shows, Reagan ran far behind Gerald Ford among liberal Republicans and somewhat behind the Michigander among moderate Republicans. Of course, Reagan more than made up for the slippage with sharp gains among Sun Belt voters, Protestant fundamentalists and conservative Catholic Democrats. But in the old Yankee GOP strongholds of New England—the best places to look for a reaction against a GOP Sun Belt, Southern or "Cowboy" strategy—Reagan in 1980 ran 30–45 points behind 1956 GOP presidential strength, and in some cases the former California governor barely ran ahead of Barry Goldwater's 1964 levels. [Table 3] illustrates the ebb. This ongoing GOP erosion in its ancestral

[TABLE 3] THE YANKEE REPUBLICAN EBB, 1956–80
Republican Percentage of Total Vote for President

County[1]	1956	1964	1980
Barnstable, Mass.	83%	43%	51%
Dukes, Mass.	83	32	34
Nantucket, Mass.	83	33	41
Hancock, Maine	87	46	54
Lincoln, Maine	86	44	52
Orange, Vermont	84	41	50
Windham, Vermont	80	33	43
Lamoille, Vermont	84	46	47

[1]*These counties, in 1956, were the Yankee Republican strongholds of their respective states.*

territory, coupled with Democratic losses in Dixie, make for yet another reason to think that the 1980s will not produce a 1930s-style traditional realignment, and another reason to think that a larger reshuffling and rearrangement of American politics is upon us.

If that sounds vague, it is. Trying to forecast the shape of our politiics during a period of global upheaval is hard enough. In 1981 the nation also found itself in the midst of a possible electoral watershed under the aegis of a President who, having turned seventy years old just after his inauguration, was deemed by many observers unlikely to seek a second term in 1984. Previous watershed elections required the Presidents involved—Jefferson, Jackson, Lincoln, McKinley and FDR—to seek and win re-election to consolidate their party's new majority status. All five did.

To summarize: my sense is that the chances for a traditional realignment of the party system are slim. Instead, what we'll probably see are short-term political coalitions and supremacies based more on communications technology than on old-style parties. In the process, our politics will become increasingly prone to plebiscitary techniques and appeals. The American party system seems a long way from overcoming two decades of weakness. In fact, that weakness is probably moving front and center.

Has There Been a Party Realignment in the 1980s?

A DEMOCRAT AND AMERICAN ENTERPRISE INSTITUTE SCHOLAR SEES
THE DISTINCT POSSIBILITY OF A REPUBLICAN MAJORITY IN THE FUTURE

Political analyst William Schneider, a Democrat, finds comfort in the data he analyzed from the 1984 presidential election, because it did not reflect a major shift to the Republicans. Reagan was highly ideological, but voters choose presidents on the basis of performance, not ideology, argues Schneider. Ideological shifts among the electorate do not occur at the initial states of realignment, but only after voters find the policies of the party in power to be effective. The first stage of realignment is a vote for *change,* the second phase an endorsement of the new majority party's leadership. The Democrats have lost many of their traditional constituencies, a process that began in 1968, but Reagan's electoral successes did not prove by themselves that a realignment occurred. Ironically, Democrat Schneider, although noting many of the same dispersive political forces cited by Republican Phillips that obstruct party realignments, sees the distinct possibility that the 1988 presidential election may finally reveal the arrival of a Republican majority that will last over the long term.

W. SCHNEIDER

8

Half a Realignment

WILLIAM SCHNEIDER

"I survived."

–Abbé Sieyés, when asked what he had done during the French Revolution.

We survived. After counting the heads that rolled into the basket, our intrepid leader, House Speaker Tip O'Neill reassured us, "There is no mandate out there." *The New York Times* backed him up with scientific evidence: POLL FINDS REAGAN FAILED TO OBTAIN A POLICY MANDATE. Even the Republicans joined in. "It was a victory for his philosophy and a victory for him personally, but I'm not sitting here claiming it's a big mandate," said White House Chief of Staff James A. Baker III. And former White House Communications Director David P. Gergen remarked, "The Republicans won the election and the Democrats are winning the interpretation."

Perhaps, but it is an interpretation that sounds suspiciously like whistling past the graveyard. The fact is, the Democratic defeat was monumental in its proportions. We lost nearly every group, nearly everywhere. President Reagan's apparent lack of coattails—the Republicans suffered a net loss of two Senate seats and gained only fourteen House seats, one governorship, and four state legislative chambers—is a fact that obscures more than it reveals. Democrats are in the same position as the French aristocracy at the time of the Bourbon Restoration. We can pretend that nothing has really happened, but the *ancien régime* is dead. Things will never be the same. The problem for the Democrats is to avoid the fate of the Bourbons, of whom Talleyrand said, "They learned nothing and they forgot nothing."

Reprinted by permission of The New Republic, © *1984, The New Republic, Inc.*

What happened is simple enough. The election was a referendum on Ronald Reagan. President Reagan's job approval ratings [held] steady at 55 to 60 percent [in 1984], which is to say that throughout the campaign most Americans felt he deserved to be reelected. Reagan's 18-point margin over Walter Mondale on November 6 [1984] was the same as it had been in January. Not a single poll taken during the entire campaign showed Mondale with a significant lead over Reagan. In the *Los Angeles Times* nationwide exit poll, almost half of the voters reported that they had made up their minds about how they were going to vote before the campaign even started last February; their decision was 2 to 1 for Reagan.

Reagan had two things going for him: the economy and foreign policy. Those are very big things. The Democrats got nowhere trying to convince people that the President had failed in either area.

The voters believed that Reagan did what he was elected to do: he curbed inflation and he restored the nation's sense of military security. As it happens, many people disagreed with the way he accomplished those things. Inflation was reduced at the cost of a severe recession. Our perceived military strength was improved at the cost of a significantly higher level of international tensions. Still, after four failed Presidencies in a row, it is rare enough to have a President who does what he was elected to do. As Reagan is fond of saying, "You don't quarrel with success."

Consider the economy. In the 1982 midterm election, the Democrats did very well with the fairness issue. Why didn't the issue work [in 1984]? Because in 1982, when the economy was bad, fairness meant *us*. In 1984, when the economy looks good, fairness means *them*.

What about foreign policy? The Democrats ran ads suggesting that Reagan was going to blow us all up. A lot of people were worried about that in 1980, but not [in 1984]. Reagan [had] been President for almost four years, and [we were] still here. The polls showed that this time the voters were demonstrably less concerned with Reagan's recklessness, his intellectual competence, and his age. That's what incumbency does for you.

A lot of Democrats thought they could use the Administration's failure in Lebanon as an issue against the President. After all, many more American lives were lost in Lebanon than were lost in Iran. But Iran is still seen as a national humiliation and a disgrace. Lebanon is not. Why? Because when it became clear that our peacekeeping mission in Lebanon was not working President Reagan had the good sense to cut our losses and get out. That, to many Americans, is leadership—the kind of leadership we did not get in Vietnam. During the Vietnam trauma, pollsters regularly asked Americans if they preferred a "hawkish" or a "dovish" policy in Southeast Asia. The answer they got over and over was, "We should either win or get out." What people didn't want was endless, pointless, escalating involvement.

Well, what did Reagan do as President? In Grenada we won. In Lebanon we got out. So much for the Vietnam syndrome.

As one election analysis put it, "He loves to display American military muscle, yet prefers to do so without there being any American victims. He supports peace from a position of American strength, but is against this strength resulting in the threat of a nuclear war." Precisely. But a policy portrayed by *Izvestia* as inconsistent and contradictory turns out to be exactly the foreign policy the American public wants.

What did not happen in the election is in many ways more interesting than what did happen. Contrary to expectation, Reagan did not sweep large numbers of Republicans into office. As House Republican leader Robert H. Michel complained, "Here the son of a buck ended up with 59 percent, and you bring in only 15 seats." The explanation, in a word, is incumbency. Incumbents have a large and growing advantage in American politics because of their dominance of the media, fund-raising, communications with constituents, and campaign technology. Americans regularly reelect over 90 percent of those members of Congress who decide to run for reelection. And most do.

Republicans actually did quite well this year in "open seats," where no incumbent was on the ballot. Open House seats were split about 50–50 before the election and ended up going 2 to 1 Republican. But they accounted for only 27 out of 435 contests. True, the Democrats gained 1 seat in the 4 open Senate races. But in the 7 open races for governor, G.O.P control went from 3 to 6.

The exit polls reveal that, nationwide, almost as many people voted for Republicans as for Democrats in House races this year. Democrats nevertheless retained a 3-to-2 lead in the House. One reason is that congressional district boundaries were redrawn by Democratic-controlled state legislatures after the 1980 census so as to protect incumbents of both parties by giving them districts with "safe" electoral majorities. It is significant, therefore, that more than 300 state legislative seats shifted to the Republicans this year. According to the council of State Legislatures, "Presidential coattails tended to work best when a seat was vacant."

It was incumbency that saved the Democratic Party from ruin. If the government had passed a decree prohibiting incumbents from running for reelection, the Republican Party would probably have gained control of both Houses of Congress and a substantial number of statehouses.

They would probably have held on to the White House too. Much too much has been made of the personality factor in the 1984 election. Yes, Americans tend to like Ronald Reagan, and he is an effective television performer. but Walter Mondale's complaint that he lost the election because he could not communicate effectively on television is entirely unconvincing. One can hardly imagine less effective television performers—or less congenial personalities—than Lyndon Johnson, Richard Nixon, or Jimmy Carter. The polls make it clear that if Ronald Reagan had run for reelection under the conditions prevailing in 1982 instead of 1984, he would have lost decisively, all his charm and amiability notwithstanding.

Several other things that did not happen:

The electorate was not, to any exceptional degree, driven by greed. Yes, people who felt better off voted for the incumbent and those who felt worse off voted for the challenger. But that was no more true this year than in 1980, or in 1976, or in any previous election. Moreover, voters' assessment of the nation's economy had a stronger and more consistent impact on their vote than their evaluation of their own personal well-being. People who felt that the country was beginning a long-term recovery voted for Reagan by a wide margin, no matter how they themselves had fared. And those who saw no improvement in the economy voted overwhelmingly for Mondale, even if they had become better off.

The gender gap did not widen. In fact, it got a bit smaller. In the end, the nomination of Geraldine Ferraro seems to have made little difference. Americans did exactly what they have done in the past: they voted for President, not for Vice President. After careful research, many voters who admired Ferraro discovered that they could not vote for her without also voting for Mondale. Women went for Reagan, Catholics went for Reagan, Italian-Americans went for Reagan, and New Yorkers went for Reagan. Even New York Italian-American Catholic women went for Reagan (54 to 46, according to one exit poll).

Mondale's share of the vote this year was no higher than Jimmy Carter's was four years ago, whereas Reagan's share went up by 8 percentage points. Does that mean John Anderson's supporters deserted the Democrats? Not at all. Anderson supporters accepted their leader's advice and voted Democratic this year, by 2 to 1. On the other hand, Reagan picked up one out of every five former Carter voters, mostly southern whites. Those who had not voted in 1980 also went heavily for Reagan.

That too was unexpected. The Democrats made a great deal of noise about a major registration campaign to expand turnout to 100 million voters. They failed dismally. Actually, those who registered for the first time between 1981 and 1983 (i.e., during the recession) split evenly between Reagan and Mondale. But those who registered in 1984—8 percent of the total vote—went 3 to 2 for Reagan. Thus the strong Republican advantage in organization and resources cancelled out gains that the Democrats might otherwise have made.

Young voters went for Reagan by about the same margin, leading to much speculation about the newfound conservatism of the young. That too was nonsense. The young are still the most liberal age group in the electorate. They supported Reagan for many reasons, all unrelated to ideology.

Last spring Mondale had a great deal of trouble with two groups of primary voters: young people and independents. They were the main elements of Gary Hart's constituency, and the evidence suggests that their motivation was more anti-Mondale than pro-Hart. (Hart substantiated this conclusion in a *Newsweek* interview last May. "[Mondale] thinks *I'm* his problem," Hart said. "I'm not his problem. *He's* his problem.") If young voters and independents had little interest in Mondale last spring, how astonishing can it be that they had little interest in Mondale this fall?

As a whole, the 1984 election was not ideological. On many issues, the voters were closer to Mondale's views than to Reagan's. These included abortion, military spending, arms control, the Equal Rights Amendment, Central America, and the role of religion in politics. The same thing was true in 1980: on a left-right scale, the voters placed themselves closer to Carter than to Reagan. Then, as now, the central issue in the election was performance—not personality or philosophy. There was widespread agreement in 1980 that on the basis of his performance, Carter did not deserve to be reelected. There was widespread agreement this year that on the basis of his performance, Reagan did.

What people were voting for in 1980 was not conservatism but change. What people were voting for this year was neither conservatism nor change but continuity. The fact that both elections were decided on the basis of performance rather than ideology is surprising only because Reagan is such an ideological figure. His achievement in 1980 was to win the support (at the last minute) of many voters who did not agree with him ideologically. He did it again [in 1984].

Which brings us to the subject of realignment. If the election was not ideological, how can anyone talk about a realignment? The answer is that, when realignment occurs, ideology is usually the last thing to change, if it changes at all.

For instance, there is little evidence that the electorate moved sharply to the left during the 1930s. In February 1936, in the midst of the Depression and only nine months before Franklin D. Roosevelt's landslide reelection, a Gallup poll found that 70 percent of the public favored cuts in governmment spending for the purposes of reducing the national debt. Voters did not accept F.D.R.'s New Deal philosophy until they were convinced that the New Deal worked.

A realignment occurs in two stages. First, the President has to demonstrate that his policies are effective. Only then do voters begin to convert to his vision of society. This year's election results suggest that the first stage has occurred. The second may be underway: the voters, when polled, revealed that they felt closer to Reagan than to Mondale on the issues—including many specific issues like abortion and Central America, where other evidence shows that people's positions are really closer to Mondale's.

The reason people seem to feel that they agree with President Reagan even if they really don't is that they believe his policies are working. The public's approach to the issues is pragmatic—whatever works must be right. Ideologues, on the other hand, believe that whatever is wrong cannot possibly work, even if it does work. Thus, many die-hard Republicans never admitted that the New Deal was a success, and many Democrats today refuse to believe there is a recovery. To pragmatic Americans, if big government policies worked during the New Deal, then they were probably right, at least for that time. If Reagan's anti-government policies are working, then they are probably right, at least for now.

The exit polls also reveal a startling shift in the partisanship of American voters. In four nationwide exit polls taken on November 6, an average of 36 percent of the voters described themselves as Democrats and 32 percent as Republicans. That is a sharp change from the 42-to-28 percent margin reported in 1980. Large numbers of Democrats seem to have abandoned their party this year, some by voting Republican, some by rejecting the Democratic label, and some by staying home.

There have been marked changes in the nature of the Democratic vote as well. Compare Mondale's vote this year to the vote for Adlai Stevenson in 1956. Both were midwestern liberals, and both got about the same share of the national vote (41 percent for Mondale, 42 percent for Stevenson). But the sources of their support were very different. Mondale did significantly better than Stevenson among black voters, college graduates, women, Jews, and professionals. On the other hand, Stevenson's support was much stronger among whites, southerners, men, blue-collar workers, union members, and Catholics.

These shifts did not happen suddenly. Beginning in the mid-1960s, two streams of voters began leaving the Democratic Party—white southerners and Catholic "ethnic" voters in the North. The first stage of this realignment occured in 1968 and 1972, when race and foriegn policy were the major issues of contention. During this period, the Democrats lost most of their "social issue conservatives," primarily but not exclusively white southerners.

The second stage, 1980–84, has been much more devastating because the party has lost its credibility on economic issues. The economic issue had always held the Democratic Party together, even when race and Vietnam were tearing it apart. Since the 1930s, the Democrats have defined themselves more than anything else as the party that protects people against economic adversity. That's what kept white working-class voters in the party despite their mistrust of its racial and foreign policy liberalism.

Gallup polls show that the Democrats' long-standing advantage as the party more likely to keep the nation prosperous has vanished. In 1980, as a result of Jimmy Carter's economic failures, the voters saw no difference between the two parties on the prosperity issue. This year, as a result of Ronald Reagan's success, the Republicans hold a 17-point advantage. If the

Democrats cannot offer people economic security, what reason is there to stay in the party?

The Democrats have become less of a populist party and more of a liberal party. As the party has lost moderate and conservative Catholics and southerners, it has strengthened its appeal to blacks and educated upper-middle-class liberals. Over one-quarter of the votes cast for the Democratic ticket this year came from blacks. In the South, blacks were a majority of Democratic voters.

Remember this old vaudeville routine?

> Doctor to patient with mysterious ailment:
> Sir, have you ever had this problem before?
> Patient: Yes.
> Doctor: Well, you've got it again.

The Democrats have had this problem before. In 1968 and 1972, to be exact. And they've got it again. Mondale's vote looks very much like the disastrous votes for Hubert Humphrey and George McGovern, both northern liberal Protestants who, like Mondale, chose northern Liberal Catholics as their running mates.

The result should be clear by now: when you offer tickets like that, you write off the South. Neither Harry Truman, nor John F. Kennedy, nor Jimmy Carter would have won the Presidency without southern electoral votes. Giving up the South wouldn't be so bad, except for the fact that the party is losing other constituencies as well. Catholics voted 59 percent for Humphrey in 1968, 48 percent for McGovern in 1972, and 44 percent for Mondale this year.

Essentially the national Democratic Party has lost its conservative wing, which used to be a considerable segment of the party. And its moderate support is diminishing fast. (Look at John Glenn's performance in the primaries this year.) To some extent, the party's losses on the right have been compensated by its gains among blacks and liberals, including liberal Republicans like John Anderson. Overall, however, the losses have outweighed the gains.

Which means the Democrats can no longer be called the nation's normal majority party. On the other hand, the Republicans cannot claim a natural majority of voters either. We are approaching a situation where the country is one-third Democratic, one-third Republican, and one-third independent. But keep in mind that with the exception of 1964, independents have given the edge to the Republican candidate in every Presidential election since 1952.

Can the Republican Party hold itself together? At least one issue, religion threatens to tear the party apart. Sure, it's a problem, but remember that in the New Deal coalition, southern racists, blacks, and northern liberals managed to stick together for thirty years, mostly by avoiding the subject of race. So far President Reagan has talked a great deal about the social issues, but has avoided placing them at the top of the Administration's agenda. If he decides to push the social issues in his second term that could damage the party's future prospects.

How will we know if a realignment occurs? During the New Deal, Republicans liked to believe that Roosevelt's majorities were personal and would vanish when he left the political scene. So what happened after four straight F.D.R. victories? Harry Truman won, and the Republicans finally had to face the fact that something fundamental had changed. If the Republicans can win without Reagan on the ticket in 1988, then we will know the same thing has happened in our time.

Can the Democrats, a party that nominated William Jennings Bryan three times, learn anything from the disasters of 1968, 1980, and 1984? Maybe, but on the other hand, many Democrats believe that they tried another approach with Jimmy Carter. And look what happened.

CHAPTER FIVE

Interest Group Power

In words that might well be used by contemporary advocates of strong controls over interest groups, particularly political action committees, James Madison stated in the tenth paper of *The Federalist* that government should strive "to break and control the violence of faction. The friend of popular governments never finds himself so much alarmed for their character and fate as when he contemplates their propensity to this dangerous vice. He will not fail, therefore, to set a due value on any plan which, without violating the principles to which he is attached, provides a proper cure for it."

Madison's views reflected the Founding Father's belief that political leaders should strive to be statesmen, subordinating private to public interests. But they recognized, as Madison pointed out in *Federalist 10,* that groups pursuing their "selfish" interests would be an inevitable part of the political process. A continuing debate in American politics concerns the role that interest groups should play in our system of constitutional democracy.

DEBATE FOCUS

Do Political Action Committees Subvert Democracy?

COMMON CAUSE LEADERS ARGUE THAT PACS UNDERMINE THE
DEMOCRATIC PROCESS

Ironically, the campaign finance laws of the 1970s, designed to control special interest influence on government, not only allowed but encouraged the formation of political action committees (PACs). Corporations, labor unions, trade associations, professional groups, and others can pay out of their own treasuries for the administrative expenses of forming and running political action committees. For their part, PACs receive voluntary contributions from employees, stockholders, and group members. PACs then contribute money directly to sympathetic political candidates, and spend indirectly in behalf of candidates and causes. The law limits direct donations to $5,000 each for a primary and general election campaign, but imposes no restrictions upon indirect expenditures.

Representatives of Common Cause argue in the following selection that PAC money flowing to congressional campaigns subverts the democratic process by giving special interests a disproportionate influence over the nation's lawmakers.

97

A. COX

9

The Choice Is Clear: It's People vs. the PACs

**ARCHIBALD COX
FRED WERTHEIMER**

F. WERTHEIMER

Our form of representative government, for all its imperfections, has served us admirably for more than two centuries. But today it is under attack. Our system of financing congressional campaigns allows special interest groups to gain disproportionate access to lawmakers in order to influence decisions in Congress. As a result, increasingly political issues are being decided not on their merits but out of deference to wealthy campaign donors.

Political action committees (PACs) are conduits for special interest money from corporations, labor unions or trade associations—groups with vested interests in the legislation Congress considers.

The problem with PAC money is that it comes with strings attached. At the very least it may buy its sponsors access to a Member of Congress—access that is not always available to others. And at worst, PAC money actually influences congressional votes.

Over the years, Common Cause has kept a close watch on the relationship between PAC money received by congressional candidates and the votes these recipients cast on matters of importance to the PACs. Time and time again, the studies show a close correlation between money received and votes favorable to PAC donors.

And the problem is getting worse. It appears that every group—except

From *Archibald Cox and Fred Wertheimer*, People Against PACs: A Common Cause Guide to Winning the War Against Political Action Committees *(Washington, D.C.: Common Cause, 1983). Reprinted by permission.*

the people—now has a PAC. The number of special interest PACs has skyrocketed, and the amount they are pouring into the political system has grown incredibly.

These are among the reasons Common Cause has decided to declare a "War on PACs." The campaign will bring together dozens of organizations and millions of Americans around the country who want to reclaim their right to elect leaders in a system relatively free of the taint of special interest money.

It will not be an easy fight: The opponents of change count among their ranks many of the nation's most influential interest groups as well as many Members of Congress who know full well that the largest share of PAC money goes to help incumbents get reelected.

Formidable as these forces are, however, there is one that is even more powerful: the American people. Thanks to unprecedented press coverage of the PAC menace during the 1982 campaigns, we have a rare opportunity to push this issue to the forefront of the political agenda, and to take up once again the historical battle for campaign finance reform that was begun so boldly a decade ago. Remember, it was in 1974 that major reforms were passed by Congress, when America took the presidency off the auction block. We must now do the same for Congress.

Archibald Cox
Chairman, Common Cause

During the congressional elections last fall, PACs showered money on candidates as never before. Now there are encouraging signs that Americans will no longer tolerate PAC tyranny. They are sending signals to Washington that alternatives are needed—and needed now.

In January, Common Cause hosted a meeting of 21 national citizens' groups that included such various interests as the American Federation of State, County, Municipal Employees (AFSCME), the Consumer Federation of America, the League of Women Voters, and Rural America. Representatives from these groups discussed problems related to PACs and possible alternatives. Sixteen of them then joined CC in signing a letter to Members of Congress stating "We . . . believe that fundamental changes in congressional campaign financing must be made. We believe that the establishment of a public financing system coupled with overall limits on PAC contributions, is essential to restoring fairness in congressional elections and confidence in our system of selecting leaders."

Groups endorsing the letter reflected an enormous diversity, and the work of this broad-based coalition will be extremely important, because this political fight is one which will need strong grassroots support before it can be fought in Congress. Despite some opposition to PACs among Members of Congress, there are many Members who are unwilling to attack a system that clearly works to the advantage of those currently in office. As one congressional champion of campaign finance reform has said, "This campaign finance issue must be won on the outside—in the press and with the public."

The stakes in this battle are enormous, and that's why Common Cause is calling it a war—a political war. We believe that representative government—a government of the people, by the people and for the people, lies in the balance.

Unless this war is won, we are facing a government of the PACs, by the PACs and for the PACs. It is truly a choice between the people and the PACs. We believe the choice is clear. We hope that millions of Americans will join with us in a successful campaign to bring an end to the power of the PAC movement in American politics.

Fred Wertheimer
President, Common Cause

A GOVERNMENT OF, BY AND FOR THE PACS

HOW POLITICAL ACTION COMMITTEES GIVE YOU THE BEST CONGRESS MONEY CAN BUY

"A government of the people, by the people, for the people"—this was the vision of one of our greatest leaders, Abraham Lincoln. Today Lincoln's well worn credo is being subordinated by a new threat—the threat of special interest money. An explosion of political action committees is robbing our nation of its democratic ideals and giving us a government of leaders beholden to the monied interests who make their election possible. If we do not fight to reclaim our government, we will find that it has become . . .

A GOVERNMENT OF THE PACS

A simple break-in at the headquarters of the Democratic National Committee in 1972 touched off a flood of revelations concerning President Nixon's abuses of power. Among the scandals that surfaced during Watergate were several concerning Nixon's campaign finances: Illegal campaign contributions by American Airlines to Nixon's 1972 campaign occurred while the airline was waiting to hear about a request it made to the White House for approval of a merger with another airline. . . . A pledge by International Telephone and Telegraph Corp. (ITT) to give $400,000 to the 1972 Republican National Convention was followed by a favorable ruling by the Justice Department on alleged antitrust actions by the multinational conglomerate.

Individuals got in on the bonanza too: Nixon's campaign received more than $1.7 million in contributions from people who were subsequently appointed as ambassadors.

In the wake of these revelations, a shocked public pressured Congress to enact sweeping campaign finance reforms. Among them was the creation of a system of public financing for presidential races, which allows major party and other serious candidates to qualify for public funds. These funds are provided by taxpayers who signal on their tax returns that they want $1 of the taxes they owe to go toward a fund established for that purpose.

To prevent any one group or individual from lavishing large sums of money on presidential or congressional candidates, Congress also placed limits on the amounts either could contribute to any one candidate—$1,000 for individuals and $5,000 for groups, per candidate, per election.

And finally, Congress established the Federal Election Commission, an independent watchdog agency, to provide the first official oversight of federal campaign finance laws.

But for all its reforms, Congress left a key piece of work undone: Members failed to institute public financing for congressional campaigns. To make matters worse, in 1974 they went along with business and labor, both of which pushed forcefully to repeal a law that barred government contractors from forming political action committees (PACs). The repeal of this law helped touch off a flood of corporate and labor PACs.

Common Cause and some Members of Congress strongly opposed allowing government contractors to form PACs, and a *Washington Post* editorial at that time labeled it "another loophole to more corruption in American politics." Once Congress had repealed the prohibition, special interest money began to pour into congressional elections.

BY THE PACS

PACs aren't new. They were formed because corporations, labor unions and professional, trade and other membership groups are prohibited from giving money directly to federal candidates. By establishing a nominally separate fund—or PAC—these groups can contribute to federal elections. PAC contributions are generally given by groups which are also regularly engaged in organized lobbying efforts; not surprisingly contributions are often given with a legislative purpose in mind.

In the past few years, the PAC system has reached disturbing dimensions. In the eight years since 1974, the number of PACs has increased from 608 to more than 3,400—an increase of more than *500 percent*. During that same time, the amount of money spent by PACs on congressional campaigns has soared from $12.4 million to an estimated $80 million—a *650 percent* increase.

Not only have the number of PACs and their total contributions increased dramatically; PACs now play an increasingly instrumental role in financing congressional campaigns. Consider these facts:

- In the newly seated 98th Congress, the average House winner received more than one third of his or her campaign funds from PACs, up from 28 percent in the 1978 elections.
- Winners in the Senate got 22 percent of their total campaign contributions from PACs. In the 1978 elections, Senate winners got only 13 percent of their campaign funds from PACs.
- More than 100 House Members received more than half their money from PACs.

If Members of Congress seem less than willing to shut the door on PACs, it may have something to do with the way PAC spending favors incumbents over challengers: In the 1982 elections, incumbents running for reelection received $48 million from PACs—quadruple the amount that challengers received. The gap in PAC receipts has widened since 1980, when incumbents got about two and a half times more money from PACs than did challengers.

In addition to the phenomenal growth in PAC contributions since 1974, there has been a dramatic increase in so-called "independent expenditures" by PACs. Under a 1976 Supreme Court ruling, PACs are allowed to spend unlimited money on behalf of a candidate, provided they do so independently of any political party or any candidate's official campaign organization. While the court's ruling—made at a time when very little money went toward such "independent expenditures"—was intended to protect freedom of speech, some PACs have used the ruling to circumvent limits on direct contributions to candidates. During the 1980 elections, "independent spending" by PACs totaled $2.4 million. In the 1982 elections, such spending reached $5.5 million.

While these expenditures comprise a small percentage of total PAC spending, they have been cause for concern, both because there are indications that some "independent" spenders aren't really independent, and because the independence of the campaigns has been construed as a license to conduct negative, mud slinging campaigns with little regard for truth or accuracy. Furthermore, unlike the parties or candidates, these groups remain outside the electoral process. They are unaccountable and, as recent history has shown, often invest their money in irresponsible attacks on candidates.

FOR THE PACS

One of the most tragic aspects of the PAC system is that money becomes more powerful than votes. "It is simply a fact of life that when big money in the form of group contributions enters the political arena, big obligations are entertained, " says Rep. Jim Leach (R-Iowa), a supporter of reform of the campaign finance laws.

One Washington lobbyist succinctly described the difference between having a PAC and not having a PAC when it came time to lobby Congress. "I won't even take a client now," he remarked, "unless he's willing to set up a political action committee and participate in the [campaign contribution] process."

PAC contributions don't always assure victory, or even support, for a special interest. But over the years, Common Cause has documented numerous instances where congressional votes in support of a special interest position corresponded closely to campaign contributions received from the special interest PACs. For example:

- An analysis of the 1981 House vote on dairy price supports and contributions from the three largest dairy PACs showed that representatives who voted for higher dairy price supports had received, on the average, nearly six times as much from those PACs between 1978 and 1980 as did representatives who voted against the dairy lobby on that vote.
- In March 1982, the House Health and Environment Subcommittee voted to weaken the landmark Clean Air Act. Members voting for the industry-supported bill received nearly seven times more in campaign contributions from the major industries affected by the bill than did the opponents of the bill.
- In May 1982, Congress voted to kill a proposed Federal Trade Commission (FTC) regulation opposed by automobile dealers. The regulation, called the "used car rule," would have required used car dealers merely to disclose to prospective buyers any known defects in their vehicles. At the time of their most recent elections, the 69 senators who voted to kill the regulation received, on the average, twice as much in campaign contributions from the automobile dealers' PAC as the 27 senators who voted against the auto dealers. The 286 House Members who voted for the dealers' position received an average of five times as much from the PAC (between 1979 and the first four months of 1982) as did the 133 House Members who voted against it.

The "coincidence" of PAC dollars and "yes" votes caused one Member of Congress to dub the defeated regulation the "used Congress rule."

- During the last two congressional elections, the PACs of the American Medical Association (AMA) and the American Dental Association (ADA) contributed more than $3 million to House Members in the 97th Congress. In December 1982, the House voted to exempt these professionals from FTC jurisdiction. The 208 representatives who voted for the AMA-ADA-backed position received more than two and a half times as much from these PACs as the 195 Members who voted against the professions. (The proposal was defeated in the Senate.)
- In December 1982, the House passed a United Automobile Workers (UAW)-supported bill which would have required that U.S. parts and labor be used in all cars sold in the U.S. The 215 representatives

who voted for the bill received $1.3 million in PAC contributions from the UAW during the last two congressional elections, 18 times as much as the $72,000 received by the 188 representatives who voted to defeat the bill. (The bill was defeated when the Senate failed to pass it before the end of the last Congress.)

Without reform of the political system, similar stories are likely this Congress. PACs poured millions of dollars into the 1982 congressional campaigns. The Members of Congress they helped elect will now be deciding on a number of important issues that affect all Americans.

Spending patterns in the last election raise a number of questions:

- How will PAC contributions affect decisions by Congress on major defense issues, such as the funding of the MX missile? PACs representing 12 of the 13 largest MX missile contractors doubled their contributions to current Members of Congress in 1982.
- Will PAC contributions influence congressional decisions in one of the most powerful committees in Congress, the House Energy and Commerce Committee? That committee has jurisdiction over such major policy areas as energy, health, communications, consumer legislation and environmental laws, including the Clean Air Act. The 42 Members now serving on this committee in the 98th Congress received, on the average, more than $100,000 each from PACs in the 1982 campaign. Energy industry PACs alone provided nearly half a million dollars to the present Members of the committee.
- Will national health policy continue to be influenced by PAC contributions from the American Medical Association (AMA)? During the last three elections, the AMA's PACs have given more than $5.5 million to candidates running for Congress. In the 1982 elections, three quarters of the present Members of the House of Representatives received a contribution from the AMA. What kind of independent judgment will these representatives exercise when an AMA-backed position comes up for a vote in Congress?

With good reason, Americans wonder if the leaders they elect are free to represent them. As a consequence, the greatest tragedy of the PAC phenomenon lies not so much in the individual victories PACs have won as the cynicism and disenchantment they engender. Americans are beginning to realize their votes aren't as important as the checks PACs sign over to a candidate's campaign.

DEBATE FOCUS

Do Political Action Committees Subvert Democracy?

A CAMPAIGN FINANCE EXPERT SEES PACS AS BENEFICIAL TO DEMOCRACY

Political scientist and campaign finance expert Herbert Alexander takes a sanguine view of PACs in the following selection. He argues that far from undermining our democracy, PACs increase political participation, act as a safeguard against excessive government power, help to finance congressional campaigns, and increase political accountability. To suggest that money is the sole ingredient of politics, and that PACs therefore control the candidates they help to support financially, is an overly simplistic view of politics. PACs should take vigorous action to improve their image by increasing public awareness of the vital role they play in our democracy.

H. ALEXANDER

10

The Case for PACs

HERBERT ALEXANDER

Seen in historical perspective, political action committees represent a functional system for political fund raising that developed, albeit unintentionally, from efforts to reform the political process. PACs represent an expression of an issue politics that resulted from attempts to remedy a sometimes unresponsive political system. And they represent an institutionalization of the campaign fund solicitation process that developed from the enactment of reform legislation intended to increase the number of small contributors.

Despite the unforeseen character of their development, PACs have made significant contributions to the political system:

1. *PACs increased participation in the political process.* The reform efforts that spawned PACs were designed to allow more voices to be heard in determining who will become our nation's elected officials. Thanks in part to PACs, that goal has been achieved.

   Although it is difficult to determine how many individuals now participate in the political process through voluntarily contributing to political action committees, some useful information is available. The survey of company PACs by Civic Service, Inc., found that in the 1979–1980 election cycle more than 100,000 individuals contributed to the 275 PACs responding to the survey, and that the average number of donors to those PACs was 388. By extrapolation, it appears that all corporate PACs active in the 1979–1980 cycle received contributions from at least 210,000 individuals.

   The largest conservative ideological group PACs, which rely on direct mail solicitations, received about 1.3 million contributions

Public Affairs Monograph, reprinted by permission of the Public Affairs Council.

in 1979–1980, though individuals may well have contributed to more than one of those groups. It is difficult to estimate the total number of persons who gave to professional and membership association PACs, though information about specific groups is available. For example, an official of the National Association of Realtors PAC estimated that his group had 80,000 contributors in 1979, 87,000 in 1980, 92,000 in 1981 and about 95,000 in 1982. It is more difficult still to estimate the number of contributors to labor PACs, although here, too, information is available regarding specific groups. According to a National Education Association official, for example, the NEA PAC received donations from about 600,000 persons in the 1979–1980 election cycle.

Surveys taken between 1952 and 1976 indicate that from 8 to 12 percent of the total adult population contributed to politics at some level in presidential election years, with the figure standing at 9 percent in 1976. According to a survey by the Center for Political Studies at the University of Michigan, however, 13.4 percent of the adult population—about 17.1 million persons—gave to candidates and causes during the 1979–1980 election cycle. Survey data suggest that the increase registered in 1980 is due to the increased number of persons giving to interest groups. Of those surveyed, 6.8 percent gave to candidates, 3.8 percent gave to parties, and 6.8 percent gave to interest groups. Since those figures add up to well over 13.4 percent, it is obvious that a significant number of persons contributed in two or all three categories.

2. *PACs allow individuals to increase the impact of their political activity.* PACs and their interest group sponsors not only encourage individual citizens to participate in the electoral process, they provide them with a sense of achievement or effectiveness that accompanies taking part in political activity with like-minded persons rather than merely acting alone.

3. *PACs are a popular mechanism for political fund raising because they respect the manner in which society is structured.* Occupational and interest groups have replaced the neighborhood as the center of activities and source of values and the ideologically ambiguous political parties as a source of political action. Individuals seem less willing to commit themselves to the broad agenda of the parties; they are interested mainly in single issues or clusters of issues. PACs, organized on the basis of specific occupational or socio-economic or issue groupings, allow individuals to join with others who share their values and interests and to undertake action to achieve the political goals they perceive as most important to them.

4. *PACs and the interest groups they represent serve as a safeguard against undue influence by the government or by the media.* By energetically promoting their competing claims and views, such groups prevent the development of

either a single, official viewpoint or a media bias. They demonstrate the lively pluralism so highly valued and forcefully guaranteed by the framers of the Constitution.

5. *PACs have made more money available for political campaigns.* By helping candidates pay the rising costs of conducting election campaigns, PACs help to assure the communication of the candidates' views and positions and thus to clarify campaign issues. They also encourage individuals without wealth to run for office.

6. *PACs have contributed to greater accountability in election campaign financing.* Corporations are legitimately concerned about public policy, but prior to the FECA they were uncertain about the legality of providing financial support to candidates who would voice their concerns. That many corporations resorted to subterfuges to circumvent the law is common knowledge. By sanctioning the use of PACs by corporations, the law has replaced the undisclosed and often questionable form of business participation in politics with the public and accountable form practiced by corporate and other business-related PACs today. However much money now is derived from corporate PACs, it is not clear that corporate PAC money today is greater proportionally than was business-derived money when there were no effective limits on giving and when disclosure was less comprehensive.

HOW PACS CAN RESPOND

PACs enjoy a growing constituency, but, in view of current anti-PAC publicity and endeavors, PAC supporters must engage in a concerted educational effort regarding their methods and goals if PACs are to avoid being restricted in their ability to participate in the political process. That effort should include, certainly, responding with specific and accurate information to criticisms made of PACs and making plain the many values PACs bring to the political process.

Educational efforts also might include using the methods of PAC opponents to the advantage of the PAC movement. For example, PAC opponents frequently correlate PAC contributions and legislative outcomes and conclude that the contributions resulted in specific legislative decisions. PAC critics publicized widely the fact that maritime unions contributed heavily to some members of the House Merchant Marine Committee who favored a cargo preference bill introduced in 1977 and supported by the unions. They implied the committee members were influenced by the contributions to report out a favorable bill. PAC supporters did little to discover and publicize the committee members' other sources of funds. The American Medical Association Political Action Committee, for example, contributed to every incumbent on the House Committee, yet AMPAC and the medical practitioners who support it had no vested interest in the cargo preference bill or in other legislation considered by the committee. Nor was much publicity given to the fact that the two committee members who received the greatest financial support from the unions represented districts in which there is a significant amount of port activity and that consequently they would understandably be responsive to maritime interests.

When critics use simplistic correlations to demonstrate undue PAC influence on the decisions of legislators, PAC supporters should endeavor to present the whole campaign finance picture: What percentage of the legislators' campaign funds came from the interest group or groups in question? Did those groups also contribute to other legislators whose committee assignments gave them no formative role in legislation of particular interest to the groups? Did groups with no special interest in the legislation in question contribute to the legislators dealing with it at the committee or subcommittee level? What factors in the legislators' home districts or states might have influenced the legislators' decisions? What non-monetary pressures were brought to bear on the legislators?

It also might be useful for PAC supporters to publicize "negative correlations," which would demonstrate that PAC contributions often do not correlate with specific legislative decisions.

PAC supporters also should question the unarticulated assumptions at the basis of much of the anti-PAC criticism.

- Money is not simply a necessary evil in the political process. By itself money is neutral; in politics as in other areas its uses and purposes determine its meaning.
- There is nothing inherently immoral or corrupting about corporate or labor contributions of money, any more than any other private contribution of funds.
- All campaign contributions are not attempts to gain special favors; rather, contributing political money is an important form of participation in a democracy.
- Money is not the sole, and often not even the most important, political resource. Many other factors affect electoral and legislative outcomes. (At the close of the 97th Congress, for example, an immigration reform bill that reportedly had widespread support in the House and the Senate died because of the effective lobbying efforts of employees, labor unions and minorities who believed they would be adversely affected by it; few, if any, campaign contributions were involved in the effort to forestall the legislation.)
- Curbing interest group contributions will not free legislators of the dilemma of choosing between electoral necessity and legislative duty. Even if PACs were eliminated, legislators would still be confronted with the sometimes conflicting demands between

doing what will help them remain in office and serving what they perceive as the public good.

- A direct dialogue between candidates and individual voters without interest group influence is not possible in a representative democracy. Politics is about people, their ideas, interests and aspirations. Since people seek political fulfillment partly through groups, a politics in which supportive groups are shut out or seriously impaired is difficult to conceive.

There is danger, clearly, in our pluralistic society if groups are overly restricted in their political activity. It is useful to recall that five of the most significant movements of the last two decades—the civil rights movement, the Vietnam peace movement, the political reform movement, the women's rights movement, and the movement toward fiscal restraint—originated in the private sector, where the need for action was perceived and where needed interest organizations were established to carry it out. *These movements would not have taken place if like-minded citizens had not been permitted to combine forces and thereby enhance their political power.*

One hundred and fifty years ago, de Tocqueville recognized that in America "the liberty of association [had] become a necessary guarantee against the tyranny of the majority." The freedom to join in common cause with other citizens remains indispensable to our democratic system. The pursuit of self-interest is, as Irving Kristol has pointed out, a condition, not a problem.

CHAPTER SIX
Interest Groups and the Law

REGULATION OF INTEREST GROUPS

Attempts to regulate interest groups date from the nineteenth century, when many states passed laws banning certain lobbying practices and requiring lobbyists to disclose their employers, tactics, and expenditures. Georgia added a section to its constitution in 1877 which provided that "lobbying is declared to be a crime, and the General Assembly shall enforce this provision by suitable penalties."[*] A California constitutional provision adopted in 1879 stated: "Any person who seeks to influence the vote of a member of the Legislature by bribery, promise of reward, or any other dishonest means, shall be guilty of lobbying, which is hereby declared to be a felony."[†]

LAWS REQUIRING DISCLOSURE OF LOBBYING ACTIVITIES

While some states banned various forms of lobbying in their constitutions, regulation was mostly accomplished through disclosure laws that more than half of the states had adopted by 1950. At the federal level, Congress finally enacted its comprehensive Federal Regulation of Lobbying Act in 1946, requiring lobbyists to register and disclose their employers, finances, and what legislation they are attempting to influence.

REGULATION OF CAMPAIGN CONTRIBUTIONS

Control over the amount of money groups can give to political candidates is another method that has been used to curb group influence. The Corrupt Practices Act of 1925 proscribed direct corporate and labor union contributions to political candidates. Also limited were the expenditures that could be made by Senate and House candidates, $25,000 and $10,000, respectively. The law contained many loopholes, however, and was never enforced.

[*]Code of Georgia, Annotated (1936), Sec. 2-205, cited in Edgar Lane, *Lobbying and the Law* (Berkeley and Los Angeles: The University of California Press, 1964), p. 27.

[†]Ibid., p. 28.

RISE OF POLITICAL ACTION COMMITTEES (PACs)

Interestingly, one way legally to circumvent the law was to create a political action committee which would receive voluntary contributions that could be used to finance candidates. Labor unions employed this device, the most notable example being the AFL-CIO's creation of its Committee on Political Education (COPE) in 1952, a PAC that helps to fund labor candidates and gives them other forms of assistance, such as appealing for electoral support and helping to get out the vote.

Revelations that many corporations were making under-the-table contributions to the Nixon campaign in 1972 spurred congressional efforts to tighten restrictions upon the flow of money to candidates. The premise of the campaign finance laws of the 1970s was that too much private money in politics would have a corrupting effect, giving wealthy groups and individuals an unfair advantage.

FAILURE OF CAMPAIGN FINANCE LEGISLATION

Campaign finance legislation in the end failed to contain the flow of private money to candidates. Moreover, the complexities of the law make it virtually incomprehensible to any but the most devoted students of its provisions. Presidential and congressional candidates alike must now have full-time legal advice to prevent them from overstepping legal boundaries. Enforcement is difficult and highly burdensome. More than one candidate has said that the enforcing agency, the Federal Election Commission (FEC), harasses more than regulates. In the meantime, campaign spending is rapidly increasing, requiring even greater injections of money. Rising costs can be attributed in part to the high price of media campaigning and the need for political consultants.*

The debate over money and politics continues, focusing upon if there is a need for tighter constraints on contributions and spending. Also a persistent issue is whether federal financing of campaigns should be extended from the presidential to the congressional level.

---

*See Larry J. Sabato, *The Rise of Political Consultants* (New York: Basic Books, 1981).

What Direction If Any, Should Campaign Finance Reform Take?

A POLITICAL REPORTER CALLS FOR STRENGTHENING CAMPAIGN
FINANCE LAWS

In the following selection, award-winning reporter Elizabeth Drew, a regular writer for the *New Yorker,* examines the importance of money in politics, and reviews new proposals that have been made to tighten contribution and expenditure restrictions while expanding political access. She supports public financing of congressional campaigns to improve the quality of candidates and to ensure political fairness.

11

E. DREW

Politics and Money

ELIZABETH DREW

There are things than can be done about the effect of money on our political system once the nature and the extent of the problem are recognized. The impact of the need for money on congressional behavior has been dramatic. First, there is no question that we have a political system in which politicans' access to money is vital and, in more cases than not, decisive. Richard Wirthlin, the Republican pollster, says, "Money not only can make the difference but can make a huge difference." He continues, "People make decisions based upon the way they see the world, and the way they see the world is conditioned by the information they have; and money can influence not only the information they have but also the perceptions they have, and therefore influences who wins and loses." Second, it is clear that the politicians' anxiety about having access to enough money corrodes, and even corrupts, the political system. It is clear that the effect on them is degrading and distracting at best. At the least, politicians increasingly consider how their votes will affect their own—and their opponents'— ability to raise money. At worst, votes are actually traded for money. It is clear that we are at some distance from the way the democratic process is supposed to work. The most fundamental question is, What kind of electoral process would give us the best kind of representation—the best at representing the public interest and producing public officials who, on the basis of experience and judgment, would make decisions that would not always represent passing public attitudes or be affected by financial contributions? Finally, it is clear that the system for funding Presidential campaigns with public money, in order to make them reasonably competitive and removed from the pressures of private interests, isn't working as it was intended to.

The broad outlines of what could be done to deal with all these things are: first, a system of public financing of congressional campaigns, which would include limits on what could be spent for the campaigns and a ceiling on the overall amount that any member could accept from political-action committees; second, a radical approach to political advertising, the costliest component of campaigns, which would include a ban on the purchase of air time and a provision for free air time; third, a reimposition of the limits on expenditures by independent committees, and other measures to close the loopholes being exploited by Presidential campaigns. Variations on all these proposals are possible, and objections to all of them are plentiful. Some of the proposals would be difficult to work out, but if the same amount of energy and ingenuity went into making the law effective that has gone into finding ways around it, the difficulties could be resolved. The point is not to try to establish a perfect political system but to try to get the system back closer to what it was intended to be.

Two of the proposals—those dealing with independent committees and political advertising—require some consideration of what the First Amendment is really about. Moreover, when the Supreme Court first ruled that limits on independent expenditures were unconstitutional, it found no history of abuse, which is understandable, since up to that point there were no limits on contributions. In the Buckley [v. Valeo (1976)] case, a prohibition on independent expenditures was held unconstitutional with only one dissenter—Justice Byron White. In its ruling in the [Common Cause v.] Schmitt case, six years after Buckley, the Court was evenly divided on the question of independent expenditures by groups on behalf of publicly financed Presidential candidates, with one member unable to participate because of an apparent conflict of interest. Therefore, it would seem that the constitutional issue is no longer the settled question that people thought it was when the Court ruled in the Buckley case.

The Buckley decision was an odd one, because at the same time that it equated money with speech and held that limits on independent *expenditures* were unconstitutional, it held that limits on *contributions* to candidates were constitutional. Its rationale was that expenditures did not pose the same danger as contributions. But if one has an absolute right to spend unlimited amounts of money for a political candidate outside the candidate's campaign, why can't one contribute whatever one wants to the candidate? Archibald Cox, the professor of constitutional law at the Harvard Law School, who also served as Special Prosecutor during Watergate and is chairman of Common Cause, argued both the Buckley case and the Schmitt case, as well as other First Amendment cases before the Court. Cox says he thinks that it is at least a fifty-fifty possibility that all that the framers of the Constitution had in mind when they wrote the First Amendment was a prohibition on prior censorship, and that some people argue that the possibility is much greater. In any event, he says, one need not resort to that argument to get at the problem of the First Amendment and independent expenditures.

Cox explains the Court's apparent contradiction in the Buckley decision by saying he believes that what the Court had in mind when it considered independent expenditures was, say, a group of professors taking an ad in a newspaper, or an individual flying around the country making speeches in support of a candidate, or even someone buying fifteen or thirty minutes of television time on behalf of a candidate. Therefore, when Cox argued the Schmitt case he suggested that the Court could limit the effect of its finding in the Buckley case by stipulating that it was not thinking in terms of large organizations making independent expenditures, which they have funded by a money-raising effort, and which, as he pointed out, "even without consultation, it's no great trick to coordinate." He suggested that one way to deal with the proposition that spending money equals free speech would be to say that there are lots of different kinds of expenditures, and perhaps money is speech in the instance of a person spending money to publish or broadcast his own thoughts, while it is an entirely different thing when an organization raises money from all over the country and spends it to broadcast. The difference, he said, is that the money is collected nationally, and that it is used for much speech but few ideas. As for the Court's argument that independent expenditures do not create the risk of corrupting public policy, Cox replied that that may be true in the case of an individual who spends for his own personal expression, or of the group of professors, but it is not true in the case of groups that raise and spend millions on behalf of a candidate.

Cox suggests a new way of looking at our elections—a way that could be most helpful in clarifying our thinking about them. He says that an election ought to be treated like a town meeting or an argument before the Supreme Court. As he puts it, there are some forums where, to have meaningful, open debate, you see to it that everyone gets an equal allocation of time and a fair chance to express his point of view. "No one considers that a restriction of freedom of speech," Cox says.

If we redefine what we mean by "freedom of speech," and uncouple the idea of "the marketplace of ideas" from the idea of "the free market," we can begin to get back to how the political system was supposed to work. It is one thing to establish a system that guarantees contending factions an opportunity to express their views, and quite another to auction off the system to those factions that can afford to pay for the most time to express them—not to mention the secondary effects that such an auction system has. Whether or not the person who has the most broadcast time always prevails, it is demonstrable that the power and the cost of political broadcasting distort the political process.

A way to guarantee contending factions a chance to have their say, turn our elections into more of a fair fight, lower the amount of money that is spent on campaigns, and raise the level on which they are fought would be to prohibit political advertising and provide the candidates with free air time. This may sound like a radical concept, but in fact America is one of the very few countries in the world that allow any purchase of television time for political broadcasts; no Western European nation does. And, while we are at it, we could consider requiring that most of the free broadcast time be in segments of not less than, say, five or ten minutes. (In Great Britain, the major parties are currently required to broadcast in segments of a minimum of five or ten minutes.) This would make it necessary for candidates to actually say something, in contrast to the one-minute or thirty-second spots, which are uninformative at best and misleading at worst. (An argument has been made that you can tell what a candidate is like from his televison spots, but that requires the public to be able to sort out fact from fiction when it doesn't necessarily have the information; and it puts the burden on the opponent to refute the spots—often something that cannot be done in thirty seconds or a minute. The answer is usually more complicated than the charge.) Arrangements would also have to be made to assure that the free time offered would be when people were likely to be watching—but this, too, could be worked out.

The essential point is that under this proposal the contenders would have a fair chance to be heard, without having to scramble to outspend their opponents for broadcasting—the most expensive and the most influential element of a campaign. Cox thinks that such a proposal could be upheld constitutionally. There would, of course, be stiff opposition to it. The broadcasters would oppose it, for obvious reasons; but the ownership of broadcasting stations is among the most lucrative businesses in America. A fallback position would be for the government to pay a portion of the cost of this broadcast time as part of a publicly financed system for congressional campaigns. (In effect, the government already does this for the publicly financed Presidential campaign.) But there is no point in adopting a fallback position until the fairest and most sensible plan has been tried. Whenever the idea of free broadcast time is brought up, a lot of sand is thrown in the air about such things as what to do in a media market like New York or Los Angeles, where there may be a number of races, or, alternatively, what to do in races where there are no media markets. Surely the mind of man can figure out some answer. When I was talking about this with Robert Dole, the chairman of the Senate Finance Committee, who, on the basis of what he had encountered in his efforts to write more equitable tax laws, is in favor of diminishing the role of money in campaigns, he said, "If they can figure out the tax code, they can figure this out." There are several paths of thinking that those trying to devise a solution might take. One is to keep in mind that the stations in the large media markets are among the most profitable ones. Another is that congressional candidates in areas like New York and Los Angeles often don't buy media time now, because they think it isn't worth it to pay for a broadcast that takes in so much more territory than their district. There is no particular reason that they should be given the means to start broadcasting where they did not do it before. But, in any case, they could be given air time without great financial risk to the stations. Another point to keep in mind is that cable television allows politicians to narrow the size of the audience they are trying to reach, and a number of politicians are already using cable, which is far less expensive than most traditional broadcast outlets. Or, in a media market with a number of candidates, the candidates could be given some free mailings instead. This, too, could be taken care of under a public financing scheme.

Common Cause has been advocating the granting of free response time to a candidate who has been attacked by an independent committee, its theory being that as long as such expenditures are allowed, this will neutralize the effect. If the attack came in the form of direct mail, the candidate could receive a subsidy to respond. But it is not out of the question that the courts will ban expenditures by the large-scale independent committees that have been springing up, especially if there is a system of public financing of congressional campaigns.

The idea of public financing of congressional campaigns has been gaining an increasing number of adherents. An aide to the House leadership said that what he witnessed during the consideration of the 1982 tax-increase bill had made him a convert to the idea. When I asked him why, specifically, he replied, "The long lines of suitors and the access they had." A number of people believed that the Ninety-seventh 1981-1982 Congress reflected the impact of the pressure of money, in its various forms, more than any Congress before it. And this sense of things led a number of people who had never subscribed to the idea of public financing of congressional campaigns to decide that the system had to be changed. A former member of Congress said to me recently, "I used to be against public financing. I thought raising money was an important way to build a campaign, to get people committed. But then I began to see how the present system was corrupting even the best of them on the Hill. And they gin each other up: they see that others are doing it, and say, Why not? It became very depressing to watch. And I changed my mind about public financing." Actually, the public-financing schemes would still allow for private participation.

A number of proposals for a system of public financing have been put forward by members of Congress as well as by Common Cause. They have been sponsored by both Republicans and Democrats. They have several common characteristics. They would provide, for the candidates in the general election, a matching system similar to that which obtains in the Presidential primary system, and would impose spending limits. (The question of public financing of congressional primaries has been set aside as something to be worked out, if necessary, once a system for the general elections is in place.) It is possible to consider spending limits without a public-financing system, but this, too, would require a change of opinion on the part of the Supreme Court; and there would always be the problem of setting the limits high enough to make candidates viable and low enough to give them a chance of not being utterly at the mercy of contributors and fund raisers. Just as the Presidential-primary system matches private individual contributions of two hundred and fifty dollars, the congressional system would match contributions of a hundred dollars. A bill sponsored by David Obey, a Democratic representative from Wisconsin and a late convert to the idea of public financing, would limit to ninety thousand dollars the total amount of matching money for a candidate for the House. Individuals would still be allowed to contribute a thousand dollars. Some of those who favor public financing would consider allowing higher individual contributions in exchange for an agreement on such a scheme. The proposals for public financing also contain a limit on the total amount a candidate could accept from political-action committees. So private money would not be driven out of the congressional campaigns—it would just be brought under control. And members of Congress would be freed from the anxiety and fear—and corruption—that accompany the present race for money. Obey's bill would limit to ninety thousand dollars the amount that candidates for the House could accept from PACs. His bill does not deal with Senate races, but others have proposed setting limits for Senate races on the basis of a state's population. A bill sponsored by Representatives Mike Synar, Democrat of Oklahoma; Jim Leach, Republican of Iowa; and Dan Glickman, Democrat of Kansas, would limit the amount that House candidates could accept from PACs to seventy-five thousand dollars, while the amount that Senate candidates could accept would vary with the size of the state—from seventy-five thousand to five hundred thousand. But the problem with simply limiting the amount that can be received from PACs, without dealing with the larger context, is that the interests that give through PACs would simply turn around and give through individual contributions— as independent oil largely does now. Common Cause and some people on Capitol Hill would also lower the amount that a PAC could contribute to an individual: from ten thousand dollars per election cycle—five thousand for the primary and five thousand for the general election—to half that amount. Obey's bill would limit campaign spending in a congressional general election to a hundred and eighty thousand dollars—a figure that seems unrealistically low and appears to be a negotiating position. The bill would also limit personal and immediate-family expenditures to twenty thousand dollars for those who participate in the public-financing plan. If a candidate chose not to accept public financing but to spend large amounts of his own money, or to exceed the spending limits, the spending limits on his opponent would be lifted, and the opponent would receive double the amount in matching funds. Obey would provide free television time for a candidate to respond to an independent group's attack, or additional public financing equal to the amount of the independent expenditures for television; and he would also offer to match other independent expenditures that amounted in the aggregate to more than five thousand dollars.

If in fact there would remain imbalances as a result of labor's efforts to get people registered and to the polls, it is not beyond the mind of man to figure out a solution to this, either. (It is to be remembered that both labor and business are now allowed to spend unlimited amounts to communicate with their own members or employees on political matters. Moreover, such organizations as the Chamber of Commerce conduct get-out-the-vote drives, and business is developing other ways to compete with labor.) The possibilities range from prohibiting these activities—which doesn't seem very healthy—to improving the registration system or designing a system under which the parties play the major role in these activities. One possibility would be to allow the parties to raise money for such activities (as was done in 1979 for the Presidential campaign)—and, in both Presidential and congressional campaigns, to impose limits and an effective reporting system. This way, soft money could be brought under control, and the two problems would be dealt with at once.

Two arguments made against public financing are that it would amount to an incumbent-protection act, since incumbents enjoy certain advantages, and that it would guarantee a challenger enough money to give an incumbent a disconcertingly stiff race. (The second argument is one that people on Capitol Hill make very quietly.) Both arguments, of course, can't be true. And if public financing amounted to an incumbent-protection act, it would have passed long since, unless Congress is an uncommonly noble institution. Moreover, most of the public-financing schemes have taken it into account that a highly restrictive spending limit would prevent challengers from competing effectively. Fred Wertheimer, the president of Common Cause, points out that the first two incumbent Presidents to run under the system of public financing of Presidential campaigns—Ford and Carter—both lost. As for the advantages of incumbency, Common Cause has brought legal action against abuse of the franking privilege. Wertheimer adds, "Incumbency has its pluses and its minuses." He says, "The key is to have a system that allows a challenger to compete. That's really all we can do, and that's all we should do."

Leach refers to the proposal to limit PAC contributions as "a kind of domestic SALT agreement between big business and big labor." In introducing his bill, Obey said, "We do not object to people accepting PAC contributions. But the size of these contributions moved around the nation by unseen hands in Washington office buildings can determine the politics of Wisconsin or Montana or Vermont or any other state in the Union. We do object to that." The lines between the representative and his constituents have been disturbed, if not yet completely cut. Elections are determined in increasing measure by forces outside the district and the state.

A number of Republicans think that it is not against the interests of their party to support a public-financing system. Barber Conable, a Republican representative from New York, who is among them, says, "Large contributions tend to come to incumbents; by the nature of things, our party will have more challengers." One Republican political consultant says, "Republicans who oppose public financing—and the great majority do—say, 'How can we overcome the numerical disadvantage of being a Republican?' I don't think that's a valid objection. It is true that Republicans are in the minority, but that is not an argument for opposing public financing. Privately, their argument is 'We can blow them out by outspending them.' My view is that if the money represents an unfair advantage it ought to be eliminated. Where is the ethics or morality in saying the system ought to be maintained because it benefits you, if the advantage is inherently unfair?"

It has been argued that the public financing of congressional campaigns would be costly. However, most of the proposals call for it to be paid for out of the voluntary dollar checkoff on tax returns, which might be raised to two dollars—so the system would be self-financed. Another dollar a year seems a small price to pay. (One estimate, based on recent campaign costs, is that the system would cost about eighty million dollars per two-year election cycle.) The more important point is how expensive it is *not* to have public financing and some limit on PAC contributions, and how risky it is *not* to restore the Presidential-election system to the way it was supposed to work. The costs are everywhere—throughout the tax code and the federal budget. They turn up in everything from the Pentagon budget to medical bills. In effect, as we go about our daily lives, buying food, gasoline, and medicine, and as we pay our taxes, we are paying for the current system of financing campaigns.

And there are less tangible but more important costs. We are paying in the declining quality of politicans and of the legislative product, and in the rising public cynicism. We have allowed it to become increasingly difficult for the good people who remain in politics to function well. What results is a corrosion of the system and a new kind of squalor—conditions that are well known to those who are in it and to those who deal with it at close range. The public knows that something is very wrong. As the public cynicism gets deeper, the political system gets worse. Until the problem of money is dealt with, the system will not get better. We have allowed the basic idea of our democratic process—representative government—to slip away. The only question is whether we are serious about trying to retrieve it.

What Direction, If Any, Should Campaign Finance Reform Take?

A POLITICAL SCIENTIST IS SKEPTICAL ABOUT CAMPAIGN FINANCE
REFORMS

The following selection critically examines proposals for campaign finance reform, pointing out that the organizational complexity of interest groups, their variety, and their different goals and strategies, complicate the task of determining both how they should and can be effectively regulated. The author challenges many of the common assumptions made about the political role of interest groups, and suggests that many proposals for change are overly simplistic.

M. J. MALBIN

12

Looking Back at the Future of Campaign Finance Reform

MICHAEL J. MALBIN

Neither public financing nor strict expenditure limits nor even the complete exclusion of private contributions from the general election can eliminate interest groups from the electoral process. The rules do not eliminate but transform interest-group politics, working to the advantage of some groups and disadvantage of others. Groups that can mobilize dispersed networks of volunteers—single- or multi-issue groups, labor unions, and a few professional associations—have been made more important in presidential elections. Groups whose members are reluctant to volunteer and in the past relied on Washington representatives and monetary campaign contributions—corporations and trade associations—have become less important because candidates are less willing to use their limited money to pay for such things as phone banks that can be staffed less efficiently, but more cheaply, with volunteers. It would be difficult to argue that an organization is less of a "special interest" because it relies on one set of resources rather than another. Whether they know it or not, therefore, people who say they want to use public financing to make congressional more like presidential elections are just saying they prefer some kinds of interest groups to others.

The examples also suggest another line of thought. The rules of campaign finance seem to encourage a situation in which Presidents and members of Congress come to office with systematically different interest-group electoral bases. It is possible—we can only speculate at this stage—that

Michael J. Malbin, "Looking Back at the Future of Campaign Finance Reform," Money and Politics in the United States (Washington, D.C.: American Enterprise Institute and Chatham, N.J.: Chatham House, 1984). Reprinted by permission of publishers.

123

this could help explain some of the difficulties Presidents have in working with Congress. Legislative-executive relations might be improved somewhat if the branches' electoral bases were made more similar. (Of course, this is an argument that could be made to eliminate presidential public financing as well as extend it.) On the other hand, it may be beneficial to have a system that gives different groups better access to each branch. But whichever view of legislative-executive relations one might prefer, the separation of powers and the permeability of the system both rest on foundations that would change only slightly with new rules of campaign finance.

PACS AND THE ORGANIZATIONAL PERSPECTIVE

Reformers who want to limit the electoral influence of PACs often seem to assume that a change in the law will produce similar effects across the full spectrum of organized interest groups. Our discussion of presidential elections disclosed the fallacy of such thinking. It is impossible to predict how an organization would react to a change in the legislative environment without considering the organization's needs on its own terms. PACs . . . are ongoing organizations, or parts of ongoing organizations, that among other things seek to maintain themselves. The perspective that informs this statement should be explored further by politicians who want to change the way organizations function politically.

The organizational perspective is a familiar one to political scientists. It leads one to expect that the precise nature of an organization's political activities will generally be chosen with an eye toward maintaining the organization's health and that the relationships between organizational maintenance and political activity will almost always be more complex than they appear on the surface. The lack of understanding among members of Congress on this point is no particular surprise; the connections between maintenance and PAC behavior have not yet been explored adequately by anyone in published research.

Some of the needed work has begun. . . . In each case, the authors found political decisions importantly influenced by organizational factors usually missed in the reformers' "who benefits?" model of legislative causation.

Independent PACs

[Political scientist] Frank Sorauf's work points directly at some questions that need further examination. He argues that among the independent PACs, there is a possibility for unaccountable, self-aggrandizing behavior by staff that would not be tolerated in a PAC that had to justify its activities to an ongoing, parent organization. Many independent PACs are "one-man" operations, with paper boards, whose geographically scattered donors exercise little control over policy. . . .

[L]et us think about how an independent, ideological PAC might behave if it operated without the slightest hint of impropriety. Vendors would still probably be chosen from among the friends and associates of the PAC directors because directors would want letters and advertisements to be cast in ideological terms, and activist ideological soulmates tend to work and socialize together in Washington. PAC directors probably would also continue to spend substantial proportions of their money on fund raising and overhead, for three reasons. First, the law makes it harder for independent groups than associations, corporations, or labor unions to raise administrative funds. Second, direct mail is a very costly way to raise money, but the best way for a group that is not part of an existing organization. Finally, expenditures for overhead that may look extravagant at first glance may seem less so when you consider organizational objectives and resources.

Independent PACs, by definition, are not created with ready-made public identities. No one in the press will pay much attention to them until they earn it. A lack of attention might not bother most corporate PACs, but it could destroy a new ideological PAC. The objective of most of these PACs is not only to help favored candidates win elections but also to influence the terms of public debate. To achieve this, it is crucial for them to gain some attention both in and outside of Washington, for themselves, and for their issues. (Such attention, not coincidentally, also helps with fund raising.) The need for attention means that these PACs must maintain a presence in Washington, either physically or through the press, and support enough of a staff to spread that presence outside. If they fail to gain attention, and fail therefore to influence the content of the substantive agenda, they will have failed as organizations. They literally have no other reasons for being and no other way to maintain themselves. Because of this, we can predict that independent PACs would react aggressively to sustain their political activities in the face of any change in the law. We can also predict that the simple internal structure of most independent PACs would facilitate their ability to adapt when they have to.

Consider now the very different, multifaceted world of PACs with parent organizations. As mentioned, little work has been done on their varying organizational imperatives. If I were planning such research, I would begin by thinking about some differences in the political interests of the parent organizations themselves. In no particular order, the following speculations come to mind. Each relates directly to the way different groups would respond to legislative limits on their activity.

Labor PACs

Labor unions rely on a broad base of very small contributors who belong for reasons that have little to do with politics. We know from James Q. Wilson's work that this produces a relatively high degree of autonomy for the professional staffs to pursue noneconomic legislative interests. The level and kind of activity, and the amount of internal decentralization, vary with a union's structure and history, but a high level of staff autonomy from the membership seems present across the board. This, in turn, permits close coordination between electoral and legislative activities.

Plenty of conflict exists among unions, of course. The American Federation of Teachers stick to a more purely educational agenda than the National Education Association, while the Steamfitters and Steelworkers disagree with the United Auto Workers on such nonindustrial issues as U.S. relationships with the Soviet Union. The different agendas produce different levels of willingness among unions to use contributions to reward or punish members of Congress for a few votes on pure labor issues, such as labor law reform, or industry-specific issues, such as auto emissions standards or common situs picketing. Construction trade unions, for example, were more willing to withhold funds from Democrats who voted against their position on common situs than was the UAW on emissions standards. . . .

Corporate PACs

Corporations are more varied than labor unions. . . .

For our purpose of assessing the potential effects of [campaign finance] reform, [several] aspects of organizational maintenance are worth keeping in mind. Corporations exist, first and foremost, to sell products or services. For this reason, we would expect that chief executive officers could not afford to let corporate political activities alienate potential customers, create interdivisional conflict, or weaken employee morale. Concern over employee morale is known, for example, to affect solicitation patterns in many companies and to lead some to permit contribution decisions to be made by politically inexpert local employees, even if they may not reflect a Washington view of how best to mesh contributions with immediate lobbying strategy. Decentralizing contribution decisions can help lobbying over the long term, of course, by getting more of a company's employees to become politically active, but that is not why many companies choose this approach. The choice seems more often to reflect a difference between Washington lobbyists and corporate headquarters over the importance of consulting employees.

We also know from interviews that some corporate officers worry about the effect of political activity on public opinion, and presumably therefore on sales. Such a concern does not show up as clearly in aggregate-level research. In fact, even though most people, and therefore most potential customers, support their incumbent House members, companies that sell products directly to the public seem to give higher percentages of their budgets to Republicans, and less to incumbents, than those selling services regulated by the government, who have an obvious stake in protecting their friends in Congress . . . Thus we have to be very tentative at this stage about the role of public opinion, employee morale, and the like because most of the research so far has not looked enough at individual corporations. Obviously, we are dealing with complex sets of interrelated interests. How corporate officers balance the partially conflicting interests of their organizations may well vary on an individual basis. So, too, would corporate reactions to future legislative curbs on PACs. In general, we can predict that internal conflicts of interest would restrain most corporations from reacting as forthrightly (e.g., with direct independent expenditures) as independent PACs, unions, or trade associations.

Association PACs

Associations, like corporations, come in many shapes and sizes. Borrowing from [political scientist] Jack Walker's recent classification, some groups have occupational and professional requirements for membership, and others have none. Among groups with occupational requirements, some have members in the profit-making sector, such as most trade and professional associations; others fall in the not-for-profit sector; and others are mixed. Because of tax rules governing nonprofit entities, most politically active associations are either trade groups, occupational groups for people in the private sector, or nonoccupational groups. The latter tend to be issue groups; when they engage in electoral politics, they are similar to ideological organizations but without the freedoms and constraints of the independent groups. Professional associations range in their political behaviour from ones that are similar to the most active trade associations, such as the American Medical Association and the Association of American Trial Lawyers, to others that engage in no direct political activity, such as the American Bar Association. Trade association PACs themselves vary in their level of political activity from the Direct Mail Marketing Association (1981-82 receipts: $1760) to the Realtors' Political Action Committee (1981-82 receipts: $2,991,732).

As a preliminary observation, it would appear that the relationships between organizational maintenance, on the one hand, and legislative or political activity, on the other, are more straightforward among associations than corporations. That is because the association needs to satisfy only one constituency, its members; the corporation has to look at employees, stockholders, and customers. For that reason, associations are better able to coordinate their electoral and legislative strategies, or engage in independent expenditures, than are corporations.

This is not to say that associations need not worry about maintenance when they get involved in politics. The character of an organization's membership base clearly affects what it does. The AMA, for example, has a large number of small individual contributors, much like a labor union, and behaves in almost an equivalent, though ideologically opposite, manner. The U.S. Chamber of Commerce has a large number of mostly small corporations as members. Traditionally, the chamber's membership has not allowed as much staff independence as a union's or the AMA's. Generally this produces operation by consensus. In recent years, it has led to support for Republicans, as the chamber has staked out broad positions about what its members believed would be good for business as a whole. Most of the chamber's political activities are indirect, but of the $16,967 the chamber contributed directly to House and Senate candidates in 1981-82, all but $736 went to Republicans, and 59 percent went to nonincumbents. In contrast, the American Bakers' Association is funded by a few large corporations with highly focused legislative interests. Its political arm, Bread PAC, contributed all but $4600 to its $50,910 in 1981-82 House and Senate contributions (or 91 percent) to incumbents; 55 percent of its money went to Democrats. Like the AMA, Bread PAC probably would be better able to respond quickly to changes in campaign finance laws than the chamber, which in turn would be in a better position than many corporations.

Conclusion

In summary, an interest group's political behavior will vary both with the professional staff's independence of its supporting members and with the particular interests, and maintenance needs, of the parent organization. Some of the distinctions among parent organizations correspond roughly to the Federal Election Commission's four largest nonparty groupings (labor union, corporation, trade/member/health, no connected organization). But these distinctions are far from airtight. Corporations run by ideologues, for example, may behave politically almost as if they were ideological PACs. (Dart and Kraft, Inc., to mention one, gave 89 percent of its $125,584 in 1981-82 House and Senate contributions to Republicans and 52 percent to nonincumbents.) In addition, the variations within each major category are far too rich to be encompassed by facile generalizations. I have chosen in this section, therefore, to present some guidelines and suggestions for future researchers who want, to borrow a phrase from [Margaret] Latus, to move beyond outrage to understanding. Until we have such understanding, we must reiterate that legislative proposals designed to curb PACs in fact would affect groups differentially in ways that we cannot foresee, but that undoubtedly would be related to a PAC's or parent group's own organizational needs. If those needs require political involvement, then political involvement there will be. In a country that protects the freedoms of association and speech, the rules may channel or shape a group's political activity, but they cannot eliminate it.

GROUPS AND ELECTIONS

My discussion of organizational maintenance . . . focused on predicting the consequences of reform. In this section, I turn to more basic questions. In what precise ways have elections, and the political-governmental environment, been affected by the professionalization of interest-group electoral participation stimulated by the campaign laws of the 1970s? After addressing this question, I consider ways in which PACs and interest groups may help further, or work against, the purposes elections are meant to serve. Finally, I indicate the kinds of legislative changes that might preserve the benefits of the present system while alleviating some of its costs.

I stated earlier that even if the existence and role of interested money is not new to elections, the proliferation of formally organized, professionally staffed groups is. What difference does it make if money is channeled through PACs instead of being given directly to candidates by interested individuals? The differences are significant, affecting actual contribution patterns, other political and lobbying activities of a PAC's parent organization, and perhaps the behavior of members of Congress. Each of those effects contributes to a concluding evaluation of the role of PACs.

PACs and Challengers

It is vitally important for a representative government to preserve a serious threat of competition in legislative elections. Since 1950, however, approximately 90 percent of all incumbent members of the House who have sought reelection have won. Since 1968, more than 70 percent have won with at least 60 percent of the two-party vote. Competition in House races was at a low level before the PAC phenomenon, in other words, and has stayed that way. Nevertheless, if it can be shown that the role of PACs significantly adds to the advantage of incumbency in this uncompetitive climate, that would be a strong argument on the side of those who see PACs as harmful.

It is well known that PACs contribute more, on the whole, to incumbents than nonincumbents. But when the distribution of PAC contributions . . . is measured against the distribution of candidates by party and candidate status . . . , it becomes clear that what is called a pro-incumbent bias in fact covers several phenomena. Labor's money is almost entirely Democratic; it tilts toward Democratic incumbents, but a fair share also goes to Democratic challengers. Very little labor money goes to Republican incumbents or challengers. Corporate PACs, in contrast, give Democratic incumbents about as much as one would expect from a random distribution of funds, but give almost as much on these terms to Republican challengers and more to Republican incumbents. Reversing labor's partisanship, corporations tend not to give to Democratic challengers. Thus, . . . , it would not be accurate to treat PAC contributions merely as if they favor incumbents. The pro-incumbent bias of the aggregate numbers results from trade associations, and from the fact that labor's partisanship exceeds that of corporate PACs. . . .

. . . On balance . . . we suspect that the effects of PAC giving may vary with the calendar. Early in the election cycle, when the bulk of organized giving goes to incumbents, the effect may be to help incumbents scare off good challengers or otherwise solidify their position. Later, when strong challengers have been identified, the overall effect may be the opposite. By concentrating their resources on close races, PACs may help to increase the net number of incumbent defeats in a campaign's closing weeks— but only after they have helped reduce the number of potentially vulnerable incumbents in earlier months.

PACs and Lobbying

If PACs are not simply seeking to improve their lobbying position by reinforcing incumbents, perhaps having a PAC helps lobbying in other ways. . . . [I]t is difficult, when talking about legislative influence, to separate direct campaign contributions from the other electoral and lobbying activities in which interest groups engage. In fact, the activities tend to reinforce each other within the group. When a group organizes itself to solicit employees or members, it is better able to stimulate its employees or members to engage in other activities, and the contributing employees or members are more likely to respond. Two business PAC representatives made this point in 1982 hearings before the House Administration Committee's Task Force on Elections. The first was Gregg Ward, director of governmental affairs for the Sheet Metal and Air Conditioning Contractors National Association:

> Simply writing a check doesn't constitute, in and of itself, much in the way of participation in the process. What we have found is that only begins their interest in the process, and to a neophytic group, an unsophisticated one largely like the one I am with, they now see that they can be involved.
>
> They want to know what has happened with their money. We try to keep them informed as to what we are doing with it, but beyond that, it stimulates and generates an interest factor. That interest factor generally then translates into them doing something about it in other manifest ways.

Don V. Cogman, vice-president of MAPCO Inc. for governmental affairs, and president of the National Association of Business Political Action committees, expanded upon Ward's point by describing some of the specific programs his company uses:

> I can tell you that coming from the political side of this game, and now being on the corporate side, that in my opinion the individual involvement, the people involvement, the volunteer involvement, its more important than money and I think you are finding in the corporate community particularly a new awareness of that. Our counterparts in the labor movement have understood that for decades. The business community has not. I think you are finding that they are beginning to understand it.
>
> In my company specifically we have a program called the citizenship involvement program, which tries to educate, promote, motivate and get involved our employees in all phases of the political system. The PAC is just part of it. I think there is a growing awareness in the corporate community of that fact.

In short, forming a PAC helps a corporation or association get its members or employees active in other aspects of politics and it helps them get members or employees to respond when it is time for grass-roots lobbying. It is possible, therefore, that legislation sharply curbing PAC contribution activity would affect these other programs. My own guess is that the effect would not be substantial and would be most felt by those organizations, a large majority, that do not as yet have a PAC or any form of ongoing political organization. Those with PACs would presumably continue soliciting, if only to involve people in other activities. Those that do not yet solicit will be encouraged through ongoing programs run by the Chamber of Commerce and others to become active in whatever way the law will permit. The campaign laws, therefore, may well have stimulated or facilitated other forms of electoral and lobbying activity when they legitimized direct campaign contributions through PACs, but PAC contributions are not necessary for those activities to continue. Thus, even though a change in the law historically may have been responsible for something, it does not follow that changing the law back will reverse what has happened. The new techniques, once learned, will not be so readily forgotten.

PACs and Members of Congress

The indirect connection between PACs and lobbying is an easy one to understand. Far more complicated is how the growth of PACs may have affected the direct relationships between interest groups and members of Congress. Here we must be even more speculative than we have been so far. I suspect that members of Congress and lobbyists both tend to look at the issue from the wrong end. Both speak of contributors directly pressuring members, using scorecards and other similar devices to get members to behave or vote *against* their inclinations. I frankly do not believe this happens very often. Direct conversion of an opponent is the most difficult of lobbying techniques, tried only in desperation and with rare success. Even when it is successful, or when it results in a slight tempering of a legislator's attitude, we would still have to separate the effect of contributions from lobbying.

But there are more subtle relationships that may be worth further thought and investigation. We know that incumbents proportionally rely more on PAC money than nonincumbents . . . This is usually interpreted by referring to what PACs hope to achieve, but would be worth considering from the members' perspective. Unless something like the McHugh-Conable tax credit bill[, providing federal income tax credits for individual contributions up to $50 to House and Senate candidates from the contributor's state, and to political parties,] becomes law and changes the incentives for members, PAC money is and will remain the easiest money for most incumbents to raise. Tens of thousands of dollars typically change hands in any of the hundreds of Washington fund raisers held every year. Far from being events at which lobbyists hold the whip hand and buy favors from members, these fund raisers normally are attended by people who either want to reward their friends for past behavior or are afraid of turning down "invitations" from members whose committees have jurisdictions over their organizations' futures. The members, clearly on top of the situation, use the events to raise $250 or so in quasi-tribute fees from people who might not otherwise support them, in modest latter-day versions of the reverse pressure techniques perfected by Herbert Kalmbach in the 1972 Nixon campaign.

If PAC contributions do not convert legislators, and if fund raisers represent reverse more than direct lobbying pressure, what effects might the current fund-raising process have on members? If we leave aside the significant changes that may come from replacing incumbents with more sympathetic freshmen, the most important effects may be very subtle and hard to trace. Opponents of the current campaign finance system like to say that contributions do not buy votes, but do buy access—that is, they help a lobbyist gain entry into a member's office to present a case. I am skeptical that a lobbyist who attends a fund raiser gets any more access than the same lobbyist would if there were no fund raisers—although I concede that when fund raisers are common, refusing an invitation can have a negative effect. I also believe that specialty bills, of the sort discussed earlier, bring out business lobbyists who are opposed to each other. Trucking bills bring out the railroads, cotton subsidies bring out the chemical manufacturers, and so forth. Whatever course the member may choose, there are plenty of PACs around to lend their support at campaign time.

What fund raisers may do is not change members' minds but change the way they spend their time. Congressional campaign costs have risen dramatically over the years, particularly for House races. As the value of incumbency grows, and elections become less subject to national or party swings, challengers have to spend increasing amounts of money in order to win. In protective reaction, incumbents raise more to preserve their safety . . . The result is that incumbents, never fully secure in their own minds despite the odds in their favor, devote more time and effort to raising early money.

The need to raise funds in turn means that members spend more of their personal time at fund raisers. If lobbyists do not "pressure" members at fund raisers, the members might still be affected by their conversations at these events. Talking with lobbyists might get the members to see and understand the problems of the people they meet and thus help shape their outlooks or their agendas. It would be difficult to prove this point. For one thing, despite their need for funds, most members do not spend all that much of their personal time at Washington fund raisers. A half dozen per year would be a good guess, and those nights are spent more on quick handshakes than on extended conversations. Let us assume, however, that Washington fund raisers play at least a small role in helping form or cement the relationships that make up Washigton's many "issue networks." If so—and I think this is the most that can plausibly be claimed for them—it would mean that this aspect of campaign fund raising helps reinforce the nationalization of interest-group politics that followed the expansion of the federal government's role. That is not earthshaking, but it is not insignificant either.

Groups and the Purposes of Elections

The nationalization of interest-group activity and of a part of campaign fund raising brings us to the most basic issue: the relationship between campaign finance and the purpose of elections. During the debate over the Bill of Rights in the First Congress, a motion was made by Thomas Tudor Tucker of South Carolina to add a clause to what is now the First Amendment that would have given people the right to instruct their representatives on specific issues. The motion was rejected then, as it was repeatedly over the next few decades, because it was based on the view that the ideal representative should mirror the wishes, feelings, and interests of his or her constituents. The alternative view, which prevailed, was that representation in an extended, diverse republic required members to come together and deliberate in a central place—talking directly to one another, sharing opinions, compromising, and thereby reaching a national consensus that would transcend the local concerns from which members would most likely begin. If the decisions displeased constituents, the constituents could change their representatives at the next election.

One assumption in the discussion of 1789 is striking for our purposes. The members of the First Congress, and most of the active Federalists in the two-year period before then, saw the national legislature as a place where members would be several steps removed from the clamor of special interests, most of which were assumed to have local bases. Today, in contrast, reformers yearn for a more locally based campaign finance system in the hope that this will help legislators escape a different sort of nationalized, interest-group clamor. The hope is fruitless. The only way to escape the current clamor would be to return to the government, policies, and environment of almost two hundred years ago. Failing that, a complex age calls not for nostalgia but for a sophisticated understanding of the multiple objectives that have to be balanced, and compromises that have to be made, to keep elections and representative institutions serving their purposes at least reasonably well.

The main purpose of elections, as mentioned, is to give voters a chance to react to government policy by replacing the people who govern them. As a corollary, elections should also serve to confer legitimacy upon those who assume office. Finally, an election system that works well should help facilitate the process of government—not necessarily by making governmental actions easier, as supporters of parliamentary regimes would wish, but by giving the elected members a sense of institutional and personal self-interest that helps each branch perform its proper function.

When we take this broad view, we can begin to see that the problems of campaign finance in the modern communications age do not lend themselves to easy solutions, for at least two reasons. First, there was always an inherent, and healthy, tension between the desire for accountability and the desire to preserve freedom for members of Congress to think about the national interest. The tension has been exacerbated in recent years. The complexity of government makes it all but impossible for voters to follow individual issues. In addition, a legislator who wants to serve the national interest cannot possibly learn about the potential effects of proposed legislation without the reaction of organized groups. In this situation, the wishes of groups should not be seen merely as nuisances. They also help confer and sustain support for people in government, and they help facilitate the process of both government and opposition by keeping the governors and governed informed.

If interest groups are not merely nuisances, neither has their proliferation been just a blessing. It may be important for people to organize on a national level, especially as the role of government expands. The proliferation of a multiplicity of interests also has some important benefits, as James Madison argued in *Federalist No. 10*. But I am not one of those twentieth-century pluralist misinterpreters of Madison who believes the public good is simply the sum of, or a compromise among, interest-group claims. Group conflict does sometimes produce legislative stalemate, and groups do sometimes win special benefits, at the expense of the general public, when the public is not looking.

It would be misleading, however, to treat campaign finance, or even lobbying, as if they were the fundamental causes of legislative outcomes. They do make a difference, but only at the margins. Lobbyists can win when their activities generally go along with what the public wants, when public opinion is divided, or when the public has no particular opinion. Lobbyists can also help lighten the burden of defeat when the public is against them. Campaign finance may modestly help reinforce the effects of lobbying. But to address the contemporary role of interest groups fully, in its most basic aspects, would force one ultimately to look broadly at the reasons institutional power has been decentralized and at the public philosophy elected members tend to believe or, at least, act upon. These considerations go well beyond the scope of this chapter. Suffice it for now to say that the problem *exists* because most people, in part of their souls, want the government to look after their special, intensely felt desires and needs. It is *perceived* as a problem by most of these same people because, in another part of their souls, they want the government to listen to their more general, less intensely felt, needs and desires when they conflict with the special desires of others. Politically, there is no easy solution because, as [political scientist] Aaron Wildavsky has noted, the Pogo Principle applies: "We have seen the enemy and they are us." All of us react strongly to our own particular concerns, and a fair number of us are likely to let those special concerns determine our vote. As long as that is true, organized interests will continue to play an important role in electoral politics, whatever the rules of campaign finance.

The second reason there are no easy solutions has to do with another byproduct of modern government and communication: the advantages of incumbency, especially for members of the House. The communication resources available to incumbent members, the fractionalization of the congressional policy process, and the long-term weakening of the importance of party to voters all make it hard to defeat incumbents without spending a great deal of money. But a system within which a lot of private money is available almost assuredly is a system in which special interests will participate on an individual or group basis. Interest-group participation may not be all that bad, therefore, if it is a necessary condition for assuring there will be enough money in the system to make the threat of subsequent accountability real.

Proposals for change

Having said this, we are now prepared to look again at some proposals for changing the law. The benefits and problems interest groups bring to the *legislative* process would not be affected greatly if groups could not contribute to candidates. The benefits they bring to *elections* would be lost, however, unless the money they provide challengers toward the end of a campaign could be replaced. In theory the job might be done by full public financing, if it were sufficiently generous to cover the country's most expensive districts. Such a form of public financing might eliminate whatever reinforcement contributions now give to lobbying, while substituting for the needed money that now comes from interested contributors. There are two problems with this approach. First, as was argued earlier in connection with presidential elections, eliminating direct contributions would not and could not eliminate the electoral role of interest groups. It would only introduce new forms of bias into the system. Second, even if the idea were good in theory, it would stand little chance of being adopted. Members of Congress are not likely ever to give their opponents enough money, solely from public funds, to permit serious challenges in expensive districts. Incumbents cannot be expected to think first about the system's need for electoral insecurity as they design the rules for their own reelection campaigns.

We return, therefore, to the real world of political practice, where some form of interest-group participation is accepted, however unhappily, as inevitable, and where the level of electoral competition and the fragmentation of the legislative process are both causes for legitimate concern. In that real world I, for one, come back to the third and fourth of the legislative approaches analyzed earlier. To the extent that fragmentation is caused partly by the role of groups, but more basically by the splits within ourselves, the institutional remedy logically seems to call for building up those political institutions and organizations that can counter our particularized interests in the name of our more general ones. In practical terms, this means increasing the role of parties.

Parties should not be considered panaceas. Excessively strong national committees could weaken Congress, as we saw. In addition, one cannot simply assume that turning all power back to the parties would weaken the power of interest groups. The strong parties of the late nineteenth century, and the national conventions of today, hardly leave one sanguine on that score. Instead of a lesser role for groups, a system in which parties were dominant could just mean better access for fewer groups. But parties are a long way from being dominant today. A great deal can be done to strengthen their role in elections without granting the unlimited spending authority Republicans might wish. Spending limits can be raised, and state and local party volunteer activities can be encouraged . . . .

In addition, the government could reclaim some of the air time it now gives freely to federally licensed radio and television stations. The stations could then be required to make 60 minutes or so of free prime time available to each party to be used in blocks of at least five minutes. In some local areas, the parties might turn the time over to candidates. In most, however, they would probably increase their generic advertising. This advertising, described [by David] Adamany, would make the parties more important for both candidates and voters, nationalizing the election in a manner that would go a long way toward countering the decentralizing effect of individualistic, candidate-centered campaigning. To the extent this happens, it would heighten the sense that elections produce mandates, adding weight to the inclinations of those members who want to resist particularized pressures in the name of a more general interest.

The second approach that deserves serious consideration is exemplified by the McHugh-Conable tax credit bill: public financing unencumbered either by spending limits or limits on a candidate's PAC receipts. As noted, public financing without limits works to the benefit of challengers, especially challengers who have not yet managed to establish themselves as serious competitors. In this respect, it serves as a perfect complement to the existing finance system, in which PACs avoid commitments to challengers in the early stage, but flock to the most serious ones at the end.

Public financing without limits also would decrease the importance of PACs by giving candidates other places to look for their funds. Not all forms of public financing would be equal in this respect, however. Matching grants would do nothing to change the mix of private givers or their importance. Flat grants—whether in cash or in such in-kind forms as postal subsidies, the frank, or free media—would decrease the importance of private money but not the mix. Of all of the bills proposed so far, only a 100 percent tax credit or voucher would change the incentives for candidates in a way that would broaden the base of participants. Interest groups would continue to play an important role, but their proportionate influence would be reduced in a way that would also reduce, rather than increase, the biases inherent in the current system.

In short, many steps can be taken to reduce the costs of interest-group participation while preserving the benefits. Nothing can be done, however, with a strategy of limits that fails to recognize that the fundamental source of interest-group power has little to do with campaign finance. Interest groups are what they are in the United States because parties, governmental institutions, communications and human nature are what they are. Any attempt to deal with what is essentially a surface symptom, the contemporary electoral role of organized groups, solely through direct regulations and limits can do little more than shift group power around and weaken electoral competition. The supposed reforms might also make a few regulators feel good for a while—but only until they glance backward at the unintended consequences of some past reforms and realize that they are looking at their own future.

CHAPTER SEVEN
The Media and the Political Process

North Carolina Republican Senator Jesse Helms, in 1985, led a group called Fairness in Media to take control of the Columbia Broadcasting System (CBS). He reputedly wanted to be Dan Rather's boss. The hostile takeover bid reflected the enduring interest politicians have in the media, because they view journalists as their adversaries. Helms and his fellow conservatives have constantly complained about the "liberal" eastern press, while for their part liberal Democrats often believe that they are under seige from a "conservative" press. Whatever the political pursuasion of the politician, he or she assumes the press will become an adversary unless properly managed.

THE PRESIDENT AND THE PRESS

The higher the level of politics the more likely the press will be considered as a potential enemy. Media paranoia is particularly acute in the White House, were both the Democratic and Republican presidents have devoted considerable energy to courting the media and managing the news. Former presidential assistant George Reedy, who served in the Johnson White House, observed that politicians understandably, but not realistically, expect reporters to support them and the national interest as they define it. "It is impossible," writes Reedy, "for newspapermen . . . to respond on every occasion with what the political leader regards as an appropriately grateful reciprocity. Therefore in the politician's mind, newspapermen are invariably guilty of 'ingratitude.' Furthermore, politicians look to members of the press to be 'constructive,' to help them put across worthwhile programs for the betterment of humanity."[*]

The press and the media, because of their power and responsibilities, have appropriately been called the fourth branch of government.[†] Political reporters serve as conduits of information within governments, and keep the public informed. An alert press helps to prevent governmental secrecy and misinformation, which undermine democracy.

[*]George E. Reedy, *The Twilight of the Presidency* (New York: The World Publishing Company, 1970), p. 114.

[†]See Douglass Cater, *The Fourth Branch of the Government* (New York: Houghton Mifflin Co., 1959).

The Press and the Media: Liberal Adversary or Conservative Friend?

AN EXPERIENCED WASHINGTON HAND CRITICIZES THE ADVERSARY
WHITE HOUSE PRESS CORPS

The author of the following selection was Vice President Spiro Agnew's press secretary, serving a boss who called reporters "effete snobs," "hopeless hypochondriacs of history," and "nattering nabobs of negativism."* Agnew in turn was reflecting the views of *his* boss, President Richard M. Nixon, who privately agreed with but publicly let Agnew be his hatchet man. Throughout his political career Nixon felt the press was out to get him. During his political campaigns and while he was president, Nixon made every effort to manage the news. "During the years I worked for him," recalled John Ehrlichman, "Nixon was usually capable of a passionless and penetrating analysis of his press opportunities. He was a talented media manipulator. I often watched him successfully plan how he or his spokesmen would dominate the evening news, capture the headlines, and right-side columns of the front page of the *Washington Post,* or the lead story in *Time* or *Newsweek.* Richard Nixon could think like an editor."†

Now a national correspondent for the *Washingtonian* magazine, the author of the next selection berates the press for its irresponsibility in constantly seeking to embarrass the president and report whatever it considers to be newsworthy even if the information undermines the national interest. Harry S Truman called presidential press conferences the closest thing to the British practice of having "question hour" in Parliament during which the opposition party asks the Prime Minister and the Cabinet any questions pertaining to the conduct of the government. Presidents have sharply reduced the number of press conferences they are willing to hold, perhaps because they view press conferences much as the author of the following selection does, more as a feast for reporters than as a forum for responsible give and take.

*See Michael J. Robinson and Moura E. Clancey, "Network News, Fifteen Years After Agnew," *Channels,* January/February 1985, p. 34.

†John Ehrlichman, *Witness to Power* (New York: Simon and Schuster, 1982), pp. 263-264.

139

V. GOLD

13

Ego Journalism: An Ex-Flack Looks at Reagan and the Adversary Press

VICTOR GOLD

It was your standard trendy Washington reception, the festive opening of the American Broadcasting Company's new headquarters in the nation's capital, and, much to the delight of the network brass, Ronald Reagan found time to drop by for a presidential blessing. He had made his little speech, shaken hands all around, and was headed toward the door, when the inevitable occurred:

"Mr. President!"

Strident, insistent . . . who else but Sam Donaldson, ABC's chief White House correspondent? Remember those first moments of the Reagan revolution? As the newly sworn President walked down the ramp following his Inaugural Address, there was Sam, bellowing that question about the release of the hostages in Iran. Vintage Donaldson, letting the new man know that, revolution or no revolution, some things weren't going to change. But that was history, and on this particular festive occasion what Sam wanted, *instanter*, was the inside word on David Stockman's future in the Reagan Administration.

To be sure, Sam's imperative tone notwithstanding, the President had an option. He could have kept on walking and been none the worse for it in terms of his image. But, being Ronald Reagan, he stopped in his tracks, half turned, smiled, and proceeded to frame a reply: Well, he said—as

From National Review, *April 2, 1982.* © *1985. National Review, Inc., 150 East 35 Street, New York, N.Y. 10016. Reprinted with permission.*

quiche and crêpes hit the floor, notebooks popped out, and recorders were activated—well, he had met with Dave a little while ago and there would be a definitive announcement later that afternoon. Another reporter was halfway through a second question before the President's hosts, much to the relief of his staff, hustled him toward the exit.

Sorry about that, said one ABC executive, fuming over his man Donaldson's having turned a courtesy call into a mini news conference. Oh, that's all right, replied the President: "Sam," grinned Ronald Reagan, "is just irrepressible."

I don't care what they say, I like Sam Donaldson. Honestly. We go back a long way, Sam and I, to the Goldwater campaign of 1964, when I was a young flack hustling press buses for my first national candidate, and Sam, then working for CBS's Washington television affiliate, was covering his first presidential race.

Do I remember what Sam Donaldson was *really* like, before he became transmogrified into an evening news superstar? Of course. How could I forget? When we first met, opening day of the campaign at Prescott, Arizona, there were only two unabashed Goldwater supporters in our traveling press party. Lyn Nofziger, then covering for Copley, was one; Sam was the other.

He was offbeat, you see, right from the start: a rambunctious news hawk not about to be intimidated by any rulemakers, least of all the doyens of the national media who set the tone and rhythm for coverage of our presidential campaigns. Offbeat, rambunctious, and yet, having said all that, I would never have guessed—not in a million news cycles—that my friend Sam would one day emerge from the pack as master of a new school of political reportage: the ultimate Ego Journalist.

Remarks of the President on the occasion of Mother Teresa's departure from the White House, June 4, 1981:

> Helen Thomas (UPI): How was your visit, Mr. President?
> The President: Just wonderful. You can't be in the presence of someone like that without feeling better about the world.
> Sam Donaldson (ABC): What do you think about the tax plan?

In the New Beginning, January 1981, there was much furrowed-browed thought given the need to develop fresh formats for the President's sessions with the White House press corps. The University of Virginia's Miller Center for Public Affairs even issues a "Report on Presidential Press Conferences," replete with observations, recommendations, and helpful hints, e.g.:

> The manner in which presidential press conferences are presently conducted on live television—with reporters jumping up, waving their hands and shouting, "Mr. President," in an effort to gain the President's eye and the opportunity to ask a question—is what many viewers (and participants) find appalling. The easiest remedy for this requires little more than an exercise in presidential leadership. The President could enforce order by refusing to

acknowledge or answer any reporter who shouts. He answers only those who raise their hands, and allows follow-up questions.

Little more than an exercise in presidential leadership? The *easiest* remedy? How ingenuous these academics. It is one thing, understand, for Ronald Reagan, like no Chief Executive in decades, to assert his mastery over Congress. But "Tip" O'Neill and his colleagues are as mere sheep to be led to a fleecing compared to Sam Donaldson's branch of government. Thus, though the Miller Center did persuade the President to insist on a degree of decorum during his *formal* news conferences, it failed utterly to deal with those techniques of jumping, waving, and shouting reportage developed by the White House press corps during the Ford-Carter years, i.e., the news conference *al fresco*, held on the South Lawn two to four times weekly, and its kindred forum, the movable media feast, held any time or place that members of the corps come within twenty feet—make that fifty—of ever-affable, ever-available Ronald Reagan.

"If you get the question within earshot," one of Sam's print colleagues counseled a newcomer to the Reagan press entourage during the 1980 campaign, "he'll answer it, because he's a decent guy."

Indeed, he would as a candidate, though it sometimes hurt his cause; indeed, he will as President, though it often results in news segments better suited to the media's than the country's needs.

"If we just let him go his own way, we'll have a perpetual press conference," Lyn Nofziger explained, after being faulted during the campaign for what many (including some critics within the Reagan camp) perceived as heavy-handed dealing with reporters trying to catch his candidate in an unguarded moment.

But, alas—or, if you happen to be a member of Sam Donaldson's school, rejoice—Lyn's heavy hand has long since been lifted, his critics having won the day. After all, we wouldn't want to go back to the Nixon Stonewall Age, would we? Of course not. Decency, in the end, prevailed.

Next question.

Remarks of the President while ambulating toward his helicopter in riding jodhpurs, July 22, 1981:

> Reporter No. 1: Any good news from the Middle East?
> The President (walking and smiling): Huh?
> Reporter No. 1 (bellowing): Any good news from the Middle East?
> The President (bellowing back): Oh, you guys know by now that I'm the most patient fellow in the world.
> Reporter No. 2 (in duet with helicopter blades): Are there any limits to your patience with Mr. Begin?

My, my, what fun and games. And if the President, not quite hearing the question correctly, had shouted back a "Yes" or a "No," what a titillating lead that might have made on the evening news. Forget the White House staff clarification that would have followed: sufficient to the deadline is the news thereof. Forget, too, whatever impact the President's errant reply might have had on the Habib mission and U.S. peace-keeping efforts in the Middle East. That, Buster, is neither the job nor the responsibility of the working press, and to argue otherwise is to suggest—with *chilling effect*—that there might be some higher calling for the White House press corps than servicing their home bureaus, every hour on the hour.

Are there any limits to your patience with Mr. Begin? Or how about this one, put up for grabs not long after: *Do you agree with General Schweitzer's assessment of a drift toward war with the Societ Union?*

In both these cases, fortunately, Ronald Reagan, while taking the bait, avoided the hook. Yet, against the day when he, and we, might not be so lucky, let's step back a few paces to examine, in the manner of the Miller Center, exactly what goes on here.

For the record, these come-as-you-are presidential television appearances—informal sportswear when he takes his South Lawn walks to and from the chopper; business suit when being queried, to the great confusion of foreign guests, about domestic affairs—are in fact scheduled as mere photo opportunities. Now, the ground rule for presidential photo opportunities has long been understood, and in former years accepted, by the White House press corps; TV cameramen and still photographers are given access to ceremonial events, e.g., bill signings, meetings with dignitaries, as well as the President's entering/leaving the White House or other site. A reporter pool can observe the proceedings, but only for note-taking purposes.

That, at least, was the rule until the coming of genial Jerry Ford, whose congenital incapacity to look a reporter in the eye and say, "No comment," led to such outlandish spectacles as the leader of the Free World galumphing down a California tarmac during the final hours of the Vietnam War, in order to avoid questions from a press corps in hilarious pursuit. Then came Jimmy Carter, whose personal dislike of the White House press corps was accompanied, with typical Cartersian consistency, by an unwillingness to enforce any rule that might incur its displeasure.

Two pliant, image-obsessed Presidents in a row: small wonder that during this period, 1974-1980, Ego Journalism came into its own, and the presidential news conference took on the Animal House ambience deplored by the Miller Center.

Clearly, Ronald Reagan's decency aside, any President who took office January 1981 was going to have his hands full exercising leadership in the White House press domain. Not only would there be the standard complaints that go with the territory—charges of news management, outcries about credibility gaps—but any attempt to curb the excesses of the Ford-Carter years, when the West Wing leaked like a sieve, would be trotted out as evidence that the New Administration, Watergate-like, was bent on obstructing the people's right to know. To know what? Why, whatever members of the corps deemed important to the national (not to mention their career) agenda.

Thus, by press corps lights, it is now an implied right under the First Amendment that a President and his staff not only be forthcoming on demand, but that the White House also be sensitive to the show-business requirements of modern journalism. For this reason, the Miller Center's recommendation that questioners at formal presidential news conferences be chosen by lot was put into effect only once, then abandoned, following protests by network correspondents. Their complaint? Not that there was anything wrong with the questions submitted under the lottery system, but that Sam, Lesley, Judy did not ask them, and consequently were not on camera reinforcing—for the benefit of employers, sponsors, and fan clubs—their certified status as six-figure-per-annum media superstars.

Tom Brokaw, *on the happy coincidence of Britain's summer riots and network coverage of the wedding of Prince Charles and Lady Diana:* "I think it's going to make a far better assignment for all of us. I don't wish ill to the British people and I certainly don't want them to burn down towns for our sake. But there has been a lot of ferment there for some time and it just happens to be breaking out now."

Judy Woodruff, *on the existential meaning of "adversary press":* "The White House staff wants order, predictability, no surprises. That makes it easier to make a President look good. But the press yearns for a little confusion, disorder, surprise—even a healthy shock once in a while. The unexpected is news, the expected is not."

Are you listening, RR? Keep in mind, they don't wish ill to the American people, and they certainly don't want us to burn down towns for their sake; but a *little* confusion, disorder, surprise, a healthy shock once in a while—is that so much to ask on behalf of a free, yearning press?

True, your constitutional duty, among other things, is to "ensure domestic tranquility." But let's be fair. My friend Sam, along with his colleagues at ABC, NBC, CBS, the *Post*, the *Times*, The *Atlantic*, aren't going to rack up any Nielsen numbers or draw down any Pulitzers phoning in, "All's tranquil on the West Wing front."

No, if there isn't any "ferment . . . breaking out," well, then, the enterprising Ego Journalist knows a few chemical shortcuts through "informed White House sources" and "high-level government officials." Understand, it's nothing personal, RR—nor even, as many of us once believe, ideological. Trendy leftism may well be the prevailing wind that blows through your White House press room, but as no less a media favorite than Ted Kennedy discovered in 1980, Ego Journalism cuts all ways. It is amoral, cynical, nihilistic—up to a point. Take the word of an ex-political flack who jockeyed press buses when Sam Donaldson was an embryo seeker after confusion, disorder, surprise; or better still, those of a prescient observer who years ago foresaw the problems your Administration would have coping with an irrepressible press:

Complete publicity makes it absolutely impossible to govern. No one has understood that better than the daily press; for no power has watched more carefully over the secret of its whole organization, who its contributors are, and its real aims, etc., as the daily press, which then continually cries out that the *government* should be quite public. Quite right: the intention of the press was to do away with government—and then itself govern . . .

All right, three guesses: Was that a) Spiro Agnew at Des Moines, b) the Miller Center, c) Lyn Nofziger? Wrong, wrong, wrong. It was—they'll have to unleash Morley Safer on this bird for the full *60 Minutes* treatment—none other than that old fascist, Soren Kierkegaard.

Funny. I don't recall that he was even middle echelon during the Nixon Dark Age.

To the point, RR—much as I hate to sound like one of those patronizing *Times* editorialists, or Bill Moyers in full cry—I'm afraid you don't quite grasp the extent of the modern media's challenge to all governing establishments save its own. In your eternally optimistic way, you still hope to plug the leakage of Administration affairs that plagued your predecessors Jerry Ford and Jimmy Carter, to put the horse of orderly governance before the media cart of "complete publicity." But to do that, it's necessary that, one way or another, you persuade those who make up your Administration that the boys and girls on the White House press bus are precisely what they claim to be—*adversaries*. Not friendly folk for sharing inner-office gossip with over the phone or, in the case of your indiscreet OMB Director, over bacon, eggs, coffee, and a live tape recorder.

Yet consider, if you will, the real question to be asked about the Stockman episode, apart from the one that interested my friend Sam. Was it simply a matter of Ego Journalist meeting Ego Politican—further proof, if any were needed, that the passion for anonymity once prized in White House aides has given way to a passion for celebrity? Perhaps. But beyond that, might it not be argued that David Stockman—along with other indiscreet Administration spokesmen in the first year of the Reagan revolution—was merely responding to the signal given by a President who casually chats up affairs of state with his "friends" in the press, anytime they can "get the question within earshot"?

Just a thought, RR, from an ex-flack. Mull it over, next time you approach the portal to the South Lawn. And believe me, it's not that I'm anti-decency or a chronic First Amendment-chiller. As I say, I like Sam Donaldson. For that matter, Brokaw, Woodruff, Stahl, and Greider aren't really bad sorts. It's simply that, where our country's foreign and domestic tranquillity are concerned, I can't say I much like their penchant for healthy shocks.

The Press and the Media: Liberal Adversary or Conservative Friend?

A WASHINGTON POLITICAL REPORTER SEES THE MEDIA MOVING TO THE RIGHT

Media Slant

The preceding selection suggests that the White House press is a presidential adversary regardless of whether or not the president is a liberal or a conservative. The Reagan White House may attack the press for its liberal bias, but Democratic administrations have been equally uncomfortable. Jody Powell, President Carter's press secretary, believes that the preponderance of reporters who are Democrats result in sharper criticism of Democratic than of Republican presidents. They apply stricter standards in judging Democrats. Powell writes:

> . . . Those [Democratic] journalists who really care about certain policy positions tend to hold Democratic presidents to a higher standard. They don't expect Republicans to do much for women or minorities or poor people, and they don't raise much hell when they don't. They expect Republicans to be a good bit laxer about conflicts of interest and other improprieties and don't pursue such stories, at least since Watergate, with as much zeal in a GOP administration.*

President Jimmy Carter, no less than Ronald Reagan, held as few press conferences as possible to avoid what he and his aides considered to be unfair coverage.

The White House press, although important, is only a tiny part of the media. Whether it covers presidents fairly or unfairly will always be a matter of debate between presidents and their aides on the one hand, and reporters on the other.

Liberal and Conservative Spin

The White House press does not exist in isolation, but is connected to a vast media network beyond 1600 Pennsylvania Avenue. Presidents may be annoyed at what they feel is the constant harping of the White House press, but their tempers rise even further when they think they are confronting a hostile national media that is not simply trying to find fault but is often opposing their policies on ideological grounds. A news summary, surveying media coverage of the White House throughout the country, is prepared for the president each day.

*Jody Powell, *The Other Side of the Story* (New York: William Morrow and Co., 1984), pp. 38-39.

146

Understandably, most presidents are more chagrined by negative stories than they are pleased by favorable coverage, for they expect the latter but consider the former to be unfair.

During the Reagan administration, the traditional Republican attacks upon the liberal national press surfaced once again. Careful studies of the media, however, suggest that it is more adversary to incumbent presidents than to challengers.* In 1980 Carter was treated more harshly than Reagan, while in 1984 the media covered the Reagan-Bush campaign far more negatively than they did the Mondale-Ferraro challenge. Ironically, Walter Mondale blamed his defeat on television, although more on his inability to master the medium than on the way it presented him.

There is indeed an adversary press, but the objects and the basis of media "spin," or "news slant," are not easily predictable. Surveys have indicated that a majority of the media elite is more politically liberal than the rest of the country.† But the media has slanted the news in both liberal and conservative directions. Moreover, as the following selection points out, a more conservative media realignment is taking place.

---

*Moura Clancey and Michael J. Robinson, "General Election Coverage: Part I," *Public Opinion*, Vol. 7, no. 6 (December/January 1985), p. 54.

†S. Robert Lichter and Stanley Rothman, "Media and Business Elites," *Public Opinion*, Vol. 4, no. 5 (October/November 1981), pp. 42–46, 59–60.

F. BARNES

14

Media Realignment

FRED BARNES

Remember the liberal press? While Senator Jesse Helms gripes about the "left-leaning media," more thoughtful conservatives have been among the first to spot the rightward drift of the press. "Conservatism isn't the regnant ideological voice of the American media, but it's on the march," says Patrick Maines, a former advertising manager at William F. Buckley's *National Review* and now president of The Media Institute. Reed Irvine, the chairman of Accuracy in Media, which has been hectoring the "liberal media" since 1969, says, "The snide carping at Reagan has been toned down. The press corps was a bit humbled by the election returns."

In fact, the press's drift began well before Reagan's reelection. Media realignment and the emergence of Reagan are signs of the same phenomenon: the conservative trend in American life that began in the late sixties and quickened in the late seventies and early eighties. Liberal ideas faded in popularity, and liberals went on the defensive for the first time in half a century; conservative ideas gained popularity, and conservatives took the offensive. The press soon began to reflect the shift in political power. A sizable segment of the press now celebrates capitalism and is unabashedly nationalistic, questions liberalism and is unapologetically complacent. This is not to say that the so-called "prestige press"—the TV networks, the newsmagazines, and the three newspapers of national influence, *The New York Times*, *The Washington Post*, and *The Wall Street Journal*—has been captured by conservative ideologues. But conservative thinkers and ideas have infiltrated what were once regarded as enemy lines.

Is this conservative trend a healthy restoration of political equilibrium, a necessary antidote to the "liberal bias" of the past? Or has the press

Reprinted by permission of The New Republic, © 1985, *The New Republic, Inc.*

succumbed to the conservatism of the times and abandoned its independence? The answers, of course, depend on one's definitions of objectivity and fairness. But however one defines them, it is clear that conservatives have a voice in the media that they haven't had before.

Media realignment has been marked by four big events and a succession of small ones. First and perhaps most important was the rise of George Will, whose surge to national influence was crowned last year when he was named the lone commentator on ABC News. Will, whose conservatism can be stuffy and pedantic as well as forceful and unswerving, now reaches the largest audience of any journalist in the country. Second and third (and almost as important) were the creation of two fresh news operations, Cable News Network in 1980 and *USA Today* in 1982. Each is more conservative than its competition. And fourth, over the last half-dozen years there has been *The New York Times*'s growing receptivity to neoconservative ideas and writers.

As for the smaller events, *The Washington Star*, which had been a voice of political moderation and the sole competitor of *The Washington Post*, folded in 1981, only to be succeeded by *The Washington Times*. The *Times*, owned by the Reverend Sun Myung Moon's Unification Church, is aggressively conservative and fiercely anticommunist. Although its circulation is a negligible 75,000, it is read widely inside the Reagan White House. Indeed, the president is said to read it regularly, starting with the funnies. "The McLaughlin Group" has raced past "Agronsky and Company" as the hot political chat show on television. "McLaughlin" has a strong conservative tilt; "Agronsky" doesn't. Though first broadcast only three years ago, "McLaughlin" is carried on 168 PBS and two commercial stations; "Agronsky" is broadcast on 37 PBS stations and five commercial stations. ("McLaughlin" is helped by the fact that the Edison Electric Institute distributes the show free of charge to any public TV station that wants it. "Agronsky" must be purchased from Post-Newsweek Stations Inc.) One of McLaughlin's regular panelists, lapsed liberal and former TNR executive editor Morton Kondracke, has become Washington bureau chief of *Newsweek*, replacing Mel Elfin, a friend of Walter Mondale's and an occasional panelist on "Agronsky." At *Time*, meanwhile, the chief Washington columnist, Hugh Sidey, once a close friend of President John F. Kennedy, has become a Reagan admirer.

And then there is the White House press corps. During Reagan's first term, reporters regularly took the administration to task. *Newsweek* called Reagan "detached" from the process of governing. After press conferences, newspapers including *The Washington Post* and *The New York Times* ran separate stories about Reagan's mangling of facts. CBS news regularly pilloried his economic program as cruel and ineffective. But none of it had any effect on Reagan's popularity.

Now White House reporters are given to lamenting their ineffectualness. Three months into Reagan's second term, Ralph Nader sponsored a seminar on "The White House Press Corps—Problems in Captivity," at which a panel of reporters flailed themselves. "We haven't been as aggressive with this president as we should have been," said Saul Friedman of the Knight-Ridder newspaper chain. "The reason is, it's difficult in this milieu . . . in which editors, politicians, folks back home . . . don't want you to go after the president."

Conservatives are far from achieving dominance over the media. Most reporters, especially those who cover national news, regard themselves as liberals. *The Washington Post* and *The Boston Globe* are still generally liberal newspapers—and adversarial in their approach to the Reagan administration. The TV news shows continue to report critically on military spending and the effects of cutbacks in federal programs for the poor. But there are more competing voices in the media now, and a few changes of heart. The result is a perceptible jump to the right in the media's ideological center of gravity.

Will is the most visible symbol of the shift. He came to prominence by writing anti-Nixon columns during the Watergate years. More than other columnists, Will reflected the deepening national conservative mood, especially on conservative and defense issues. He led the promilitary bandwagon that emerged in reaction to Jimmy Carter. And he was reliably conservative on social issues like abortion. In 1980 he attached himself to Ronald Reagan. By the time Reagan was inaugurated, Will was ubiquitous— a syndicated column twice a week, fortnightly pieces on the back page of *Newsweek*, appearances on ABC news shows, the hosting of a well-publicized dinner party for Reagan. Finally in 1984 came his position as commentator on ABC's "World News Tonight," where he appears two or three times a week.

Will is the first conservative commentator on network television (you can't count Howard K. Smith, who was a hawk on Vietnam but liberal on most other issues). "I dare say I'm the only person on network television regularly who in 1964 voted for Barry Goldwater," Will announced on the air last March. Will's boast aside, this is a big breakthrough for conservatives. "Will reflects change all right—in America and in the perception of America by media moguls," wrote columnist Ben Wattenberg last July. "But it is important to note that in an electronic age this sort of decision not only reflects change but engenders it. An articulate and attractive conservative voice in so many homes will switch some opinions. More important, such a voice tends to rally and energize those who will say, 'Well, that's what I've believed all along.' Finally, it influences other voices in the media: they will have to deal with some arguments that could have been previously ignored or trivialized."

Wattenberg touches on the central issue of media politics: the balance between engendering political change and reflecting it. Conservatives obviously welcome Will's appearance on network television; if he engenders change as well as reflecting it, so much the better. They are less sanguine about broadcasting decisions by network executives that might influence opinion in liberal ways.

Many conservatives have worried that Will might feel compelled in his TV commentaries to soften his views to accommodate a nonconservative audience. If anything, he has been more hard-line than ever. He has argued to an audience of ten million that the MX should be authorized; Edwin Meese III confirmed as attorney general; Jeane Kirkpatrick named *Time's* Woman of the Year; Libya punished harshly for promoting terrorism; a war launched against users as well as dealers of cocaine; the Soviets denounced for the shooting death of Major Arthur Nicholson in Berlin in April. What's more, he has called for overthrowing the Sandinistas and warned against economic pressures on South Africa. Far from passively embodying the conservative mood, Will is actively promoting it.

At *The New York Times* such forthright conservatism is not in vogue, but a close cousin—neoconservatism—is. This is not really surprising. Neoconservatism is the creation of New York intellectuals, some of them friendly with *Times* editors, including executive editor Abe Rosenthal. Next to *Commentary*, *The New York Times Magazine* is now the most reliably neoconservative publication in the country. Virtually every issue contains an article by a neoconservative—Michael Novak assaulting liberation theology, Robert W. Tucker calling for a new Reaganesque brand of détente with the Soviet Union, Morris Abram zinging racial quotas, John Vinocur touting Clint Eastwood as a serious actor and filmmaker.

In recent months *The New York Times's* Op-Ed page has been studded with conservative columns by people like Norman Podhoretz, the editor of *Commentary*, and David Smick, spokesman for supply-sider Lewis Lehrman. The paper's foreign news coverage often takes an anticommunist tack. Raymond Bonner, who had covered Central America for the *Times*, was called back to the United States in 1982. He had regularly reported on discrepancies between the administration's public version of events in El Salvador and information contained in the embassy's classified cable traffic. Conservative media critics, expecially Reed Irvine of AIM, had singled out Bonner for being overly critical of the Salvadoran government, and welcomed his transfer. There has also been a significant change in the *Times'* s cultural reporting. The paper, for example, recently hired Richard Grenier, the movie critic for *Commentary*. In one of his first pieces, Grenier skewered what he called "treason chic," the whitewashing of spies for the communist bloc in a spate of plays and movies such as *Pack of Lies* and *Another Country*. (Grenier, though, may not be the most reliable ideological ally. Geoffrey Stokes of *The Village Voice* notes that Grenier's review of *Apocalypse Now* for *Commentary* criticized the film's "unmistakably sophomoric, not to say, semi-educated quality." But in *Cosmopolitan* Grenier proclaimed the same film "so gorgeous, so technically magnificent, so ambitious and laden with meaning, that—whatever side you take—you must see it.")

Cable News Network and *USA Today* represent efforts to outflank the journalistic establishment. CNN, formed in 1980 by Ted Turner, offers 24-hour news to 29 million subscribers. "It's a conservative network," says Patrick Maines of The Media Institute, all the more so since CNN decided recently to drop Daniel Schorr, its chief correspondent and house liberal. CNN's news coverage is straight, but its emphasis on economic issues, with five separate business shows, is supportive of unfettered capitalism. Still, the source of CNN's reputation comes from two other shows, "Crossfire," the network's most popular program, and "Evans and Novak."

Patrick J. Buchanan, the new White House communications director, made his name as one of two panelists on "Crossfire" (with Tom Braden as his liberal counterpart). Buchanan brutally questioned liberal guests, a task taken up now by columnist Robert Novak or Cal Thomas, a Moral Majority official and columnist. Novak and his partner Rowland Evans also do a twice-weekly "Insider Reports" on CNN. Not long ago they hammered Democratic national chairman Paul Kirk for urging the party to reject special interests while refusing to name any of them. "You don't consider blacks a special interest group," said Novak. "I am sure you don't consider women a special interest group. What about homosexuals, gays? Is that a special interest group?" Kirk ducked the question.

The celebration of capitalism is even more pronounced on three other cable networks. The USA network, which reaches 23.5 million homes, features "BizNet News Today," produced by the U.S. Chamber of Commerce, as its main morning show. The Financial News Network, which goes into nearly 16 million homes, tracks daily business activity lovingly. On ESPN, a sports network that reaches 30 million subscribers, early mornings are devoted to "Business Times," which provides cheerful features on companies, corporate leaders, and new technology, as well as regular financial reports. And there is the Christian Broadcasting Network, created by evangelist Pat Robertson. It offers its own news programs, all on conservative and fundamentalist themes.

USA Today began publication as the Gannett chain's national flagship in September 1982, in the dark days of the recession. But from the start it was proclaiming the coming of the recovery with front-page stories on signals of a burgeoning economy. It did this well before the rest of the national press got wind of the turnaround. It remains relentlessly upbeat about the economy. One day it spotlights a boost in auto sales, the next an increase in industrial output. *USA Today* can clearly be accused of cheerleading, which is something the "prestige papers" and the networks can't. Last fall *USA Today* raved about its buying power for consumers. "Our Dollar Pounds the Pound," declared a headline. About the same time, *The Washington Post* was reporting on the role of the strong dollar in driving down foreign sales of American-made equipment. *USA Today* is also fervently nationalistic. It openly rooted for American gold medals on its front page during the Olympics last summer.

USA Today was initially given little chance for survival, even by Wall Street business analysts. It appealed mainly to sports fans, who were said to toss away the front, business, and features sections. "Everybody was skeptical [in 1982]," says John Morton, a newspaper industry analyst. "We didn't perceive there was any appetite for the publication. I'm a lot more optimistic now than I've ever been about its chances of making it." The paper has 1.4 million readers daily, and its ad linage has soared from 6.5 pages a year ago to 15.5. It lost $100 million last year, but according to Morton, "If they keep going, they can possibly be in the black in 1987." It would seem that the immediate future of this fourth national newspaper, more conservative than the others (though not more conservative than the editorial page of *The Wall Street Journal*), is all but assured.

Tom Brokaw of NBC and Hugh Sidey of *Time*, both media superstars, reflect the press drift in different ways. Brokaw now appears in an ad for "NBC Nightly News" in which he implicitly defends the network against charges of liberal bias. He says firmly that he knows "of no more patriotic group than television journalists." But people shouldn't rely on them, he continues, to "get all they need to know in this complicated world. They must read books, good newspapers and quality magazines, listen to the radio, talk to their neighbors, go beyond what information is easily available. That's the best check on any potential abuse of power." This is a remarkable concession of network fallibility.

Sidey, who has written a column on the presidency since 1966, is not so defensive. He made his name in journalism first as a friend of John Kennedy, then as someone who was close to Lyndon Johnson and Hubert Humphrey. But he concedes that he's changed his political outlook. "You call it what you want," he says. "I've changed. Yes, I've changed. The problems have changed. The world has changed. I say you have to sort through it." When he sorted through the election results last fall, Sidey sneered at the "pundits, academics, and campaign theorists" who debunked Reagan, at the "network commentators gamely trying to disguise their preference for Mondale," at the elitism "in the newsrooms of the big liberal papers, in the salons of trendy Georgetown." The world "beyond the Hudson and Potomac rivers" was no longer beholden to the Eastern elite for its political views. The "ordinary people" went with Reagan. In fact, Sidey's view might well be seen as the "trendy" one today. Now conservative bias is applauded just as vigorously as liberal bias was once denounced. Media realignment confirms the press's continuing susceptibility to political fashion.

CHAPTER EIGHT
The Presidency

The president stands at the pinnacle of the political system. Elected by all of the people, albeit through the Electoral College filter, the president's role and responsibilities have grown enormously since the founding of the Republic.

THE NOMINATING PROCESS

Presidents are elected nationally, but political parties must first nominate candidates to run. Party nominating procedures can have a profound impact upon the character, quality, and political orientation of presidential nominees. Candidates tend to represent the party constituents who choose them. Brokered conventions, in which party bosses and elected leaders meet in "smoke-filled rooms" behind the scenes to select candidates, strive to choose nominees that have wide electoral appeal within and without the party. On the other hand, candidate selection through grass-roots primaries may produce more ideological nominees who appeal to the relatively small number of party activists who turn out to vote in the primaries or participate in caucuses. Candidates who are popular with party activists, such as George McGovern was in 1972, often have little chance of winning the general election because their extreme ideological views have little national appeal.

EVOLUTION OF PRESIDENTIAL NOMINATING PROCEDURES

The presidential nominating process is periodically in a state of flux as party leaders and members attempt to adjust selection procedures to ensure the choice of representative nominees who can win the general election. In the early nineteenth century, congressional party caucuses nominated candidates for both the presidency and vice presidency. However, the caucuses soon became unrepresentative of the party as a whole, and by 1828 parties began to use conventions to nominate presidential candidates. Andrew Jackson and the Democrats held the first full-fledged nominating convention in 1832.

Throughout the remainder of the nineteenth century, the national nominating conventions satisfactorily represented party activists and interests in choosing nominees. State and local party members and leaders participated in caucuses and committees to select convention delegates.

154

The introduction of presidential preference primaries in 1912 once again reformed nominating procedures by allowing rank-and-file members to express their candidate preferences. Fewer than twenty states, however, adopted the primaries, making it impossible for candidates to win the nomination simply by running in primaries. Moreover, some of the primaries were merely "beauty contests," in which voters expressed their preferences without choosing delegates. Candidates nevertheless often chose to run in a number of primaries to boost their vote-getting credibility with the party leaders who would decide on the nominee. Prior to 1972, when running in primaries became necessary to capture the nomination, seven Republican and ten Democratic nominees had been winners of the most primary elections in the years in which they were nominated.*

RENEWED EMPHASIS ON THE GRASS ROOTS

The quest for broader party representation in the choice of presidential candidates once again resulted in party reforms in the 1970s that expanded preference primaries to 37 states and the District of Columbia by 1980. Begun by the Democrats, the reforms also affected the Republicans, and no candidate of either party could win the nomination without victories in a majority of the primary states.

RETURN OF PARTY LEADERS TO THE NOMINATING PROCESS

Turmoil within the Democratic party, whose members seem to relish conflict over procedures as well as ideology, led to a retreat in 1984 from the reforms of the 1970s. The Democratic party's elected national and state leaders, who had largely been excluded from the nominating process during the 1970s, were understandably unhappy. The Democratic National committee (DNC) chose North Carolina Governor James Hunt to head yet another party reform commission after the 1980 election. The commission was stacked with traditional party leaders, including members of Congress, governors, mayors, and a variety of state and local officials. Attempting to reverse the grass-roots trend spurred by the McGovern commission in the 1970s, the new panel recommended, and the DNC adopted in 1982, new rules for the 1984 convention. These rules provided that 14 percent of the delegates would be uncommitted party officials, mostly drawn from members of Congress. The number was not high, but in a close contest the party leaders' votes could determine the outcome. The leadership bloc stood mostly behind Walter Mondale in 1984, and helped him to capture the nomination, although he also had to win a majority of primary and caucus delegates.

*Nelson W. Polsby, *Consequences of Party Reform* (New York: Oxford University Press, 1983), p. 11.

CONTINUING STRUGGLE FOR CONTROL

The magnitude of the political stakes guarantee that debate over party reforms will continue. Essentially this debate involves who will control the nominating process. It is not simply a conflict between party power brokers and the rank and file, but among different party leaders who feel that their individual power within the party will be augmented more by one system than by another.

DEBATE FOCUS

Should the Rank and File or the Power Brokers of Political Parties Choose Presidential Nominees?

A DEMOCRAT AND REPUBLICAN JOIN IN PROPOSING A NEW NATIONAL
PRIMARY TO SUPPLEMENT CONVENTIONS IN THE PRESIDENTIAL
NOMINATING PROCESS

The authors of the following selection address a number of concerns about contemporary nominating practices, including the decline in importance of the national conventions, the reduced role of party officials, and the general circumvention of the party organization which helps to undermine the party system itself. Media politics dominates the present system, emphasizing images over substance as reporters focus more on the political horse race than on the issues. Qualities of presidential leadership are not adequately tested in the grueling primary and caucus process.

    A national preprimary convention system is recommended in which each party would hold a *national* primary *after* its national convention to nominate both presidential and vice presidential candidates from among the top two or three contenders at the convention. State presidential preference primaries for the selection of delegates to the convention would be abolished, to be replaced by local party caucuses followed by state conventions. Designed to strengthen both the parties and grass-roots participation, the plan is a fascinating and provocative compromise of the party reforms of the 1970s and efforts in the 1980s to put party pols back into the driver's seat.

15

T. E. CRONIN

R. D. LOEVY

Putting the Party as Well as the People Back in President Picking

THOMAS E. CRONIN
ROBERT D. LOEVY

Our nomination process has changed dramatically since the 1960s when John F. Kennedy had to enter just four contested state primaries. Once shaped mainly by state and national party leaders, it is now as much or even more shaped by single-interest groups and the media.

The formal nominating process begins with the Iowa caucus in January of each election year and lumbers through more state caucuses and conventions and thirty-six primary elections before candidates are finally selected at national party conventions in July and August.

Nobody, with the possible exception of Ronald Reagan, seems happy with the present nominating system—especially the patchworky maze of presidential primaries. The process strains the patience of most Americans. Isn't there a better way, ask most Americans, to test a candidate's mind and integrity and encourage quality voter participation?

Critics say the main thing primaries do is eliminate good candidates. The late Adlai Stevenson, a three-time presidential candidate said the primary system is "a very, very questionable method of selecting presidential candidates. . . . All it does is destroy some candidates." Walter F. Mondale, a few years ago, wrote, "I am convinced . . . that the system itself is becoming

The Presidential Nominating Process: Volume I, Kenneth W. Thompson (Ed.), "Putting the Party as Well as the People Back in President Picking," Thomas E. Cronin and Robert D. Loevy, pp. 49–64. Copyright 1983 by University Press of America, Inc. Reprinted by permission.

increasingly irrational, self-defeating and destructive of the ultimate goal of electing the most important political leader in a free society in the world." Last election season, friends and supporters of Senator Howard Baker (R-Tn.) came away thinking the New Hampshire primary was an unfair as well as unreal test of their candidate's promise as a national leader.

The current primary system plainly favors well-heeled out-of-office individuals who can spend full-time campaigning in selected early state nominating battles. Thus Carter, in 1976, and Reagan, in 1980, could spend up to a hundred days in Iowa, New Hampshire and Florida while the office holders such as Udall, Baker, Anderson, Kennedy and Presidents Ford and Carter had to remain on their jobs as legislators and executives in service to the nation.

Our present nominating process has become a televised horse-race focusing more on rival media consultants and advertising executives than on the competing ideas, programs or even character of the candidates. More voters, to be sure, take part in primary elections than in caucuses and conventions. But what about the *quality* of that participation? Primary voters often know little about the many candidates listed on the ballot. They may drop in at the primary election booth between a trip to the drugstore and the local supermarket and give little more thought to choosing candidates than to choosing among brands of toothpaste and canned vegetables. Popularity polls, slick spot ads, and television coverage of the early primaries offer episodes and spectacles, and the average citizen is hard pressed to distinguish significance from entertainment.

"Winners"—sometimes with only twenty percent of the vote—in the early small state nomination contests are given significant and undue media coverage—and this fact becomes an important part of any savvy campaign strategy. Jimmy Carter's victories in Iowa and New Hampshire in 1976 and the outpouring of cover and feature human interest stories on him are a prime example of this momentum fever.

Voters in New Hampshire and a few other early primaries often virtually get the right to nominate their party's candidate. Candidates who do not do well in these early stages get discouraged and their financial contributors and volunteers desert them. In practice, voters in later states often get presented with just one or possibly one and a half surviving candidates—which leaves many voters in California or Colorado feeling that they have been both cheated and disenfranchised. The final result is that, in most presidential years, the nominees of both major parties are decided much too early in the process.

Critics of the present nominating practices are also concerned, rightly we believe, about the declining importance of the Democratic and Republican National Conventions. Now that nominations are often "sewed up" by winning early primaries, the national conventions have become *ratifying* rather than *nominating* conventions. Most delegates, "bound" by various state and party election rules to vote for a specific candidate, are no longer expected or able to negotiate, bargain and compromise the various diverse interests within the party and work toward nominating a candidate with broad party support. Instead of having real work to do, most delegates have little more to do than cast their predetermined required vote, enjoy a round of cocktail parties, pick up local souvenirs, and then go home. It's all pretty empty and a bit of a charade and it is little wonder that the networks are moving away from gavel to gavel coverage.

A further complaint is that the current nominating system has diminished the role of party and public officials, and concomitantly increased the role of candidate-loyalists and issue activities. Primaries bypass the local party structure. They encourage the candidates and their managers to form candidate-loyalist brigades to support their candidacy several months in advance of the primaries. Elected officials generally are unwilling to become committed to one candidate or another until well along in the election year and hence they are often, in effect, frozen out of the present process. But does this make sense? Hardly. Because most serious candidates for national office hold elective office, or did so in the recent past, the views of their peers who have served with them in Congress or the National Governor's Association can be particularly insightful. Congressman Gillis Long (D-Louisiana) says the rise of primaries and the requirement that delegates be "bound" to a candidate has had the effect of excluding many of the elected officials who in the past would have participated in the nomination of their party's nominee. "We have paid a terrible price for that," Long says. "Most elected officials are attuned to mainstream concerns. For the health and vigor of our party, they need to be involved in the party process. They know the political waters. They know the shoals, and prevailing currents." Because elected officials, especially members of Congress, have some obligation to implement the goals and platform of their party, they should participate in the development of party positions.

The plea from elected officials is as follows: Bring us back into the system; give us incentives for involvement; give us responsibility in selecting our candidates and writing our platform. Let us integrate the national presidential party and the congressional party as one working unit where the various components have some status and voice in the processes and outcomes of the other components.

Those who want to strengthen the party role in the nominating process do not think elected or party leaders should dominate or control nominations. Rather they want to encourage peer review and insure that a reasonable number of elected officials are allowed to participate in the single most significant activity performed by a national party. Political scientist Everett Ladd suggests that the person who successfully "passes muster in a peer review process, if elected, comes into office with contacts and alliances that he needs if he is to govern successfully."

U.S. Senator Alan Cranston (D-Calif.) raises yet another objection to the present system when he says few if any of the qualities that bring victory in primaries are the qualities the presidency demands of its occupants. Cranston may overstate the case, but here is how he thinks:

> Primaries do not tell us how well a candidate will delegate authority. Nor do they demonstrate his ability to choose the best people for top government posts . . . Primaries don't tell us how effective a candidate will be in dealing with Congress, nor how capable a candidate will be at moving the national power structure, nor how good an educator of the American public a candidate would really be as President. And, most important, primaries don't tell us how good a candidate would be at Presidential decision-making. Primaries do not adequately test courage and wisdom in decision-making—yet those are the ultimate tests of a good President.

What follows is a proposal for a pre-primary convention system at the national level—or a national pre-primary convention plan. Our proposal is a recombination of certain state practices fused with some contending "reform" or "rereform" suggestions.

We are more than a little aware that no procedure is neutral, that any system has various side-effects and unanticipated consequences. Further we know that no method of nominating presidential candidates guarantees good candidates or good presidents. (The nominating method used in selecting Lincoln also gave us Buchanan. The nominating method that nominated Eisenhower and Kennedy nominated Richard Nixon as a member of the national ticket on five different occasions.) Plainly, no procedure can substitute for rigorous screening and the exercise of shrewd judgment at every step of whatever system is used.

Still, we want to suggest what we think is a bold, comprehensive and novel better way to select presidential nominees. We offer it as an antidote to the tinkering that characterizes most of the conventional remedies currently being suggested. This is not to say we disagree with many of the suggested incremental changes usually proposed. Rather we think a fresh approach might be even better. We trust it will provoke readers to rethink the existing process and to join the national dialogue on this subject.

The national preprimary convention system would reverse the present order of things. It would replace the present glut of thirty-six individual state primaries with a caucus and convention system in all states, to be followed by a national convention, which in turn would be followed by a national Republican presidential primary and a national Democratic presidential primary to be held on the same day in September. The sequences would look something like this (with illustrative dates):

1. May 1st—Local Precinct Caucuses Throughout the Nation
2. May 14th—County Convention Day Nationwide
3. May 21st—Congressional District Caucuses Nationwide
4. June 1st—State Conventions Nationwide
5. July—National Conventions
6. Sept 10th—National Primary Day

Although this proposal runs counter to the present established thinking that the presidential primary should occur before the convention rather than after it, there are working precedents at the state level. The State of Colorado, for example, holds Democratic and Republican party precinct caucuses in early May, in which any registered party member may attend and vote. These precinct caucuses elect delegates to county conventions held in early June, and the county conventions in turn elect delegates to the state party convention, held in early July.

At the state party convention in Colorado, any candidate for statewide office who receives twenty percent or more of the delegate vote is automatically placed on the ballot in the early September primary election. The candidate who gets the highest number of votes is listed first on the ballot, the candidate who gets the second highest number of votes is listed second, and so on down the line. Candidates work hard at the state convention to receive the so-called "top-line" designation, and convention delegates have real work to do in deciding who will be on the primary ballot and in what order their names will appear. In the September primary election, the plurality winner receives the party nomination and runs against the opposition party candidate at the regular general election in November.

A few other states have preprimary caucus and convention systems similar to Colorado's, among them Connecticut, Utah, and New York. The proposal thus is new and innovative only when applied at the national level. At the state level, it has been well-tested. Colorado, for example, has used this system since 1910 and has found it to be a good system for retaining the strengths of both the party convention and the party primary election.

A national preprimary-convention plan starts with party caucuses nationwide on the first Monday in May of the presidential year. Any citizen would be eligible to attend a particular party caucus, but all those who vote at the party caucus would have to first register at the caucus as members of that political party. By national law, those who register in a political party at the precinct caucus would be allowed to vote only in that particular party's national primary the following September.

Party members at the party caucus would be eligible to run for delegate to the county party convention. Those candidates for delegate who wished to identify themselves as supporting a particular candidate for President could do so, and they would be bound to vote for that candidate when they attended the county convention.

The county convention would be held on county convention day on the second Saturday in May. County convention delegates would elect delegates to the state party convention, which would be held on state convention day on the first Saturday in June. The state convention would elect the state delegation to the national party conventions, which would be held in July.

Similar to the procedure at the precinct caucuses, candidates for delegate at the county and congressional district conventions would state their preferences to remain uncommitted at this time. Those stating a preference would then be committed or "bound" on the first ballot at the national conventions. After the first ballot at the national conventions, however, these delegates could exercise their personal judgment in voting for the remaining candidates of their choice.

We propose, and the national preprimary convention plan would readily accommodate, the selection at the state party convention of twenty-five percent of the state's delegation to the national convention as unbound delegates. These persons so designated might be nominated by the state central committees from available state elected and party leaders who have demonstrated strong commitment to their party. Such officials might include several members of the state's congressional delegation, statewide elected officers such as governor and attorney-general, a few big city mayors and state legislators as well as state party leaders. These unbound delegates would sometimes mirror local and state caucus results. But they would have an obligation to exercise their best political judgment, not simply to abide by public opinion and the temporary wishes of their supporters. Their presence and their perspective should help make national conventions more deliberative and more an occasion for party renewal than has been the case in recent years. These officials could also take into consideration late breaking events or reflect current opinion in July as opposed to the public moods earlier in the spring.

It is important to note what would not be allowed in the process outlined here. States would be prohibited by national law from holding any form of official pre-convention presidential primary election. Throughout the entire process, the emphasis would be on selecting party members as delegates. Less than seventy-five percent of the state's delegation will be bound to specified candidates in advance of the convention.

Voting procedures and other operational details at the party caucus, the county convention, congressional districts, and the state conventions would be left to individual state laws and national political party rules. The structure, organization, and scheduling of the Democratic and Republican national conventions would be the same as they are now, with the exception that both conventions would be held in July instead of one convention in July and the other in August.

The major task, as always, of the national convention would be to nominate candidates for the national party primary the following September. There would be two ballots. On the first ballot bound delegates would vote for their declared choice, and unbound delegates could vote for any candidate. After the first ballot, all candidates except for the top three finishers would be eliminated. The top three candidates would then run off against each other on the second ballot, at which time *all* delegates would be unbound and could vote their individual preference.

The authors are of two minds as to what should happen at this point. One of us believes that only the top two remaining candidates (so long as each receives a minimum of thirty percent from the convention) should be placed on the national primary ballot.

The other believes the threshold endorsement should be lowered to twenty-five percent with the possibility that three candidates be allowed on the national primary ballot. If three candidates are placed on the primary ballot, a procedure called "approval voting" would come into effect. Under approval voting, voters can vote for as many candidates as they like. Thus if Reagan, Bush and Baker were on the national Republican primary ballot in September 1984, a moderate Republican might vote for both Baker and Bush, while a conservative Republican might decide to vote for Reagan, or to vote for both Bush and Reagan. Approval voting is, in part, an insurance plan preventing an unrepresentative or least preferred candidate from winning in a three person race. Two centrists can sometimes split the centrist vote between them only to find they both lose to a candidate decidely on the right who wins thirty-five percent of the vote to their combined sixty-five percent (as happened in somewhat similar circumstances when James Buckley won in a New York Senate race in the early 1970s, or as George "Your Home Is Your Castle" Mahoney did in a Maryland Democratic primary for governor back in the mid-1960s).

Regardless of which formula is used to get two or three candidates on the party's national primary, only those candidates among the top three who received twenty-five percent of the vote or more on the second ballot would appear on the September primary ballot.

On the first ballot, a number of delegates will have voted for candidates who did not finish in the top three. On the second ballot, these delegates will have the opportunity to vote their preference for the party nominee front-runners. The system thus allows delegates to vote their first choices, no matter how weak, on the first ballot, but it also allows all the delegates to participate in the final ranking of the strongest party candidates on the second ballot.

In certain presidential years, a candidate may be so strong at the convention that he will not have to face a national primary election. This will occur when, on the second ballot, one candidate is so strong that neither the second-place candidate or the third-place candidate has twenty-five percent of the convention vote (or under our other alternative, when the second of two top finishers has less than thirty percent). Some states which use the pre-primary convention plan also declare that a candidate who receives seventy percent of the state convention automatically receives the party's nomination, and thus a primary is not needed. This same stipulation would also sensibly apply at the national level. It would be expected, for instance, that a popular incumbent president with strong support within his own party could avoid the strain of a September primary.

The final duty of the national party convention would be to create a pool of acceptable vice-presidential prospects from which the eventual presidential nominee could make a final choice following the national primary in September. All of the candidates who qualify for the second ballot at the convention would automatically be in this vice-presidential pool (although one of them would eventually be removed by winning the party's presidential nomination). The convention could add up to three more vice-presidential candidates to the pool. Immediately following the party presidential primary election in September, the winning candidate would select his vice-presidential nominee from the candidates in the pool. The presidential nominee thus would make the final selection of his vice-presidential running mate, but all the vice-presidential eligibles in the pool would have received "party approval" at the national convention.

The National Democratic Presidential Primary and the National Republican Presidential Primary would both be held on the same day, the second Tuesday after the first Monday in September. This date is suggested because all voters will have returned from August vacations and will have had one week to recover from Labor Day, the three-day holiday annually scheduled for the first Monday in September.

Any voter who was registered in a particular party by July 1 of the presidential year would be eligible to vote in that particular party's national presidential primary election. The date of July 1 is suggested because it is late enough that those citizens who have had their partisan interest stimulated by the local precinct caucuses, the May county conventions, and the June state conventions, still will be able to register in a particular political party. The first of July is early enough to prevent partisan voters from switching from one party to the other after they see which candidates are going to be nominated or which parties are going to have national primaries. The goal here is to prevent partisan voters whose party is not having a presidential primary in a particular year from switching their registration in order to vote for the weakest opposition candidate.

If there are, or should be in the future, any states that do not provide under state law for voter registration in the two major political parties, the United States Congress should pass any necessary national laws to guarantee that all United States citizens have the right to register in a particular political party and vote in the September presidential primary.

The one candidate who gets the most votes in the September primary will be the party candidate in the November general election. A plurality of votes rather than a majority will be sufficient to declare the winner. In case of an exact tie vote, or in case of a close race where large numbers of ballots were contested, or if the winning candidate dies or becomes functionally disabled, the party national committee shall decide the official party candidate for the November election. National law passed by Congress would provide for the details of these procedures.

As noted above, the first official event following the national primary would be the selection of the vice-presidential candidate by the presidential nominee. Notice that the presidential candidate will have considerable latitude in selecting his party running mate. If it appears propitious to select one of his defeated opponents and thereby mend party fences, he is free to do so. If he wishes not to choose a defeated opponent, however, he has three candidates available (one or two of whom he might have pushed for the post) who have been officially approved by the convention.

SOME ADVANTAGES OF THE PREPRIMARY CONVENTION PLAN

The National Preprimary Convention Plan is designed to eliminate the more criticized characteristics of the present presidential nominating system and also to provide some positive additions not found in the present system:

1. This plan would eliminate the present series of thirty-six individual state primary elections which are so exhausting to the candidates, and, eventually, boring to both the news reporters and the average voter. These thirty-six state primaries would be replaced by a single national primary election campaign that would last only six to eight weeks— from the end of the party national convention in July until the early September presidential primary election.
2. The present series of thirty-six individual state primary elections is sometimes unrepresentative of true voter sentiment because turnouts for presidential primaries are relatively low, averaging around thirty percent of registered party voters. The tremendous national interest that would be created by a single national party primary election, held in every state on the same day of the year, would increase voter interest and, accordingly, voter turnout. Turnouts for national presidential primaries often might exceed fifty percent of registered party voters.
3. The present system of thirty-six individual state primaries creates a situation in which candidates who win early primary election in small and often "unrepresentative" states enjoy a tremendous media advantage in succeeding primary elections. Instead of being noticed because of their personal characteristics or their issue positions, candidates are evaluated mainly on the basis of how they did in previous primaries and how they are likely to do in future primaries. Political "momentum," not character and issues, becomes the main focus of the present pre-convention campaign. The National Preprimary Convention Plan would eliminate this problem of early primaries in small states being so important relative to later primaries in large states.

4. The present thirty-six state primary system creates artificial regional advantages for those candidates who are lucky enough to have strong support in states that just happen to have early primary elections. The current process which begins in New England and gradually moves south and then elsewhere also minimizes the importance of certain regions such as the Rocky Mountain west and as a result minimizes the need for presidential candidates to respond to the problems of certain regions. The National Preprimary Convention Plan would eliminate these regional advantages by having all Americans in all regions of the country vote in a single national primary on a single day.

5. The present primary election system has reduced the national party conventions to the status of "ratifying conventions" rather than deliberative "nominating conventions." The National Preprimary Convention Plan would revitalize the national convention and give the delegates to the convention real work to do. On the first ballot, the convention delegates will make the first cut in narrowing the field of party presidential hopefuls. On the second ballot, they will determine who will get into the national presidential primary and the order in which the candidates' names will appear on the ballot. As the field of potential winners progressively narrows, from the first ballot to the second ballot, delegates who were bound to first ballot losers will be able to switch their votes away from early losers and to make choices among the finalists. There will also be the issue of the order in which the final nominees are going to finish and the responsible task of creating a qualified and politically-appealing pool of vice-presidential candidates. The dull and boring party national conventions that currently exist will once again become true nominating conventions at which delegates are significant and are lobbied by the various candidates, and have important and challenging decisions to make.

6. The current presidential primary system de-emphasizes the importance of political party membership and the influence of party caucuses and party conventions. Would-be presidential nominees bypass the official party structure by filing directly in preferential primaries and going straight to the voter with techniques such as direct mail, telephone canvassing, and radio and television advertising. In many cases, candidates use hastily-assembled organizations of outside volunteers to defeat the established party hierarchy in the presidential primary.

The National Preprimary Convention Plan would help to restore the importance of the official political party structure while at the same time strengthening the average voter's role in the final decision. In the first stage of the nominating process, candidates would have to make their main appeal to the party activists who are most likely to attend party caucuses and get elected to county conventions and state conventions. People who had not previously considered participating in local party activities might begin doing so in order to be able to advance their preferred presidential candidates. Also increasing the importance of party caucuses and county and state conventions would be the fact that these events would be scheduled on the same day throughout the entire nation.

The broader party electorate would not be side-stepped completely, however. After the party activists have made the first cut at the state level and the national convention has further refined the field, the national party membership will make the final decision in the national presidential primary election.

7. Another problem with holding thirty-six presidential primaries at differing times in thirty-six different states is the fact that the main focus tends to be on local issues in the individual states rather than on national issues of concern to the American people as a whole. This local and state emphasis would continue to exist under the National Preprimary Convention Plan, but only prior to the national convention. After the national convention had limited the field to two or three finalists, these top finishers would have to campaign nationally before the national party electorate in order to win the national presidential primary. National issues would thus often take precedence over local state issues from the time of the convention to national presidential primary day.

8. The current presidential primary system is often criticized for having made contemporary presidents very independent of their own political party organizations. Since the incumbent president's renomination is mainly dependent on support in popular primaries rather than support from party regulars, so the argument goes, the president no longer cares much whether his own party professionals are behind him or not.

    The National Preprimary Convention Plan would increase the incumbent president's responsibility to his own political party without reducing the influence of the average party primary election voter. Every incumbent president will want to win "top-line" designation for the primary by finishing first in the second ballot at the national convention. In order to do this, the president will want to cultivate the support of the party activists. Most presidents will thus become more responsible to their own parties.

9. The current thirty-six primary system has been characterized as being unduly influenced by television. Candidates aim their main appeals, so the argument goes, not directly at the voters but at the television cameras through which the vast majority of political information is now filtered to the voters.

Rather than denying the rise of television-politics, the National Preprimary Convention Plan accepts this reality and endeavors to enhance the television-voter relationship. One of the reasons for holding all the party caucuses in the nation on the same day is to make the party caucuses a "super" event that will be thoroughly covered by the news media and thus impart a maximum of political information to the voters. The same thinking applies to the scheduling of a single day for county conventions and a single day for state conventions. The hope is that the tremendous increase in television and other media coverage of the presidential nominating process will result in significantly increased amounts of citizen participation in the nominating process, particularly in terms of increased voter turnouts for the national presidential primaries.

POSSIBLE OBJECTIONS

No plan is perfect and there are some possible defects to the national preprimary convention system. Here are some likely concerns and our discussions of them:

1. The present system has one arguably positive feature that would be less present under the national preprimary convention system. The present series of state primaries that begins with a few smaller states gives lesser known but qualified challengers a chance to make themselves known, and pick up steam (and money) as they move on to some of the larger states. Having all the local caucuses and state conventions taking place at the same time will make it more difficult for less known and less well-financed candidates.

   We acknowledge that lesser known candidates will have a somewhat more difficult time under our plan. On the other hand, the cost of entering caucus states is significantly, perhaps five times, less than entering primary states as a serious candidate. Second, a candidate need only do well in a handful of states to prove his or her abilities and capture at least some national attention. Since the nomination will not usually be decided on the first ballot, a number of worthy candidates will be able to survive and thus obtain peer review and political scrutiny before the convention makes its final determination.

2. Some will contend that the national preprimary convention system is too national, too rigid and too mechanistic. They might add that it diminishes federalism, at least to the extent it tells states when and how they will select delegates.

   Our response is that the presidency is a national office. Further, it is clear that the national parties have both the responsibility and the authority to decide on the procedure for the nomination of the President. Finally, this new plan will strengthen the party at the state level and it treats all states as equals. No advantage will be given to those living in a particular state just because their state has an early primary or caucus.

---

3. Critics are likely to say that the national primary feature of this new plan will encourage television and media events of the worst possible kind.

Our response is that our plan will actually diminish much of the negative influence of television in the first and crucial phase of the nominating process—the preconvention state. It will require presidential candidates to meet with party and elected local leaders and to build coalitions at the grass roots level—not just appear on television spot ads. After the convention, the endorsed candidates will have to rely heavily on television. They will have to appear in debates, or on talk shows, or in addresses to the nation. This is as it should be, for presidents can no longer govern unless they are effective users of electronic media. Thus our plan requires party renewal and party coalition-building skills as well as effective media campaigning.

4. Some critics may fear this will diminish the role of minorities and lessen the affirmative action gains of the past decade—especially gains made in the Democratic party.

We do not think there is evidence that this will be the case. Existing affirmative action rules may just as easily apply. Indeed, the increased turnout at the national primaries should enhance minority participation. And surely this will allow for substantially more minority input than is gained by leaving this crucial decision to the people in a few small unrepresentative states such as New Hampshire.

5. What about its impact on third or minor parties?

Third parties would still have their national conventions. But they would seldom have a need for a national primary. Perhaps some rule could be worked out so that any national party receiving at least five percent in the last presidential election could participate in the national primary arrangements—if they wished to do so.

6. Wouldn't the national primary be an even greater expense to the states?

Perhaps. But nowadays we are already conducting thirty-six primaries and these include most of our bigger states. Conducting the national primary in fifty states in the fall as opposed to thirty-six in the spring is not really much of a difference.

Doubtless there will be additional objections. Our purpose here is not to solve all the technical problems or anticipate all the political side effects. We want to present an alternative that has thus far been overlooked.

Here is a plan, we think, that shortens the formal election season and simplifies it so the average voter can understand its operations. More than the present system, it will test the political coalition-building skill of serious candidates, those skills so needed to win the general election and to govern.

More than the present system, it allows for sensible participation from all segments of the party. More than the existing system, it would promote responsible parties that at the same time are subject to popular control. More than the existing system, it would facilitate and encourage the best possible candidates, including busy office-holders, to run for the presidency. And more than the existing system, it would facilitate and encourage thoughtful participatory caucuses and conventions at all levels of our system, and it would go a long way toward rescuing the all but doomed national conventions and help make them more of an occasion for reflective societal leadership.

Should the Rank and File or the Power Brokers of Political Parties Choose Presidential Nominees?

A SEASONED POLITICAL SCIENTIST VIEWS SKEPTICALLY THE USE OF PRIMARIES TO NOMINATE PRESIDENTIAL CANDIDATES

In the following selection, Austin Ranney, American Enterprise Institute political scientist, examines how far popular participation should go in presidential nominating politics. He questions whether grass-roots democracy at the nominating stage can produce good candidates, educate people on the issues, or prepare contenders to become president. He suggests that a return to the brokered nominating politics of the past might best serve the nation by strengthening party responsibility and producing candidates who have honed their political skills far beyond those required simply to win popularity contests.

A. RANNEY

16

Candidates, Coalitions, Institutions and Reforms

AUSTIN RANNEY

... [P]olitical scientists usually describe the form of government of the United States as a presidential democracy. By that they mean a system in which the head of government is a president directly elected by the people and not a prime minister indirectly selected by a parliament. But most political scientists would also go beyond this. They would say that the presidency is the key element in our whole system of government, and that the system works well only when the presidency is working well. Many would also say that the presidency has not been working very well for at least twenty years now, not since Dwight Eisenhower, the last President to serve two full terms of office and the last President to be generally regarded as successful. John Kennedy was assassinated before he could do very much, either good or bad. Lyndon Johnson was driven from office for his identification with an unpopular war. Richard Nixon resigned to avoid almost certain impeachment. Gerald Ford became the first incumbent since Herbert Hoover to be defeated for reelection, and Jimmy Carter became the second. And as I speak tonight the polls show that Ronald Reagan has even less popular approval for his handling of the presidency than any of his predecessors have had at comparable stages in their first two years.

Now, this discouraging record has led many people to ask why our presidents, on whom we depend for so much, seem to do so badly, regardless of whether they are Republicans or Democrats, conservatives or liberals. It is surely one of the most critical questions we face as we approach the

The Presidential Nominating Process: Volume I, *Kenneth W. Thompson (Ed.), "Candidates, Coalitions, Institutions, and Reforms," Austin Ranney, pp. 68–80. Copyright 1983 by University Press of America, Inc. Reprinted by permission.*

200th anniversary of our constitution. It is being investigated by many of our most skilled and dedicated analysts, some of the most distinguished of whom, as I have already said, are hard at work right here at the Miller Center at the University of Virginia. And it is of course a question with a multitude of aspects, far too many even to be listed in these brief remarks. I therefore propose to focus on just one aspect, namely, the presidential nominating process. I do so without apology, however, for I believe that the kind of people we select to be our presidents has a great deal to do with how well or badly the office works. Not everything, of course, but a great deal. And I also believe that the nominating process by which we choose our major parties' nominees is more important in deciding who will occupy the office in November than deciding whether it will be the Democrat or the Republican. To be concrete, it seems to me that in 1980 the process by which the Republicans settled on Ronald Reagan rather than John Anderson, Howard Baker, George Bush, John Connally, Philip Crane, Robert Dole, or Gerald Ford—plus the process by which the Democrats chose Jimmy Carter rather than Ted Kennedy—eliminated more possibilities and made more important choices than the process by which the voters in November chose Reagan over Carter and Anderson. That is why I shall focus tonight on the presidential nominating process. I propose to ask four questions about it. First, is the process well designed to produce good candidates? Secondly, does the process give those candidates the kind of experience and connections that will help them be effective presidents? Third, does it help to strengthen those other institutions that our nation needs to be governed effectively? And finally, what are the prospects for improving the process?

. . . [A] great many people have offered answers to those questions in newspaper columns, television commentaries, political magazines and so on. I think I have read and heard most of what they have said and I find that you can divide the commentators in this question into two big groups. One group seems to have as its motto the old saying, "Virtue is its own reward." Typically these people are quite satisfied with the process. They point out quite correctly that in 1980 about 32 million people participated in selecting the nominees, whereas in every other country in the world only a small handful of party leaders have anything to say about who is going to head the parties. So, these people say, our system is the most democratic in the world, the most open, the best; so it is just fine, leave it alone. To quote a great assistant of another great President, "If it ain't broke, don't mend it."

The other group of commentators on the presidential nominating system seems to have as its motto another old saying, namely, "By their fruits ye shall know them." These people tend to ask not so much is the system intrinsically fair or participatory or open or democratic; they ask instead, does it produce good results? Does it produce good candidates? Does it give the people good education on the issues? Does it give good preparation for those candidates to become Presidents?

It should be evident from the way I have described both of these groups that I identify myself with the second, and so all of the questions that I intend to deal with tonight are concerned with the results of the process rather than with its intrinsic fairness or the degree of participation in it or whether it makes good entertainment or anything else.

So I turn then to the first question. Is the process well-designed to produce good candidates? Most people, I suppose, have probably answered this question in terms of whether they are enthusiastic about Carter or Reagan or both. And it might be very difficult to find a large number of people that we could analyze, as social scientists like to do, because there is a good deal of evidence that there was a higher level of dissatisfaction with the two major party candidates in 1980 than there has ever been in any previous presidential election since modern public opinion polling first started. The best evidence of this is provided by the Center for Political Studies at the University of Michigan, which has been conducting studies of the presidential electing process going back to 1952. In each of its surveys it has been asking its respondents to rank the presidential candidates on a scale from zero (awful) to one hundred (absolutely perfect). And in 1976 the average ratings given by the voters to the two candidates were by far the lowest they had ever been. They averaged in the low 20s for the two candidates as compared with, for example, in the 50s and 60s when Eisenhower was running against Stevenson. There is other evidence as well. A number of the states in the 1980 primary elections had on their ballots a "none of the above" line where you could vote for Carter or Kennedy or for "none of the above." And there were actually two states in which "none of the above" finished second—the first time in history in which that has happened.

I recognize that many people when they hear evidence of this sort, will say, well yes, but after all under the earlier system there were a lot of pretty poor candidates, too. After all, look at Harding and Coolidge and . . . Grant. They certainly were poor nominees and poor presidents, so there is merit to that argument. I would add that there is no system that is guaranteed always to produce good candidates nor is there any system that is always guaranteed to produce bad candidates. In moments of nostalgic longing when I am asked what system do you really favor, Mr. Ranney?, I sometimes say that I favor the congressional caucus system, which produced such candidates as Thomas Jefferson and James Madison and James Monroe, and then we got rid of it because it wasn't democratic and participatory enough. Then they say seriously now, what kind of system, do you favor? I think the answer to that has to be that it is beyond the human mind to produce a system guaranteed always to produce great candidates and, equally, there is no way of producing the system that is guaranteed always to produce bad candidates. It seems to me the question is properly asked, rather, are there particular systems that tend to favor certain kinds of candidates rather than other kinds of candidates?, and I would say that the real test of any system is the kind of candidates it produces *most* of the time.

In trying to answer that question it seems to me that we have to recognize that certain aspects of our current presidential nominating system advantage certain kinds of candidates and disadvantage others. One . . . is the absence of what might be called "peer review." That is to say, the present nominating system provides no regularized process by which the government and party leaders, who know the potential aspirants to the presidency on the basis of having dealt with them in legislatures or in executive positions, have any special say about who is good presidential timber and who is not. The fact is that presidential nominations are made by ordinary voters voting in the primaries. It is also the fact that most of the knowledge that most voters have about the presidential nominees is knowledge they have gained exclusively from the mass media, especially television, and not from any kind of face to face contact.

If I may indulge in a slight aside, I think that that has real consequences about the kind of candidate we have. I am a citizen of Maryland but because the Washington television market is what it is, I followed the recent Virginia gubernatorial campaign as closely as most citizens of Virginia did, at least as far as TV advertising is concerned. And my main difficulty was that I had difficulty remembering as each ad came on which candidate was which, which one was Robb and which one was Coleman, because they seemed to me to be almost indistinguishable. Both were good looking young men, well dressed, rather cool, or, as they say in California, "laid back," and difficult to distinguish from each other. It occurred to me that perhaps we have here the answer to one of the greatest mysteries of presidential politics in 1980—the mystery of what happened to John Connally. Connally, as you know, refused to accept any federal money for his campaign so that he could spend any amount of money that he could raise and he is said to have spent over eleven million dollars in return for which he got one delegate. If I may paraphrase the late Sir Winston Churchill, never in the history of human politics has so much money been spent by a candidate for so few delegates. Yet when John Connally was speaking to live audiences in auditoriums he was a great stump orator—one of the best in present day politics. He regularly got cheering, stomping, whistling ovations from live audiences. He entered a number of primaries, spending most of his money, as candidates do these days, on television campaigns, and he was a terrible failure. Why? I am not a total believer in all of the works of Marshall McLuhan, but I do believe in his famous insight that the television is a "cool" medium, whereas others—for example, stump speaking—are "hot" media. And the kind of politician who comes across well through the flickering light of the tube in people's living rooms is a very different kind of politician than one who comes across well through the hot medium of speaking to two or three thousand people in an auditorium. In my opinion, that is the main thing that happened to John Connally: he is a hot personality, he campaigned largely on the cool medium of television, and as a result he failed miserably.

Much the same case could be made about Ted Kennedy, and my suspicion is that one impact of television on the future of politics is that there are going to be more and more Robbs and Colemans doing well, and fewer and fewer Connallys and Lyndon Johnsons and Hubert Humphreys and Ted Kennedys. That may be wrong but it is at least an interesting hypothesis well worth looking at.

In any event it seems to me that it is quite clear that we do not have any peer review and that most of the screening of candidates that goes on, goes on through the electronic media, and that most of the people who select the candidates, the people who vote in the primaries, select on the basis of what they have seen on the tube.

The second characteristic is a characteristic which is being very vividly illustrated now. A number of political scientists were shocked by the fact that Jimmy Carter started all-out campaigning for the 1976 Democratic nomination almost two years before the Democratic convention met. Unprecedented to start that early, they said. It may have been unprecedented then, but in the strictest legal sense of the term, Walter Mondale and Ted Kennedy began campaigning for the 1984 Democratic nomination within a matter of a few weeks after November 1980. Carter's concession speech had hardly ceased tinkling in the ears of the national audience when Mondale and Kennedy started beating the bushes. In fact, the Mondale organization has been registered with the Federal Election Commission (and campaigning and raising money) ever since February of 1981. So in effect, presidential campaigns nowadays never cease.

Why? I think the answer lies in what many commentators call the "front-loading" of the primaries; that is, the fact that what happens in Iowa and New Hampshire at the beginning of the campaign is twenty times more important than what happens in the much bigger states of California and Ohio and New Jersey at the end of the campaign. Hence it is critical for a candidate to do well in the early primaries and caucuses, because if he does well there the media will announce to the world that he is the front runner, the candidate to beat. Given that kind of momentum and given the proportional allocation of delegates in the later primaries the candiate can ride that early momentum to victory as indeed has been the case with all of the winners in recent years.

Now, the kind of politics that enables one to do well in Iowa and New Hampshire is what political scientists call "retail politics." That is, the candidate does not so much appear on the tube and give great speeches to large audiences. Rather, he emphasizes meeting with small groups in coffee clatches and school rooms where there may be no more than twenty or thirty people present and the object is personally to shake the hand of every individual voter. And Mr. Mondale is already very well launched on such a campaign.

Does that favor certain kinds of politicians over others? I think it does, at least in one regard. After he withdrew from the 1980 contest for the Republican nomination, Howard Baker, one of the most effective leaders of either party in Washington, said rather ruefully that he guessed you had to be an unemployed politician to make a serious bid for the presidency. One indeed wonders if it is a coincidence that Mr. Carter and Mr. Reagan were able to campaign fulltime as ex-governors holding no other position when their leading opponents were either incumbent presidents or incumbent senators who had to stay at home in Washington, at least a certain amount of time, and tend to their governmental knitting. It seems to me that in the current contest Mr. Mondale has a considerable advantage, assuming that he has overcome his historic aversion to Holiday Inns. He is able to campaign fulltime, something that his other leading opponents, such as Senator Hart and Senator Glenn, are not able to do. Such a system does not guarantee that outsider candidates are always going to win, but it seems to me undeniable that the system, as it now works, tilts in favor of the outsider.

Although there is no way of proving it, I think that Ronald Reagan might well have been nominated under the old system as well as under the new system because, after all, he was a well-known figure in the Republican party and had run for the presidency on two previous occasions, almost winning the presidential nomination in 1976. But it is inconceivable that Jimmy Carter could have been nominated under the old system where only people who were well-known to a large number of the national leaders of their party could hope to win its nomination. Some people will regard the fact that the present nominating system makes it possible for a Jimmy Carter to be nominated as a strong argument in its favor, while others may regard it as a strong argument against the system. I am not going to make either of those arguments. I am simply going to say that, given the frontloading of the primaries, the ability of the outsider to come in and, by early victories, build up a kind of a momentum which, with a boost from the media, will ultimately carry him to the nomination, is possible under the new system in a way in which it was not under the old system. So, deciding whether the system produces better candidates or worse candidates depends on how you feel about Reagan and Carter. But if one asks, does the system make it easier for outsider candidates by giving them advantages that they did not used to have, the answer, it seems to me, is yes.

We turn now to the second question: does the process give the candidates the connections and experiences they need to govern effectively? I have a little story to tell that illustrates my views on that question. It took place in 1977 after the Democratic party's Winograd reform commission had met. The newly-elected President Carter called in the commission for a reception in the White House to thank its members for their labors, and he made a little speech. The basic point of the speech was that the thing of which he was most proud was that he owed his nomination to no organized interest group, but only to the people: the people had given him the nomination in the primaries, the people had elected him over Ford and he felt indebted to nobody other than the people. I remember thinking at the time, well, Mr. President, I hope that when things begin to get difficult for you you will find that 'the people' out there will give you support you need because you will find that the organized groups, the congressmen and the pressure groups and the labor unions, are not going to feel any more indebted to you than you feel to them. This is not the occasion for me to discuss what went well and what went badly in the Carter administration, but it would be fair to say that he got precious little help from those groups, and that made effective governing a lot more difficult for him.

The point is that in the old days before the "reforms" of the 1970s, presidential nominations were won primarily by presidential aspirants and their representatives talking to the powerful governors, mayors, senators, state chairmen and the like. The aspirants got know those influential people well in that process, and later on, when they became presidents, they had already developed substantial networks of relationships that they were able to use to build up the support they needed to get their programs adopted. Under the present nominating system that is no longer the case. An aspirant does not win the nomination by lining up endorsements of the parties' leaders. Senator Edmund Muskie went that route in 1972, he got the endorsements of almost all of the party's leading members, and it turned out to be worth absolutely nothing when he did not do as well in the New Hampshire primary as the media expected him to do. And George McGovern, who had a few major leaders' endorsements swept to the nomination. Jimmy Carter won the 1976 nomination in the same way, and that was substantially the case with Ronald Reagan in 1980. So, endorsements by party leaders are not only useless, in fact there is a rather substantial advantage, if the truth were known, for running *against* the "party establishment," for making it clear that you are an outsider, a new broom, and have not had any part in that mess in Washington.

In short, we have succeeded in separating the process of building the coalition needed to win a nomination from the process of building the coalition needed to govern. Nominating politics and governing politics are two quite different operations in a way that they never have been in the past. And it just may be that the kind of politician and organization that is best for nominating politics may not be so good for governing politics. History may reverse the judgment, but it is quite common for people now to regard Jimmy Carter as not a very successful president, as politically inept, as ineffective at handling his relations with Congress. What we tend to forget is that, from at least one point of view, Jimmy Carter is one of the greatest politicians in American history. I would argue that Jimmy Carter's feat of winning the Democratic nomination in 1976 as an almost total unknown and outsider is one of the great political feats of history. Then in 1980, even though the early polls showed him running 25 and 30, he won the nomination again—with, to be sure, a little help from the Ayatollah Khomeini. So he was magnificent at nominating politics, and the fact that he could be one of the great nominating politicians in history and one of the least effective governing politicians in history strikes me as a vivid illustration of how much we have separated nominating politics from governing politics. This does not mean that no one who ever wins a presidential nomination is ever again going to be an effective president. It does mean that if that does happen it will be because we are lucky, not because there is anything in the nominating process that produced the kind of people likely to be good at governing.

That leads to my third question: has the presidential selection process strengthened the *institutions* we need to govern effectively? It is well to begin answering this question by remembering that our constitutional system was deliberately and brilliantly designed by the fifty-five men who wrote it *not* to produce effective government capable of taking swift and purposive action. It was designed to make it dificult for government to act at all if it has to against the strong objections of any significant part of the community. Thus, separation of powers; thus, federalism, thus checks and balances and all those other institutions that were designed not to make it easier for government to get good things done but make it difficult for government to do bad things. Yet, every government on occasion needs some way of focusing its powers so that it can develop and implement effective policies, particularly in emergencies like great depressions or wars. Over the years American government has developed a series of institutions, political parties for one, a strong presidency for another, a powerful bureaucracy for another, as ways under certain conditions of bypassing the built-in centrifugal tendencies, of our governmental system.

How has the new nominating process affected those institutions? Very clearly it has played an important role in weakening our political parties. In fact, I would say that as far as presidential politics is concerned we now have in this country effectively a no-party system. Do not misunderstand me—into the indefinite future a person will have to be labeled either Republican or Democrat to have a serious shot at the Presidency. But the point is that those labels are going to be won by the individual entrepreneurial candidate organizations who win the primaries. The labels certainly are not going be awarded by groups of party bosses meeting in smoke-filled rooms deciding to whom they will give the honors. Certainly no set of bosses is now meeting or will ever meet to decide that the 1984

Democratic nominee is going to be so-and-so, or, for that matter, the Republican nominee is going to be so-and-so. Political parties used to play important roles in raising money for presidential campaigns. Now they play very minor roles. Political parties and their national chairmen used to be the main organizers of presidential campaigns. Now the campaigns are run by the candidate organizations, and the parties have little voice in strategy or tactics.

As a result, the national political parties have just about disappeared, except as labels, from presidential politics. With regard to the power of the presidency, as a result of the Vietnam war and as a result of the Watergate scandals, the formal powerful bureaucracy. Efforts were made by President Carter to reduce the power of the bureaucracy. Efforts by President Reagan are being made along the same lines and efforts by the next President and the President after him and the President after him will undoubtedly also be made and no doubt that power may even be eroded a bit. But of all of the classical institutions for making up for the weakness of our fundamental political agencies of government, the bureaucracy is the one least changed in recent years.

These, I believe, are some of the consequences of the new presidential nominating process. Some would say that the new process is still an improvement on the old one: it is more open and more democratic and more participatory, and these virtues are their own reward. Others, including me, say that the new process is worse because it is less likely to produce candidates who have the kind of experience and know-how that will make them effective Presidents. It is less likely to give them the kind of experience and the connections that they need in order to be effective Presidents and it has a strong tendency to weaken those institutions of government that any President needs to govern effectively.

My final question is: what are the prospects for improving the process? In recent years, especially since 1980, a number of commentators and organizations have studied the process and have sought ways of improving it. The most notable so far have included the commission headed by former Governor Terry Sanford of North Carolina, the Miller Center Commission co-chaired by Melvin Laird and Adlai Stevenson III, the Democratic party's fourth reform commission chaired by North Carolina's governor James Hunt, and a commission headed by Chancellor Alexander Heard of Vanderbilt University which is going to spend several years studying the problem before it makes its report. The recommendations that have been made by the commentators and the commissions are remarkably similar in their diagnosis of what is wrong with the current presidential nominating process and in their suggestions about what might be done about it. For example, all three commission reports argue strongly that the absence of any element of peer review is a great deficiency in the presidential nominating process and they recommend a variety of measures for restoring some element of it, of which the most notable, made by all three commissions, is that ex-officio, uncommitted official delegate voting slots be given to the parties' elected officials, to the parties' governors, senators, representatives, perhaps mayors, perhaps state party chairs,—in short, to a large number of the people who under the present rules are denied any kind of ex-officio seats.

They also all agree that the delegates ought to be given a chance to make up their own minds. They all strenuously object to Rule 43c that was adopted by the Democrats in their convention in 1980, which required every delegate to vote for the candidate on whose slate he was elected in the primary to support, and provided that if the candidate had any reason to believe that the delegate would not faithfully honor his pledge that candidate had the right to remove that delegate. All three commissions voted for the rescinding of any such rule on the ground that, given the long time between the first and last primaries, the candidate who looked marvelous in the snows of Iowa and New Hampshire in the late winter may look very different in terms of desirability in the heat of New York or Kansas City or Chicago or Philadelphia when it comes time actually to cast their votes in the conventions.

A third conclusion on which all agree is that the financial restrictions that presently place such a premium upon a candidate's ability to raise money in small contributions—which only candidates who have a very strong ideological following on either the far left or the far right can hope to have—encourage extremists and disadvantage moderates. So all recommend raising the ceilings on campaign contributions by individuals.

The University of Virginia Miller Center Commission report is the only one that so far has directly tackled one of the most difficult of all of the problems: the proliferation of the presidential primaries. It has recommended that the number of primaries be reduced to a maximum of sixteen and that those states that do choose to have primaries must hold them in regional primaries organized by time zones, and that furthermore, the order in which those primaries are held should be determined by lot rather than one particular time zone always coming first.

What are the prospects that all or some of these reforms will be adopted? Of course the Hunt Commission's reforms have already been adopted. What about the Sanford Commission's suggestion and the Miller Center Commission's suggestions? We can be hopeful, but I do not think we can be confident that, for example, of the present thirty-six states holding primaries enough are going to drop them that we are only going to have sixteen primaries in 1984. In fact, in mid-1982 more states are considering adding presidential primaries than dropping them. It seems to me that the next logical step down the road, one that I would not welcome but that I think is a real possibility, is the adoption of a one day national presidential primary and the complete abolition of the conventions—something that according to the most recent Gallup polls, is favored by seventy percent of the American people.

If adopted, will the reforms help? My feeling is that at the most they can only have a marginal effect. They may, particularly in the Democratic party, have a beneficial effect upon the platform writing process because they will involve in the platform-writing process some of the senators and congressmen and governors who have a real stake in seeing that the platform is something more than what Stuart Eizenstat called the 1980 Democratic platform: "the sum total of the maximum demands of every interest group represented at the convention."

But it seems most unlikely that if a particular candidate has "swept through the primaries" or has been declared by the media as "the clear winner of the primaries," no convention, however unbound by formal pledges and however many party leaders attend it, is going to deny that candidate the nomination. You can just imagine the howl that would go up from the media if that should happen. On those rare occasions where we have closely contested conventions of the Reagan-Ford type in 1976, the new rules might make a difference; but that kind closely-contested convention will not happen very often.

So I conclude that the new reforms will make, at the most, only marginal improvements in what I have been describing. And if that is the case, it seems to me appropriate to end these remarks with the famous phrase with which the Supreme Court opens each of its sessions: "God save the United States."

CHAPTER NINE
Congress

Ralph Nader called Congress the "broken branch"; Common Cause charges that special interests through their political action committees buy congressional votes; the FBI sets up sting operations to ensnare congressmen in bribery; David Brinkley tells his audiences that on Capitol Hill instant coffee takes 30 days to make; political scientists regret legislative inefficiency and the lack of collective responsibility; and congressmen themselves campaign against the institution in their bids for reelection. It is no wonder that the public holds Congress in low esteem, ranking its prestige somewhere near another maligned group—used car salesmen.

REELECTION OF INCUMBENTS

While the public, stirred up by the media, criticizes Congress as an institution, it steadily reelects incumbents at almost a 90 percent rate. Political scientist Richard Fenno has explained the "incumbency effect" by pointing out that legislators carefully cultivate constituents through effective homestyles while they often publicly disparage the institution in which they serve.* David Mayhew argues that Congress is set up to reelect its members, giving them the freedom and opportunity to advertise their names, claim credit with constituents for concrete benefits, and take whatever positions they find acceptable in their districts.† Congress, concludes Gary Jacobson, reflects "great individual *responsiveness*, equally great collective *irresponsibility*."‡

*Richard F. Fenno, Jr., "If, As Ralph Nader Says, Congress Is 'The Broken Branch,' How Come We Love Our Congressmen So Much?"—reprinted in Peter Woll, *American Government: Readings and Cases,* Eighth Edition (Boston: Little, Brown and Co., 1984), pp. 477–485. See also by the same author *Homestyle: House Members in Their Districts* (Boston: Little, Brown and Co., 1978).

†David R. Mayhew, *Congress: The Electoral Connection* (New Haven: Yale University Press, 1974).

‡Gary C. Jacobson, *The Politics of Congressional Elections* (Boston: Little, Brown and Co., 1983), p. 189.

EFFECTS OF POLITICAL PLURALISM

Congress mirrors the pluralistic politics that exists beyond Capitol Hill. Whatever is "wrong" with Congress is also a defect of the broader political system, not the result of scheming and incompetence by legislators. Attributes of Congress frequently criticized are weak parties, a fragmented committee structure, the abiding quest for personal power by members and staffers, and subordination of the national interests to constituent and special interests. Critics suggest it is amazing that Congress can accomplish anything at all, and when it does, it is more often than not serving the selfish interests of its members, constituents, and private groups rather than dealing with pressing national concerns.

SERVING MEMBER GOALS

There seem to be few defenders of congressional politics, perhaps because politics itself is often misunderstood. Richard Fenno said that reelection, internal power and influence, and good public policy are member incentives that largely determine how congressmen will behave. The incentives are not mutually exclusive, as members of Congress attach different degrees of importance to each one depending upon their positions and priorities. The decentralized organization of Congress facilitates reelection and the personal quest for internal power. Because congressmen do not have to toe a party line, they have maximum flexibility to take positions that will appeal to constituents. Moreover, the diffusive committee system enables them to exercise influence on behalf of constituents, channeling pork barrel projects to their districts. The many committee and subcommittee chairmanships available to members also give them important symbols of internal power.

Although political forces dictate congressional behavior, the debate over what is "wrong" with Congress continues. Recommendations for change are constantly made from both within and without Capitol Hill. The following selections illuminate the nature of the controversy.

Is Congress a Mess or a Responsible Institution?

A POLITICAL JOURNALIST FINDS CONGRESS TO BE INEFFICIENT,
INEFFECTIVE, AND IRRESPONSIBLE

Revealed in the following selection is much of the rhetoric, often used by members themselves, that is critical of Congress. Quoted are many legislators from both sides of Capitol Hill who willingly voice their criticisms, even though they draw many political benefits from the very system they deplore. Also examined are all facets of the institution in need of "reform."

G. EASTERBROOK

17

What's Wrong with Congress?

GREGG EASTERBROOK

Representative Michael Synar, of Oklahoma, swears that this actually happened: He was addressing a Cub Scout pack in Grove, Oklahoma, not far from his home town of Muskogee. Synar asked the young boys if they could tell him the difference between the Cub Scouts and the United States Congress. One boy raised his hand and said, "We have adult supervision."

Is anyone in charge on Capitol Hill? October's two-week-long melodrama over shutting down the government was not an isolated instance. Recently Congress voted for a $749 billion package of tax cuts, and only a few months later was locked in debate over a constitutional amendment for a balanced budget. The House voted in favor of Ronald Reagan's plan to almost double the number of nuclear warheads in the U.S. arsenal, and not long after voted in favor of the nuclear freeze. Only once in the past six years has Congress finished the budget appropriations before the beginning of the fiscal year; many spending bills have not been completed until months after the spending they supposedly control has begun. Long periods of legislative stalling are followed by spasms in which bills are passed with wild abandon, and these often contain "unprinted amendments" whose contents congressmen have never had an opportunity to read. Many provisions of "tax leasing" became law that way, as, in 1981, did the phone number of a woman named Rita. Rita's number had been scribbled in the margin of the only copy of an amendment being voted on, and the following day it was duly transcribed into the printed copy of the bill.

"The system is a mess, and what's amazing is how many members of Congress are fully aware that the system is a mess," says Alan Dixon, a senator from Illinois. Congress has, of course, seemed out of control at many

From The Atlantic, December 1984. Copyright ©1984 by Gregg Easterbrook. Reprinted by permission.

points in the past. During the late 1930s, as signs of war grew, Congress was synonymous with irresponsibility; during the McCarthy era, with cowardice. In 1959 it ground to a halt over the minor issue of Dwight Eisenhower's nomination of Lewis Strauss as secretary of Commerce and the even less important issue of an Air Force Reserve honorary promotion for the actor Jimmy Stewart. Through the 1960s it huffed and puffed about the Vietnam War, but never failed to approve funds for the fighting. In 1972, after hours of acrimonious debate, it voted to raise the federal debt ceiling for a single day. A degree of built-in vacillation was part of the Founding Fathers' plan for the legislature. But have recent changes in the structure both of U.S. politics and of Congress as an institution pushed Congress across the fine line separating creative friction from chaos?

"Congress today is a totally different institution from what it was when I arrived, in 1961," says Morris Udall, of Arizona, one of the House's senior members. "The magnitude of change is no illusion." The end of the seniority system; the arabesque budget "process" and other time-consuming new additions like the War Powers Act; the transformation from party loyalty to political-action-committee (PAC) loyalty; the increased emphasis on media campaigning; the vogue of running against Washington and yet being a member of the Washington establishment; the development of ideological anti-campaigns; a dramatic increase in congressional-subcommittee power and staff size, and a parallel increase in the scope and intensity of lobbying—all are creations of the past fifteen years. Some have served to make the nation's legislature more democratic and to improve its contact with the public. Others have made congressmen more frantic and timorous. But every change has in some respect caused Congress to become more difficult to run. Right now there isn't anyone in charge, and there may never be again.

EVERYWHERE A MR. CHAIRMAN

Hardly anyone laments the dismantling of the seniority rules—not even people like Udall, who would benefit if the old system still existed. From roughly the turn of the century until 1975 rank was based solely on how many years a member had been in Congress. The chairman of a committee could create or disband subcommittees, choose the subcommittee chairmen (often choosing himself), dictate when the subcommittees held hearings and whether bills were "referred" to them, hire the committee staff, and exert total control over when the committee itself would hold hearings or report bills to the floor. All these powers rested exclusively with twenty to twenty-five men in each chamber; others in Congress could wield power only by outvoting the senior members on the floor, and then only when the senior members permitted such votes to occur.

Seniority had long been considered unassailable, for the reason that senior members would use their powers to block any reform. But by the late 1960s the resistance of the southern committee chairmen to the obvious need for civil-rights reform had eroded seniority to the point at which challenges became possible. Every two years, as a new Congress was convened and new internal rules were passed, younger members would press for further concessions. "In 1971 we managed to pass a resolution saying that seniority would not be the sole criterion for chairmanship and that there ought to be a vote," Udall explains. "It was vaguely worded and we didn't try to take the issue any further. In 1973 for the first time, we held such votes. Every chairman was retained, but it established the precedent—that there had to be a vote. Then in 1975 we won."

It was a pivotal year for the structure of Congress. Ninety-two new representatives, mostly Democrats—the "Class of '74"—had been elected to the House in the wake of Watergate. Government institutions in general were in a state of low regard. Conservative southerners had been shamed by how long they had stood by Richard Nixon; and two powerful old-school committee chairmen, Wilbur Mills, of the Ways and Means Committee, and Wayne Hays, of the House Administration Committee, were going off the deep end. The Class of '74 provided the extra margin of votes needed to end seniority in the House. Three entrenched chairmen—Wright Patman, of the Banking Committee, F. Edward Hebert, of Armed Services, and W. R. Poage, of Agriculture—were overthrown. More significant in the long run, a "subcommittee bill of rights" was passed. Essentially, subcommittees won the right to hold hearings on any subject at any time. Committee members would be able to "bid" for subcommittee chairmanships; full committee chairmen could no longer control these slots or hold more than one subcommittee chairmanship themselves. Each subcommittee chairman would get funds for at least one staff aide who would work for him personally, not for the committee. The total number of subcommittees would be expanded. A similar though more genteel sequence of change took place in the Senate.

The autocracy of the chair broken, Congress was transformed from an institution in which power was closely held by a few to an institution in which almost everyone had just enough strength to toss a monkey wrench. In 1964 there were forty-seven meaningful chairmanships available in the House and Senate. Between the dispersion of subcommittee posts and the increase in the total number of committees and subcommittees, 326 Mr. Chairman positions were available in 1984. Allowing for those who hold more than one chairmanship, 202 of Congress's 535 members—38 percent—are now in charge of something.

More than any other factor, the deregulation of subcommittees has increased Congress's workload and decreased its cohesion. In 1970, before the change, congressional committees [collectively] held an average of twenty-three meetings a day. By 1982 the figure was thirty-seven meetings a day, and it remains at that level today. Senators now average twelve committee and subcommittee assignments each. With the trend toward "government in the sunshine" the number of closed committee hearings has dropped substantially—from 35 percent of all hearings in 1960 to seven percent in 1975. This serves the public's right to know but also increases the amount of time congressmen spend posturing for public consumption instead of saying what they think, which is practical only in closed hearings. The subcommittee bill of rights established "multiple referral," under which several subcommittees could consider the same bill or topic. The result is increased redundancy, more speechifying, and almost unlimited potential for turf fights.

According to John Tower, chairman of the Senate Armed Services Committee, "Our committee spends a large proportion of its time trying to fend off competition from other committees and monitoring what the other committees are doing." In the Senate the Armed Services, Appropriations, Governmental Affairs, Budget, Foreign Relations, and Veterans' Affairs committees all have an interest in military legislation; subcommittees of the same committee may also have overlapping jurisdictions, such as the Arms Control and European Affairs subcommittees of Foreign Relations. Multiple subcommittees each with multiple jurisdictions are a primary cause of the dizzy progression of non-events in Congress. Headlines like SENATE MOVES TO BAN IMPORTS and HOUSE HALTS FUNDS often refer to subcommittee actions that will be modified many times before they take effect or, more likely, vanish without a trace. Some sort of milestone was achieved last June when both the International Economic Policy Subcommittee of the Senate Foreign Relations Committee and the International Trade Subcommittee of the Senate Finance Committee held hearings covering the same topic—Japanese auto imports—on the same day, at the same time, with many of the same witnesses.

Driving the system is the unleashed desire of congressmen to be in command of something—anything. Culture shock for new congressmen arriving in Washington can be severe. Having just won a grueling electoral test and bearing the status of big wheels at home, in Washington they discover that they are among thousands of potentially important people competing for influence and attention. Young congressmen also find themselves assigned to cramped, dingy offices with Naugahyde furnishings and no majestic view of the Capitol dome. The yearning for a Washington badge of recognition and the additional perquisites that would make Capitol Hill life what they imagined it to be can set in almost immediately.

A chairmanship is particularly important because television is permitted in hearing rooms. Almost from the onset of television, congressmen have realized the promotional potential of the carefully scripted hearing: the

McCarthy and Kefauver hearings of the 1950s, which were among the first "television events," made their eponyms famous.

Fame may be an elusive goal, but publicity is not. The proliferation of networks and newscasts meshes perfectly with the proliferation of Capitol Hill hearings. Congress itself is difficult for television to cover, because no single person is in charge and few actions are final. A well-done hearing, in contrast, has a master of ceremonies, a story line, and an easily summarized conclusion when a witness commits a gaffe, announces a "policy shift," or clashes angrily with committee members. Hearings, unlike floor action, also allow congressmen to introduce props—the masked witness being a perennial favorite, piles of money or gimmicks like chattering teeth being reliable avenues to television coverage.

Once created, a subcommittee takes on a life of its own, if for no other reason than that the staff must justify its existence. In 1970 the House Committee on the District of Columbia had fifteen staff members; today it has thirty. The Senate Rules Committee had thirteen staff members in 1970 and today has twenty-seven. The House Appropriations committee has more than twice as many staff members as it had in 1970, and the Merchant Marine and Fisheries Committee's staff has risen from twenty-one to eighty-nine. Debra Knopman, a former staff aide to Senator Daniel Moynihan, says, "The staffs are so large everybody wants to have his say and leave his own little stamp. Pretty soon the weight of people wanting attention becomes greater than the force moving the legislation, and the whole thing grinds to a halt."

Staff allegiance is to the subcommittee chairman rather than to the overall purpose of the legislature, and bickering with members of other staffs becomes a primary means of self-advancement. While the top jobs in congressional offices pay well—$46,000 to $56,000 a year—the average pay is only $25,000; between the low salaries and hectic working conditions, turnover in congressional offices runs at a rate of 40 percent a year. A staff of bright, inexperienced people will work harder and produce more good ideas per salary dollar spent than older, trained staff, but it will also lack an institutional memory, demand more attention, and make more mischief, mostly in the form of turf fights.

The proliferation and redundancy of committees has produced a proliferation of redundant committees to study the problem. In the past decade the Senate has appointed three internal-reform study groups: the Stevenson Committee (named after the former Illinois senator Adlai Stevenson III), the Pearson-Ribicoff Group (run by retired senators James Pearson, of Kansas, and Abraham Ribicoff, of Connecticut), and a committee now meeting under the chairmanship of Senator Dan Quayle, of Indiana. Stevenson recommended a simplified system that would combine overlapping committees. Pearson and Ribicoff recommended that all subcommittees be abolished; that committees like the Small Business Committee and the Select Committee on Aging, which exist mainly to mollify interest groups, be subsumed into larger committees; and that the pairs of committees most frequently at each other's throats—the Armed Services and Foreign Relations committees, and the Budget and Appropriations committees—be merged.

None of the major Stevenson or Pearson-Ribicoff recommendations were enacted. The feudalistic system may prove in the long run more resilient that the seniority system, because now the number of congressmen with a stake in preventing change is much greater. Merging the Armed Services and Foreign Relations committees, for example, would eliminate one of the glamorous "A" committee chairmanships that are tickets to instant prominence, to say nothing of eliminating about ten subcommittee chairmanships. When Howard Baker, the retiring majority leader, appeared before the Quayle committee last July to present a summing up of his years of leading the Senate, only two senators were present to hear him. All the rest had schedule conflicts.

THE BUDGET THAT WOULDN'T DIE

The way Congress spends money was converted into a "process" with the passage, in 1974, of the Congressional Budget and Impoundment Control Act. Its immediate purpose was to prevent Richard Nixon from "impounding," or refusing to spend, money that Congress had appropriated. But the Budget Act also had a long-term goal: solving a structural defect in Congress's spending machine.

Before 1974 the House and Senate each had three kinds of committees involved with the budget: authorizing, appropriating, and revenue. The authorizing committees, like Agriculture, Transportation, Energy, and Interior, are the most familiar; they "authorize" federal activity by writing legislation in their subject areas. But though they can start or end programs, they cannot approve expenditures—only the two appropriating committees can do that. Since the amount spent on a program usually determines that program's effect on policy, the potential for overlapping and disputation is boundless. Neither authorizing nor appropriating committees, meanwhile, have the power to raise the money that backs up the checks—only the Finance Committee, in the Senate, and the Ways and Means Committee, in the House, do. Because of this separation it became all too easy for authorizing and appropriating committees to ignore the fiscal consequences of their actions—getting the money was somebody's else's job—and for the revenue committees, in turn, to demand that the other fellow crack down on spending.

During the 1950s and 1960s, when deficits were relatively stable, this state of affairs was tolerable. According to Robert Giaimo, who served in the House from 1958 to 1980 and was the Budget Committee chairman in the late 1970s, "No one, including myself, in Congress in the 1960s ever asked what anything would cost. All we thought about was, Does this sound like a good program? Can we get it through?"

The budget process was intended to bring together the questions of how much to spend, how to spend it, and where the funds would come from with a single resolution that would both guide Congress and impose a series of spending ceilings to control the deficit. Congress would have, say, a certain ceiling for transportation, and if it wanted to add funds to subway construction, it would have to remove a like amount from highways.

Ideally this would have been accomplished through some merging of the authorizing, appropriating, and revenue committees. But merger would have required that at least two powerful chairmen, plus many subcommittee chairmen, surrender their posts. So an entirely new procedural tier, the budget committees, complete with two important new chairmanships, was set on top. The result is what Howard Baker calls "a three-layer cake." In theory, on receiving the President's budget requests, in early winter, the budget committees quickly produce a nonbinding first resolution to set general ceilings. Then the authorizing committees write policy-setting legislation within those ceilings, and the appropriating committees—after learning of the authorizing committees' policy objectives—award the money. Near the end of this cycle the budget committees produce a second resolution to reconcile the inevitable differences between what the budget ceilings allow and what the committees are actually spending. This resolution is binding, and after it is passed, in theory the reamining pieces fall smoothly into place.

In practice the budget process isn't working anything like that. Budget resolutions have become the subjects of such contention that this year the first resolution, due on May 15, wasn't passed until October 1—even though it was nonbinding. Appropriating and authorizing committees work concurrently and nearly year-round, the appropriating committees choosing dollar amounts before, from the standpoint of policy, they know how the money will be used. The Budget Act breaks down spending into functional categories different from those employed by the committee structure, so when a budget resolution is being debated, wrestling goes on over which portion of which ceiling should apply to which committee, a procedure known as "crosswalk." Thus the process leads to a continuous frenzy of activity but few decisions that count.

In order to prepare the fiscal 1984 defense budget, the Senate Appropriations Committee held seventeen days of hearings, producing about 5,300 pages of testimony. The Senate Armed Services Committee held twenty-seven days of hearings on the defense budget and called 192 witnesses, many of whom also appeared before the Appropriations Committee to make the same statements. The Senate Budget Committee held hearings on the subject as well, producing two resolutions that had to be debated and voted on by the full Senate.

Meanwhile, in the House, the Armed Services, Appropriations, and Budget Committees were duplicating this work, and the full chamber was voting on a different budget resolution. And none of it was final.

When the defense bill itself came to the Senate floor, it sparked weeks of debate; the (different) House bill caused a similar swirl on the floor. Even after that the defense budget wasn't finished. A House-Senate conference committee had to be created to resolve the discrepancies between the two versions, and then the conference-committee bill had to be debated and voted on by both chambers. Spending levels for the Defense Department weren't finally set until mid-November of 1983, seven weeks after the fiscal year had begun.

Last summer Howard Baker was negotiating simultaneously with various factions on the defense authorization bill and the defense appropriations bill and with a House-Senate conference committee deadlocked on the defense sections of the budget resolution. In other words, he was trying to arrive at three different versions of the same number—none of which would be final. "This is crazy," Baker told the Quayle committee, in a plaintive tone. "It makes absolutely no sense."

The endless budget deliberations have also been a driving force behind a dramatic increase in the number of recorded votes on the floor. In 1960 the House staged 180 roll-call votes, or 0.7 votes per working day. In 1970 there were 443 votes, or 1.3 per working day, and in 1980 there were 1,276 votes—3.9 each day. (In the Senate roll calls have increased from 1.5 a day in 1960 to 3 a day in 1980.)

The sheer logistics of staging four roll-call votes a day are imposing, because congressmen are rarely on the chamber floor, or even in the Capitol. When roll-call votes are signaled, congressmen must drop what they are doing (usually attending committee meetings at one of the congressional office buildings several hundred yards from the Capitol), race to the floor, vote, and race back. It is considered political suicide to miss roll-call votes, even when the subjects are trivial (in recent years the House voted 305 to 66 to establish Mother-in-Law Day and 388 to 11 to permit the International Communication Agency to distribute a slide show called *Montana: The People Speak*) or when the votes are likely to be overturned later. Since low attendance has an instant negative connotation, one of the easiest ways for a challenger to attack an incumbent congressman is to hammer at a "bad attendance record" on floor votes—a tactic that avoids the issue of whether the congressman might have made more meaningful use of his time.

Because of the regularity with which redundant floor votes occur, Congress "never finishes anything, never arrives at a decision," according to Senator Ted Stevens, of Alaska. "Always they are just preliminary decisions that will be addressed again later anyway. It's totally confusing to the public, and even to ourselves." By my count there have been thirty-six "test votes" in the House and Senate on the MX missile since Reagan took office, most of them necessitated by some whorl of the budget process. These test votes have been accompanied by tension, packed press galleries, ringing debate—all the drama of decision, but no decision. On a Tuesday in December of 1982 the House worked late into the night debating whether to cut nearly $1 billion from MX funding. The vote was headline news nationwide and was played as HOUSE KILLS MX. Then, on Wednesday— *the following day*—the House voted to retain $2.5 billion for MX research and development.

The MX is far from unique as a source of marathon voting. In 1981 the Senate staged twenty-five roll-call votes on the budget-reconciliation bill (an interim step) and fifty-five on the tax-cut bill. In 1983 there were eight Senate roll-call votes on what language to use in condemning the Soviet destruction of Korean Air Lines flight 007. During three months in 1983 the House took twenty-seven recorded votes on the nuclear freeze, including eleven in one week.

Often in recent years the United States has technically not had a budget at all but rather has operated under a "continuing resolution" that keeps the money flowing but avoids an official legislative confrontation over the deficit. Continuing resolutions are popular, in part because they are one of the mechanisms that allow congressmen to seem to be voting for both sides at once: they can vote No on the budget itself ("I'm opposed to these deficits") and vote Yes for individual programs on the continuing resolution ("I brought increased federal spending to this district"). Similarly, the frequent votes to raise the federal debt ceiling are technically "temporary" legislation, so that congressmen can claim that each vote was merely for an emergency stopgap, not an endorsement of the debt itself. A temporary vote results in the need to have another showdown over the same subject a short time later, even though it was known all along that the "temporary" increase would not provide enough time to make substantial reforms in spending practices. "We are forever staying up all night to extend the debt one month, doing nothing for a month, and then staying up all night again," says a highly placed officer of the House.

In recent years there also has been an increase in the use of supplemental appropriations bills, which are in effect end runs around the stagnated budget process. A case study in how Congress now works is this year's summer-jobs supplemental. In March of 1984 the House overwhelmingly passed a bill providing $60 million in emergency aid for African drought victims. The bill was sent to the Senate, where immediate passage was expected. Realizing this, Senator Dixon—who had been looking for means to enact a $100 million increase in federal summer-jobs for high-unemployment states like his, Illinois—decided to attach his proposal as an unrelated amendment, or "rider," to the famine-relief bill. (In the House, amendments must be germane; there is a similar rule in the Senate, but it is rarely enforced, meaning that in effect any rider can be attached to any piece of legislation.) In early April, Dixon's jobs amendment was added to the relief bill without opposition.

All aboard! The train was about to leave the station. A noncontroversial philanthropic bill—who could be against food for drought victims and summer jobs for youth?—was ideal as a carrier of baggage. Within ten days the Senate had attached no fewer than thirty-five more riders to the bill. Among them were $14 million for the Cumberland Gap Bypass Tunnel; $5 billion for the Commodity Credit Corporation; $845 million for two child-nutrition programs; $2.3 billion for the Rural Housing Insurance Fund; $850,000 for recreation in Nassau County, New York; $70 million for the Corporation for Public Broadcasting, providing "that none of the funds appropriated under this paragraph shall be used to pay for receptions, parties, and similar forms of entertainment"; $1 million for abandoned-mine reclamation grants for Montana; $50 million for crop insurance; $25 million for United States Customs Service airplanes; $62 million for military aid to El Salvador; $21 million aid to the *contras* in Nicaragua; extra money for the Senate Stationery Revolving Fund; and a "sense of the Senate" section praising the Navy's Seabee construction teams as "elite units of unprecedented mobility and versatility."

Soon the House made known that it wanted the Senate to drop all the riders, including the summer-jobs provision; Jamie Whitten, of Mississippi, the House Appropriations Committee chairman, said that the Senate had "overstepped its prerogatives"—that is, gone wild. Then the mining of Nicaraguan harbors by *contra* forces was revealed and became a media event. Congressmen began to compete to see who could express the most outrage, even though Congress had supplied the funds with which the mining was carried out. Talk increased of using certain provisions of the War Powers Act, which would set in motion another new "process." Passed in 1973, the act was catalyzed by Nixon's "secret" bombing of Cambodia and invasion of Laos, but its origins go back to President Truman's decision to commit U.S. troops to Korea without consulting Congress and to President Johnson's use of trumped-up evidence to trick Congress into passing the Gulf of Tonkin Resolution. The War Powers Act creates a sequence of deadlines that so far have served mainly to generate meetings, testimony, and the appearance of action; its serious provisions, involving the withdrawal of troops, have never been acted upon.

During the harbor-mining flap, the House held ten hours of floor debate on an anti-mining resolution, not because there was any doubt about the outcome—the resolution won 281 to 111—but because so many members wanted a chance to make a speech with the cameras rolling. The Senate also held a long-winded debate before voting 84 to 12 to condemn the mining. The votes were headline news—even though neither was a decision but merely a nonbinding expression of concern. This "done," Congress adjourned for the Easter holiday.

By mid-May the House had passed a new version of the famine bill, removing some of the Senate riders. A conference committee was called to resolve the differences, especially over the now controversial aid to El Salvador and the *contras.* In early May, José Napoléon Duarte was elected president of El Salvador. He met with House leaders and persuaded them of his sincerity, and House objections to the $62 million in extra aid for his country were dropped. But the $21 million for the *contras* remained in dispute. White House lobbyists said that they would not support the bill unless aid to the *contras* was included. Stalemate was reached. Famine relief and the summer jobs measure were now being held up by a political non sequitur.

In mid-June, Dixon appeared before the Senate's Democratic caucus with a spending breakdown showing that although the jobs measure was intended mainly for industrial states, almost every state—forty-four of fifty—would get some share of the money. This seemed to increase senatorial enthusiasm. Then at a televised press conference, President Reagan was asked whether he felt that employment for the poor should depend on aid to the *contras.* Reagan seemed only dimly aware of what was at issue, but the question had been phrased in such a way that he came off sounding hard-hearted. A spate of bad publicity resulted, including editorials in most of the nation's papers.

In late June there was another round of floor debate in the Senate. Aid to the *contras* was dropped from the bill, as were a few of the other riders. When finally approved, the supplemental, which had started with a single provision worth $60 million, contained twenty-two provisions worth $1.1 billion. Reagan signed it on July 2—with the intended summer-jobs recipients already well out of school, and an unknown number of African drought victims, if anyone still remembered *them,* added to the death toll.

MOUNTAIN PEAKS

When seniority was in flower, the personal prospects of most congressmen were limited. There was nothing a congressman might do to speed his ascendancy to the chairmanship of a committee. He could only wait. If he wished to be able to deliver appropriations for his district or constituency, his best chance lay in cultivating the good will of a few older chairmen and leaders—the speaker, the majority and minority leaders and their assistants, and the party caucuses, which made and revised committee assignments.

The main way to win the favor of this small group was to keep quiet. Make no special demands, vote as directed, and never challenge a leadership position or a senior chairman's bill on the floor. Challenging the power structure might work on occasion—but the senior members were around for the long haul, and they had excellent memories for those who crossed them. Stepping out of line might also cause a congressman to lose the financial support of his party, and that might cost him his job.

As the tenor of American politics changed—and as, through Watergate, internal Washington came to be associated with disgrace rather than dignity—Congress changed. "Today each senator is his own mountain peak, with his own staff, his own source of financing, his own pet issues, and his own agenda," says Nelson W. Polsby, the author of several standard texts on Congress.

With the seniority system gone, the rewards of patience are fewer—there's no guarantee that playing by the rules will lead to a prominent position. The prominent positions themselves have been devalued, and the penalties for being a glory-seeker have been all but eliminated.

At the same time, with the expansion of television coverage, playing to the crowd has become much more rewarding than playing to the club. In 1964, 1,649 journalists were accredited to cover Congress. Today 3,748 are: seven journalists for each congressman. By far the largest increase has been in the number of radio and television journalists. While Congress itself is difficult for the networks to cover, individual congressmen make ideal subjects for television. They hold important positions; they speak in catchy phrases that clip into twenty-second bites; they eagerly seek exposure, and thus are willing to cooperate with television's requirements; and they have opinions on nearly everything. Congressmen, in turn—particularly senators, because of their extra prestige—have found that they can use television to cultivate national followings that will supply them with fame, donations, and a power base, should they run for President. Self-promotion has always been a factor in Capitol Hill affairs, but the advent of television has made it convenient to a degree never before possible.

The shift in campaign financing toward direct mail and PACs has an obverse effect that is often overlooked: the shift away from political-party structures as a source of funds. In 1982 candidates for the House received, on average, only six percent of their funds from Democratic or Republican party organizations. Almost all their money came from PACs and from individuals, most of whom were PAC-affiliated or solicited by direct mail. Oil-company PACs alone gave more money to Democratic candidates in 1982 than did the Democratic National Committee. Party discipline has always been weak in U.S. politics; there is nothing in the United States that rivals the bitterness and intensity of Western European party feuds, for example. The two restraints that congressional leaders have traditionally used on members are the promise of campaign funds and the threat of seniority freeze-out: with the former more readily available outside Congress and the latter lacking credibility, mountain peaks are heaving up in every direction.

This change affects the substance of government as well as the style of Congress. Subcommittee hearings held primarily to showcase the chairman waste not only subcommittee members' time: someone must testify at those hearings. Secretary of State George Shultz was called to Congress for formal testimony twenty-five times in 1983, or every other week; all told, high State Department officials made nearly 400 appearances. Senator Robert Kasten, of Wisconsin, says that officials appearing before redundant committees not only discuss the same topics but use the same words. "Often I'll say to myself, Where have I heard that before? and realize that it's the exact same speech that was read by the same man, the week before, at another hearing. If you miss part of his speech, just go to the next hearing, because he'll be giving it again."

Constantly going up the Hill to testify—and constantly having to defend budget requests, which in the multi-tier system are subject to some kind of challenge somewhere almost daily—affects the efficiency of executive agencies. Administration officials come to view a good day of committee testimony as representing the successful fulfillment of their duties. This is an essential element of Washington make-believe. In turn, congressmen often view an official's relations with Congress as in itself the measure of success (it was Anne Gorsuch Burford's refusal to release documents to Congress, not her policies at the Environmental Protection Agency, that caused her downfall). And reporters come to view accessibility to the press as the chief test of an official's worth. The question of what goverment is actually doing is often lost in the shuffle.

PRISONERS OF TRIVIA

Trivia, even to the most dedicated congressman, has its pull. When there are a thousand small things that demand attention—hearings. floor votes, hands to shake, parties to attend, and speeches to deliver—the mind tends to focus on them, and larger purposes are forgotten.

The development in the 1970s of computerized direct mail, for example, may have given congressmen a powerful new tool with which to raise money, but it also gave interest groups a powerful new tool with which to bury Congress in trivia. In 1972 members of the House received 14.6 million pieces of mail; last year the figure was 161 million, and this year mail is running at a rate of 200 million pieces. That comes to 459,770 pieces of mail for each representative. On a single day this fall Tip O'Neill, the speaker of the House, received *five million pieces.* One staff aide, who worked for Hubert

Humphrey in the 1960s and now works for one of the Senate's lesser-known members, recalls, "During the height of the debate on the Civil Rights Act of 1964, Humphrey got 3,000 letters. This was considered astonishing. Now we can get 3,000 letters a day even when there's nothing going on."

Most of the letters are sparked by mass-mailing campaigns made possible by computers and targeted address lists: it is not unusual for a congressman's office to receive in one day fifty handwritten letters all of which have exactly the same wording. But the fact that few of the letters are spontaneous does not diminish their importance to congressmen; each letter represents both the concerns of a citizen and a lost vote should the congressman fail to reply. Failing to answer a letter—even with a form letter—is riskier than missing a roll-call vote, since the letter constitutes the most direct contact the average voter will ever have with a political leader.

"People write to us to complain about the expansion in congressional staff, then get mad if someone isn't standing by to answer their letter," says Janet St. Amand, the legislative director for Representative Thomas Carper, of Delaware. Form-letter computers that spew out paragraphs in response to key words have been installed in congressional offices, and the offices of senators from large states now more closely resemble mail-order outlets than legislative enclaves. Senator Dale Bumpers, of Arkansas, was embarrassed a few years ago when it was revealed that his computer contained a form letter designated "late apology to friend" that began, "It was good to hear from you, and I hope you'll accept my apologies for my delay in getting back to you. I had put your letter aside to answer personally. . . ." Capitol Hill interns and lower-level staffers now find that their lives consist almost entirely of opening letters, flattening the contents, and stuffing envelopes with the responses.

Robert Rota, the postmaster of the House, says he sees no end in sight for the increase in congressional mail: "The stamp will always be the cheapest form of lobbying, and as long as the enthusiasm for lobbying keeps building, so will the volume of mail."

One new distraction that members of Congress dare not complain about publicly, but nonetheless feel, is the physical presence of constituents in Washington. The increase in travel by average Americans is among those measures of society's wealth that do not fit neatly in the consumer price index but are unmistakable. In 1970, 2.8 million people visited the Capitol grounds; the figure continued to build even through the recent recession, and in 1983 it hit five million. Crowds are such that it is now sometimes difficult, even during the week, to walk through the Capitol Rotunda; in the summer, tourists even abound in the unmarked (purposely, to discourage the curious) underground passageways that link the functional parts of the Capitol.

When the Philip Hart Senate Office Building was completed, two years ago, there was a minor revolt among senators who were ordered to move in, in part because the Hart Building lacks the traditional unmarked doors that allow senators to slip in and out of their private offices unnoticed.

THE CAMPAIGN THAT NEVER ENDS

Along with the shift from seeking success within Congress as an institution to seeking national attention and interest-group financial backing went a shift in corporate campaign contributions in the 1970s—away from incumbents and toward challengers.

The great bulk of business contributions had always gone to sitting congressmen, even liberal Democrats, on the "bird in the hand" theory. During the 1970s, as seniority broke down, conservative chairmen lost their ability to control liberal younger members, who at times seemed out of touch with the reasonable requirements of business. Concurrently, oil companies were finding both that they had huge sums of money at their disposal and that they were under political attack, by means of the windfall-profits tax and other measures. Having the money to spend and the desire to spend it, oil companies broke tradition and began to funnel money to challengers; they hoped either to defeat the incumbents or to make them so nervous that they would fear their own shadows. Other business groups joined in. By the time a few "safe seat" senior members who had always played by the rules lost re-election bids, a new type of electoral anxiety was created.

As it happened, the attack by business on incumbents had less effect than anticipated: congressional "mortality rates" are about the same today as they were in the 1950s, and as the anti-business mood of Congress has dissipated, corporate funding has returned to its traditional patterns. In 1984 business contributions favored incumbents by a wide margin. Another force has arisen to feed the anxiety: an explosion in single-interest groups and independent negative-campaign organizations like the National Conservative Political Action Committee, which specialize in attack. NCPAC may not be the juggernaut it once appeared. Its track record of defeating incumbents is modest, and in several races NCPAC's efforts have backfired. But the proliferation of groups like it, armed with millions of dollars, has kept the re-election anxiety level on the high plane to which business first raised it. In the 1982 congressional elections the largest single pool of money was the $64.3 million spent by "nonconnected" ideological PACs. Total corporate PAC spending, in contrast, was $43.3 million.

Most of the money spent by ideological PACs is used to attack someone or something, rather than to propose constructive solutions. Negative views sit well with the public in the wake of two Presidents in a row—Carter and Reagan—who have campaigned "against Washington." "Americans are by nature skeptical of authority, and inclined to believe the worst about government," Representative Willis Gradison, of Ohio, says. "This makes an anti-Washington or anti-Congress campaign the easiest type of campaign to sell to voters." It also profoundly affects the tone of politics, making congressmen feel that they must endlessly justify themselves by endlessly campaigning: merely being in Washington renders them guilty until shown innocent.

This campaign trend and the growth of television interact with each other in a diabolical way. "Today, if you can't sell an issue in twenty seconds, you can't use it," Representative Synar says. "It only takes twenty seconds to say 'Your congressman is against prayer.' It takes me five minutes to explain why that's wrong. But television won't give me five minutes. Television demands that I boil everything down to a single sentence." Synar adds that the only way he can reply to a negative charge within twenty seconds is with another negative, knocking the ball back into his opponent's court. This need to be negative suits perfectly the internal imperatives of television, which congressmen are increasingly aware of and anxious to satisfy. Television producers assume that they are struggling to grab viewers' attention every second the set is on: most viewers are eating, reading, talking, or otherwise distracted. Emotional facial expressions and confrontations tend to make them look up from dinner, and thus are prized.

Confrontations also have human story lines that can be grasped by someone who just walked into the room. Even the viewer who wants to be well informed about public policy, if he walks in when a complicated discussion is in progress, may assume that he has already missed too much and change channels, whereas the viewer walking in during an argument can immediately pick up on what's happening. Whether Gary Hart's "new ideas" were good or bad, television reports tended to skip over them during his presidential-nomination campaign, because they were complicated and took too long to explain. The fact that Hart had changed his name and signature, however, could be communicated in a single sentence, and called forth emotional reactions that made for lively television. During the much-publicized Roger Mudd interview, Mudd addressed seventeen questions and comments to Hart. Only one of the seventeen concerned an issue. All the rest were about style or were confrontational questions designed to provoke emotional responses. "Why do you imitate John Kennedy so much?" would embarrass any candidate who was imitating Kennedy and anger any candidate who wasn't—the perfect television question.

Congress has made a seemingly minor internal-policy change that fuels the endless campaign: it now pays for members to shuttle back and forth between Washington and their districts. In the 1960s congressmen were allowed up to twelve trips home a year. Now they get expense accounts sufficient to pay for about forty trips. Between government-financed trips and those financed by trade associations and other groups, most members of Congress now go home almost every weekend.

The fact that congressmen are out of town on weekends had led to a significant decrease in personal contact among them. Congressmen who don't know one another are more likely to believe the worst of one another's motives, and to lack a sense of common purpose. The introduction into the House, in 1974, of an electronic voting system that employs magnetic key cards has also played a role in this change. Jack Gregory, an official in the Office of the Clerk of the House, says, "Before electronic voting, it took the House forty-five minutes or so to read the rolls. Members were physically compelled to be in the chamber during that time, and they didn't have much to do, so often they would chat and get to know each other. With electronic voting, they can breeze in and breeze out."

Representative Udall recalls how different it was when his brother, Stewart, was a congressman, in the 1950s: "He used to drive here from Arizona with the kids in January, and then in June they'd drive home for the summer. If there was a fall session, Stewart would drive back here alone and the kids would go to school in Arizona through the fall; then he'd drive back home at Christmas to get them. That was all—two trips a year at the most." Now, Udall says, he himself flies back to Arizona thirty-five weekends a year, and sometimes during the week. "From a campaigning standpoint, it means you no longer have that excuse, when someone wants you to appear, of saying you won't be back in town for three months. They know you can get on a plane." Congressmen from the western states spend about one day a week in transit, flying back and forth. To accommodate them, congressional schedules are arranged to be light on Mondays and Fridays, and thus are all the more hectic in the middle of the week. Another result of all the traveling and campaigning is simply exhaustion. Synar says, "I am tired, physically tired, all the time, and so are most of the members I know. Tired people do not always make clear decisions."

BIG MONEY, BIG ANXIETY

Money rarely buys elections. In 1982 the Republican Party raised five times as much money as the Democratic Party, but the Democrats won more seats. Money can, however, buy individual congressmen's votes on a bill, or distort congressmen's thinking on an issue—normally all an interest group needs to achieve its ends. Most important to the structure of Congress, the velocity at which campaign spending has increased over the past ten years has engendered a permanent state of anxiety in which congressmen can never stop worrying about fund-raising and the compromises it entails.

In 1974 a total of $73.5 million was spent on congressional races. In 1982 the amount had risen to $289 million, a 300 percent increase during a period when the consumer price index rose 96 percent. In 1974 the mean expenditure per candidate for the House was $53,000; by 1982 it had risen to $228,000. Those running for senator spent an average of $437,000 apiece in 1974, $1.8 million in 1982. Most of the new money came from PACs, from direct-mail solicitations, and from individuals giving at the behest of PACs—business executives who "voluntarily" made individual contributions to candidates designated by their firms, for example. Most of the new money has been spent on television, usually for ads that say little or nothing about matters of substance.

These numbers are impressive enough in themselves, but they represent only part of the picture. Two almost entirely new categories of campaign spending came into being in the 1970s—the nonconnected negative spending of ideological PACs and the "soft money" spending by groups that in order to get around campaign laws are not officially tied to candidates (most of the big money spent in 1982 for conservative Republicans fell into this category, as did Walter Mondale's "delegate committee" spending in the Democratic primaries). Of the $190 million spent by all PACs on the 1982 congressional campaign, only $84 million went to candidates; the rest went to negative spending or to soft-money commercials in support of candidates who theoretically had no idea that the commercials were being made. In many races the amounts of nonconnected negative and loosely connected soft money spent were greater than party contributions to the candidates; for example, direct contribution to 1982 Republican candidates by the Republican Party averaged $18,000, but soft-money expenses to assist them averaged $264,000.

The rapid acceleration of political spending has taken place for many reasons, among them changes in the campaign laws, an increased focus on Washington as both a cause of national problems and a source of lavish bailouts, and the greater use of ever-more-expensive television time. When the campaign-reform laws of the early 1970s were passed, the pattern of political giving was for unions to collect small sums and donate them to Democrats through proto-PACs like the AFL-CIO's COPE; for small contributors on both sides to send money more or less spontaneously, usually to addresses they found on campaign brochures or at the end of television appeals; and for wealthy businessmen to give large sums to Republicans, in order to receive tax advantages and to win reputations as players. After Watergate left many large donors either indicted or humiliated because their contributions had wound up in the hands of the burglars, businessmen were happy to take a lower profile and find an impersonal means—the PAC loophole in the new laws— for their gifts.

Between PACs and direct mail it has become possible to raise very large sums on a routine basis, and the new political environment of obsession with Washington makes it likelier that companies and individuals will respond when asked. New money-raising tends to appeal to the lowest common denominator, relying on negative pitches, scare tactics, and exaggeration—all political standbys, but refined with targeted marketing techniques.

Political expenditures now function roughly like an arms race in which neither side wants to keep raising the stakes but each is afraid that if it stops, its opponent will not. (Like most weapons, most political contributions serve mainly to cancel each other out.) With expenses constantly rising, there is no telling how much will be needed for next year's race; several of the congressmen I spoke to said they had lost track of what a "reasonable" total campaign expense might be. So, in the manner of the protagonists in an arms race, congressmen feel compelled to stockpile.

It's there for the asking—who could resist? Representative Henson Moore, of Louisiana, had $332,000 left over when he won re-election in 1982 by 87 percent of the vote, and he has continued to raise money at an unflagging pace, adding another $273,000 through 1983 and the first six months of 1984. Representative Dan Rostenkowski, of Illinois, raised $519,000 for the 1982 campaign, although he ran nearly unopposed, and raised another $168,000 in 1983. Rostenkowski is the chairman of the tax-writing Ways and Means Committee, whose members, along with those of the parallel Senate Finance committee, have the easiest time obtaining donations, since they are in the best position to do specific money favors for specific industries.

That campaign-law reforms accidentally encouraged PACs is widely known, but the greater irony is that they have made congressmen *more likely* to sell out, and to do so on a wider range of issues. Contributions are now limited to $1,000 for individuals and $5,000 for organizations. What is $5,000 to a congressman who must raise $228,000? Not much, unless he can snare every offer of $5,000 that comes along. No individual contribution is particularly significant; only many gifts from many interests will suffice.

In years past a politician like Robert Kerr, senator from Oklahoma, might be in thrall to the oil interests but a free man on other issues. Two or three checks from the right bank account would have been enough to fund his campaign. Similarly, in 1974, the year of the reform laws, two or three checks from wealthy sources could have supplied the mean of $53,000 spent in a House campaign. Today, to raise a large number of contributions, each small compared with the total amount required, a congressman takes advantage of every possible PAC source, and that means making promises to every special interest at every turn.

As a result, congressmen now owe their first loyalty to PAC interests rather than to party or public interests. Corporate lobbyists generally want small favors—a vote on a bill, sometimes as little as a few words inserted into a regulation or a different effective date on a tax provision. Because the favor requested is small and specific, congressmen know that lobbyists will be watching closely to make sure it is delivered; and they know that, by the same token, very few voters will notice or care whether a commodity-straddle exemption is retroactive to 1982 or 1981. This makes possible a relationship between PAC donations and specific votes that is not possible between PAC donations and general-election returns.

Best congress money can buy stories have grown so familiar in recent years that they have lost their power to scandalize and are now thought of as the naive complaints of good-government wimps. What kind of national government is it where selling out is so widespread, so generally *accepted*, that it no longer causes outrage? In the House recently there have been two rival versions of the Superfund bill for the cleanup of toxic wastes; studies by the Congress Watch organization recently discovered that representatives who sponsored the mild version, favored by business, averaged $4,784 in contributions from chemical-company PACs; those who sponsored the strict version averaged $532 from such companies. Since 1981, another public-interest group has found, representatives who regularly voted for bills favored by nuclear-power interests have averaged nearly four times as much in donations from companies in nuclear fields as those who regularly voted against. These are but two of many examples.

There is another reason that congressmen are so concerned with campaign fund-raising: sometimes they can keep the money. Campaign law allows retiring congressmen to convert unspent contributions to personal use, as a sort of informal retirement bonus. So the more a congressman raises, the more he can make—an exceptionally powerful financial incentive not to rock the boat and upset interest groups. When Representative Ray Roberts, of Texas, retired, in 1981, he took with him $13,014 from his campaign fund. In 1979 Congress amended the campaign laws to end such "closeouts" for future congressmen, but those voting took pains to exempt themselves: any congressman first elected before 1980 will be allowed to keep his campaign funds when he retires.

Congressmen who raise more than they need can also use their money to make contributions to each other. Many now have their own personal PACs—Rostenkowski; Stephen Solarz, of New York; and Henry Waxman, of California, among them. Congressmen make donations to assist congressmen of like philosophical slant and to increase their own influence in Congress and within their committees. Well-heeled congressmen competing for the affections of other congressmen through internal PACs have become another force for congressional fractiousness.

An interest group wishing to make a cash payment to a congressman need not resort to the roundabout means of investment in a retirement fund: it can simply give an honorarium for a speech, money that goes straight into the congressman's pocket. Eleven senators earned more in 1983 from speaking fees than from their salaries. Richard Lugar, of Indiana, netted $129,065 (after contributions to charity) from honoraria; Robert Dole, of Kansas, netted $106,917; and twenty-one senators took in more than $50,000.

Corporations pushing a bill that limits product liability paid $34,000 to Senator Paul Laxalt, of Nevada, $30,350 to Senator Orrin Hatch, of Utah, and $26,250 to Senator Kasten from 1981 through 1983. Similar fees have been paid by other lobbying interests to other congressmen for speeches, and *paid* is the proper word: while congressmen use the word *honoraria* to make their appearances sound like some lofty philanthropic activity, anyone else who makes a speech in return for a fee is referred to as paid.

Honoraria are possible because Congress excluded itself from the conflict-of-interest regulations it imposed on others. If a White House aide accepted $34,000 from a company trying to influence the Administration's stand on the product-liability bill, there would be loud calls in Congress for the aide's head. Edwin Meese's nomination as attorney general was thrown into limbo because Meese borrowed less than congressmen routinely take.

Congressmen also suffer from anxiety relating to their own salaries. Inflation has reduced the buying power of congressional pay by about 40 percent since 1972, while the salaries of corporate executives have gone into orbit. Both senators and representatives make $72,600 and have an honoraria limit of $21,780 (a law limiting honoria to 30 percent of a congressman's salary was passed recently, after bad publicity about the huge fees).

Yet congressmen spend their time determining the fates of people who make substantially more—lobbyists earning $150,000 to $500,000 a year solicit them, television newscasters pulling down six-figure salaries (thanks in part to monopoly licenses Congress gave the networks) interview them, corporate executives beg them for tax favors and import restrictions that will translate into higher executive bonuses. The resentments that arise may not reflect favorably on those who profess to be public servants, but they are nevertheless real and they prey on congressmen's minds, especially since congressmen tend to view themselves as executives of the world's largest and most important corporation. So whereas $72,600 a year is a lot to the average person, it can easily seem paltry to a congressman; the resulting salary anxiety both distracts congressmen from the people's work and encourages the type of rationalization according to which there's nothing wrong with taking $5,000 from a chemical company and voting on its bill the following day.

Congress voting itself a raise is among the most charged of all political topics, yet the public might find it far cheaper in the long run to give congressmen a sizable increase—say, to $100,000—while barring them from outside income of all kinds. The extra few million could be a bargain compared with the money that would be saved if congressmen no longer had an incentive to avert their eyes from billions in cost overruns and sweetheart deals, just to be able to skim a few thousand off for themselves.

MULTIPLE LOBBYING

There are so many lobbyists today largely because there are so many opportunities to lobby. The breakdown of the seniority system and the weakening of congressional leadership has drastically increased the number of people on whom the touch must be put.

A well-informed veteran lobbyist says, "There used to be two to five guys on each side [House and Senate] who had absolute control over any category of bills you might want. All you had to do was get to them. Now getting the top guys is no guarantee. You have to lobby every member on every relevant subcommittee and even [lobby] the membership at large."

Another lobbyist, Eiler Ravnholt, who was for twelve years the administrative assistant to Senator Daniel Inouye, of Hawaii, and who now represents the Hawaiian Sugar Planters Association, adds that it has become necessary to lobby the expanded staff as well. "In the present environment congressmen spend so much time campaigning that they have no choice but to cede much of the legislative authority to their staffs," Ravnholt says. "During the 1960s it was not unusual to walk into the Senate library and see Sam Ervin sitting at a desk, researching a bill. Ervin was an exception, but not that much of an exception; until fairly recently many congressmen played active roles in the legislative detail work. Now they can't. Nobody can. The staff does the detail work and so you must lobby the staff." And where before there were a few important individuals on the House and Senate staffs, now there are thousands.

And thousands of lobbyists. There are 6,500 registered lobbyists in Washington (twelve for every congressman), but the figure does not include trade-association officers, lawyers working on retainer to clients, or liaison officials of corporations with Washington offices. The generally accepted total is about 20,000, or thirty-seven lobbyists for every congressman. Determined interest groups often hire several lobbyists, whose contacts grant access to different sectors of Congress. Brewers pressing for a beer-distribution-monopoly bill have, for example, hired the firm of Wagner and Baroody (all-purpose lobbying), Kip O'Neill, son of Tip O'Neill (access to Democrats), the former congressman John Napier, of South Carolina (access to Republicans), and Romano Romani, a former aide to Senator Dennis DeConcini (access to senators). So many lobbyists in Washington now represent so many overlapping interests that a subspecialty has sprung up—lobbying among lobbyists.

The budget process has been a veritable boon to the lobbying profession. With multiple votes, there is a steady progression of brush fires for lobbyists to stamp out—increasing their clients' anxiety and willingness to pay high fees—and also many more opportunities for a lobbyist to make his case. "Now they can wear you down," Senator Patrick Leahy, of Vermont, says.

"You might be able to hold out for the public interest on the first, second, third, fourth, fifth votes, but on the sixth vote they're back again, and many give in."

Unlike the public, whose attention fades from an issue when it appears that the struggle has been fought and finished (HOUSE KILLS MX), lobbyists have an interest in duplication. Billing by the hour, they are only too happy to have the process drag on interminably. And their attention does not wander: the many minor budget votes that become a blur even in the minds of congressmen are a perfect vehicle for quietly winning concession after concession. Representative Udall says, "The more fragmented the system is, the easier it is for pressure groups to exert control. This is a side effect of our reforms no one anticipated."

When a House-Senate conference committee working on the "deficit down payment" bill went into all-night session last June, the other congressmen went home, but the lobbyists stayed. As Rostenkowski and Senate Finance Committee Chairman Dole emerged with an agreement at 5:30 A.M., they found about a hundred lobbyists still sitting outside the conference room. Among the 282 provisions of the bill, which was supposed to *reduce* the deficit, was a new $1.4 billion tax break for insurance companies; $600 million in reduced capital-gains taxes; $300 million in extra benefits for commodity traders, mainly in Rostenkowski's home town, Chicago, who had used tax straddles (the benefits were for "professional" traders, not ordinary citizens—only for the people who were supplying the money Rostenkowski doesn't need), and other favors.

So pervasive are lobbyists in Congress that it is not uncommon to see them crowded outside the main chamber doors in the House and Senate giving thumbs-up or thumbs-down signals to congressmen rushing in for roll-call votes. Photographers are forbidden to take pictures by the chamber doors, so they cannot capture this spectacle. Lobbyists became upset recently when, in the wake of the Senate bombing, Capitol security passes were issued. The lobbyists were granted access privileges, but their passes were blue, whereas staff passes were red or yellow and press passes green; this made it easy to tell when a congressman was in the company of a lobbyist. Fortunately for lobbyists, it has become fashionable on Capitol Hill to wear one's pass tucked into one's shirt pocket.

Ideological lobby groups have increased in number since the early 1970s; most specialize in anti-politics and take pride in bringing Congress to a halt. The increases in roll-call voting have been caused partly by ideologically extreme congressmen who demand recorded votes even when they know they will lose, in order to create a record they can run against—a sort of anti-Washington index. In the winter of 1984, when the school-prayer issue was at its peak, many senators felt that a silent-prayer amendment stood a good chance of passing. But Reagan Administration lobbyists were adamant that a silent-prayer amendment not be allowed on the floor, for the very reason that it might succeed. They were hoping instead to lose a roll-call vote on vocal prayer and thereby create a convenient list of "against prayer" Democrats for Republicans to attack during the fall campaign.

Like expanded staffs and extra subcommittees, interest groups, once they are formed, take on lives of their own. Senator Leahy explains, "Say a group is created to campaign for an issue, like school prayer. Once it has a director, a staff, and a mailing list, it is not going to go out of business if the staff has anything to do about it. They will look for another issue. Half of the interest groups are really running on self-interest, the interest of the staffs in keeping their jobs." Jesse Helms's National Congressional Club, as the journalist Tina Rosenberg has documented, raised $9.3 million during the 1982 election cycle, ostensibly to aid conservative causes, but gave away only $150,000; fully 98 percent of the contributions went to salaries and overhead.

Congressmen have many money-related reasons to be tolerant of lobbyists, among them that an increasing number of retired or defeated congressmen are staying in Washington to become lobbyists themselves. Of 856 living former congressmen, roughly 25 percent are still in the Washington area—although fewer than one percent came from the Washington area originally. Every longtime Washington observer I have spoken to agrees that the percentage of congressmen staying in Washington is much higher today than it was in the past. Even the percentage of offspring and siblings in lobbying is up, as Bill Keller, of *The New York Times*, has written. Besides Kip O'Neill (whose firm lobbies for sugar and cruise-ship concerns in addition to beer), there is Robin Dole, daughter of Robert Dole (a lobbyist for Century 21), Jamie Whitten, Jr. (steel, barge, and cork interests), Virginia Brown, daughter of House Majority Leader James Wright (National Association of Homebuilders), Michelle Laxalt, daughter of Paul (oil, Wall Street, Hollywood), John Laxalt, brother of Paul (South Korean industry), James Schroeder (Israeli interests), and others. Everybody's doing it—why not me? Or my family?

Even the number of Congress's internal lobby groups, or caucuses, has risen. Today twenty-seven formal caucuses have staffs and receive federal funds; another sixty operate informally out of members' offices. Current caucuses include the Senate Copper Caucus, the House Footwear Caucus, the Congressional Port Caucus, the House and Senate Steel caucuses, the Senate Tourism Caucus, the Congressional Crime Caucus (not a fund-raising group), the Senate Rail Caucus, the Congressional Coal Group, the Congressional Jewelry Manufacturing Coalition, the Congressional Alcohol Fuels Caucus, the Senate Children's Caucus, and the Congressional Mushroom Caucus.

NO FUN ANYMORE

"I often feel that by the time I arrived in Congress, in 1974, the fun was over," Representative Gradison says. "All the landmark legislation, the laws that were exciting and glorious to take part in, had been passed. Now the bills were beginning to fall due, and there would not be glorious work for us, just the struggle to pay those bills."

Through the 1960s and early 1970s Congress made history time and again: the Civil Rights Act; the Voting Rights Act; the Clean Air and Water acts; Medicare and Medicaid; the Resource Conservation and Recovery and Toxic Substances Control acts, which started federal action against toxic wastes; new federal housing programs and aid to education; the successful battles against Nixon and the seniority system; public financing for presidential races; disclosure laws for federal candidates and officials—the list goes on.

Twenty years ago a congressman looking at the nation saw *wrongs*, like legally sanctioned discrimination, that could be righted simply by changing the law. It can be argued that today's political horizon is far different. There are many intractable dilemmas, but few open-and-shut cases such as raw pollution being pumped into a stream. Most current social problems don't have self-evident solutions of the type that Congress could codify in bills and announce tomorrow. Stopping the poll tax against blacks was one thing; moving an entire generation out of the ghetto and into the economic mainstream is quite another, and it's not at all clear how that can be done.

Congressmen face, instead, the tasks of reining in dramatic programs of previous Congresses and cutting the deficit, which are neither politically glamorous nor pleasant tasks. "They build statues and name schools after people who promote great programs," Representative Bill Frenzel, of Minnesota, says. "They never build statues for people who have to say no."

Indeed, what with the fragmentation of Congress, the inherent unpleasantness of cutbacks, and the eye-glazing vista of deficits of $172 billion, it becomes difficult for congressmen to take seriously the idea that any one particular cut matters. Everybody's taking what they can get—why should my program be the one to suffer when the deficit is so vast? What difference could another few hundred million possibly make?

Traditionally, congressmen find it easiest to advocate a bold new spirit of austerity in someone else's state or district. But there is a sense in which congressmen do not even mind excessive spending in other districts: it creates an atmosphere in which overspending is the norm and money for pet programs is less likely to be challenged.

In June, when the $18 billion water-projects authorization bill was about to go to the House floor, James Howard, of New Jersey, the chairman of the Public Works Committee, circulated a roster of the House with black spots next to the names of members in whose districts were programs he planned to attack if they voted against the water bill. Included in the Public Works Committee's bill was $189 million for a dam in the district of the committee's ranking Republican, Representative Gene Snyder, of Kentucky. Representative Harold Wolpe, of Michigan, who got a black dot, told T. R. Reid, of *The Washington Post*, "You always hear rumors in the cloakroom that they'll kill your project if you dare to oppose anybody else's, but this is the first time I've ever seen them put it on paper. . . . It's extraordinarily blatant." The more spending in general, the more for my district: everybody does it. Any congressman who goes after another congressman's program knows his will be attacked in turn, both by the congressman and by the program's PACs and lobbyists. Even a congressman who might be willing to accept a cut in his own district knows that in the present undisciplined environment he would be played for a sucker; no other congressmen would join in the sacrifice.

This attitude helps explain why, for example, nearly every congressman favors cutting the defense budget in the abstract but votes to preserve the individual programs that make up that budget. In 1983 Congress *added* $4.6 billion to the Pentagon appropriations that President Reagan had asked for. Defense lobbyists in particular are adept, when budget showdowns approach, at avoiding any discussion of whether their projects are the efficient or otherwise proper choice, and at framing the issues strictly in terms of jobs: Congressman, this vote represents 2,000 jobs for your district. Any government expenditure creates jobs—the question is what jobs are best for the nation when national needs, finances, and policies are weighed. But this question is seldom posed to an individual congressman. The question posed is, Do you want these jobs in your district today or not? Do you want your name on them or not?

These considerations apply to most government spending decisions, but they do so with unusual force in defense because of the twenty-second rule. A congressman who presses to reform specific defense programs will win little political credit. Few voters know or care what, say, an AGM-65D is; there's no reason why a voter should, and the benefits of Pentagon reform—lower deficits and greater national readiness—are long-term and directly felt by no one. At the same time, any congressman who challenges a military-spending program exposes himself to the twenty-second charge of being "against defense."

Cutting back and slowing down giveaways has never been fun. For example, it took a public outcry in the late 1940s to kill the excise tax and color restrictions on margarine, which were bald favors for the dairy lobby. But now the congressional agenda seems to consist almost entirely of no-fun issues, and there is no indication that Congress is ready to face them.

The results of the 1984 summer session are suggestive. Congress went into the session having passed the "deficit down payment" bill, which included $50 billion in tax increases over a three-year period but only $13 billion in spending cuts—mostly from Medicare payments, although $1.6 billion of the "cuts" came from postponing payment of military retirees' cost-of-living adjustments (COLAs) so that they would fall in the next fiscal year. (On the same day that the House Budget Committee was making its "down payment," the full House was approving initial funding for the space station, which makes for a dramatic election-year announcement, and costs little now, but commits the nation to spending at least $8 billion over the next few years to build the project and many billions more to operate it.)

During August two of the leading boondoggles at present, the Synthetic Fuels Corporation and subsidized operation of the Hoover Dam, came up for votes. There was a chance to kill synfuels subsidies, but only limited cuts were made, and $8 billion was left in the program. Meanwhile, power subsidies for the Southwest, where electricity from federally financed dams costs about one twelfth what consumer-financed power costs in the East, were preserved and extended until 2017 at a cost of at least $6 billion. These two acts alone wiped out all the cuts in the "deficit down payment."

Through the summer congressmen continued to try to have fun, passing new spending bills: $1 billion extra for college financial aid, $175,000 to study promotion of Iowa commerce, $2.5 million for the city of Oakland to restore a presidential yacht, $1 million for business loans in Queens, $12 million for a highway-safety "demonstration" program in Michigan, increases in the Corporation for Public Broadcasting's budget, then $130 million, to $270 million a year by 1989, an extra $350 million in postal subsidies, $500,000 for a golf course near Capitol Hill. Congress was only following the example of the President. At a news conference on July 24 he had condemned Congress and blamed its "do-nothing Democrats" for failing to pass a balanced-budget amendment. He went on to ask for a $5 billion bonus Social Security benefit increase, a new IRA tax break, extra tax benefits for business in enterprise zones, and more tuition tax credits for private schools.

1920s, 1980s

Henry Bellmon, a senator from Oklahoma, retired in 1980 to return to his farm near Billings, grow wheat, and raise cattle. He had been the ranking Republican on the Budget Committee; had he stayed, he probably would have become chairman. When I spoke with him, the latest Congressional Budget Office estimates had just been released. There would be a $172 billion deficit this year (the all-time record, before Reagan, was $66 billion). Federal borrowing would be $175 billion, about the same as the deficit. Interest on those loans would account for $110 billion, or close to twice the highest pre-Reagan deficit for interest alone: little principal would be retired.

The CBO projected that *even if economic growth continues unabated*, the deficit will be $263 billion in 1989. If growth is moderate, the deficit will be $308 billion. The CBO didn't calculate what might happen if there is another recession. "There simply aren't enough discretionary cuts left to affect deficits like that," Bellmon said. He proceeded to recite the basic breakdown of present federal spending:

- Entitlements (mainly Social Security, Medicare, military and civil-service pensions): 45 percent
- Welfare: less than one percent
- Defense: 28 percent
- Interest on the federal debt: 14 percent
- Everything else: 13 percent
- Percentage of present federal spending that is deficit spending: 20

Bellmon explained, "That means that if you cut out absolutely everything government does that is not related to entitlements or national defense, you would still have a deficit." Absolutely everything would include closing down the FBI, the State Department, the CIA, and all other federal agencies; ending all education grants and revenue-sharing grants to states and cities ("fiscally sound" local governments are financed in part by the federal deficit, although mayors and governors usually forget to mention that when they condemn the big spenders in Washington); stopping all farm price supports and all federal construction and maintenance of highways, bridges, waterways, subways, and dams; ending Federal Deposit Insurance Corporation protection of bank deposits and cutting off all federally subsidized mortgage loans; closing down the National Aeronautics and Space Administration, the National Science Foundation, the Centers for Disease Control, the Smithsonian, and the National Transportation Safety Board; ending all border patrols and abolishing the Immigration and Naturalization Service; ending all air-traffic control, all inspection of nuclear-power plants, all monitoring of stock fraud through the Securities and Exchange Commission, all federal arts funding, all federal courts, all national parks.

"Under these conditions we have only three choices," Bellmon continued. "What must happen is either a major arms-reduction agreement with the Soviets that will allow us to cut back drastically on defense. Or a major reduction in the COLAs for everybody. Or a major tax increase. Those are the choices."

In other words, except in the unlikely event of a new détente, the message of politics in the 1980s must be, Expect less—either less Social Security and Medicare and lower pensions or less income after taxes.

In the 1920s society lived well beyond its means and pretended that tomorrow would never come. Is the United States Congress, in its present state, able to deal with tomorrow? Can it take the message to the voters that they should in every way expect less?

In early January the Ninety-ninth Congress will prepare to convene. The first few days, in which the party caucuses will meet to make committee assignments and alter rules, will set the tone for the next two years. Here are some possibilities congressional leaders might consider:

Committee structures should be combined and simplified; particularly, the quadruple budget/appropriations/authorization/revenue sequence should be reduced by at least one phase. The most logical and least turf-destructive reductions would be to combine the budget committees with the revenue committees, putting the combined groups in control of overall revenue-versus-appropriations ratios, and to eliminate the appropriations committees. Money and policy amount to the same thing. Why must congress pretend otherwise?

Seniority-system reforms should be reeled back somewhat—not to return to the stagnant old days but to stop the tail from wagging the dog.

Congressmen should receive a substantial raise and in return be required to forsake all forms of outside income. They are supposed to function as judges of society's needs; they should be as far above reproach (and influence) as judges.

There should be an absolute freeze on present federal-spending levels, extending to all entitlement programs and defense. If Congress wanted to allocate more money to one program, it would have to take some away from somewhere else. Congressmen cannot hope to reverse the "everybody does it" mentality of deficit increases without a political tool—a means by which they can argue to constituents (in simple, twenty-second terms) that they would like to give them more but just can't. There is nothing in the original social compacts of Social Security and other entitlement programs that confers a "right" to perpetual increases or to benefits for those who don't need them; those "rights" are political creations of Congress, and can be reversed.

A pay-as-you-go law should be enacted. Advocated by Senator John Glenn and others, pay-as-you-go would be a direct means of accomplishing what the budget process attempts to accomplish indirectly: tying government revenues to spending. Any legislation allocating new funds would at the same time have to provide a source for those funds, in the form of either a tax increase or a deduction from another program. When a person buys something, he considers the purchase not in the abstract but in light of how much he has to spend and what will be left over for other purchases. Businesses act the same way. Only government separates the question of what to spend from what is affordable. Pay-as-you-go would have far more teeth than the strictly symbolic balanced-budget amendment, which would require Congress to balance the budget unless, on an annual basis, it voted otherwise. The balanced-budget amendment would add another showy "process" but no actual discipline.

Budgets should be drawn up on a two-year cycle to reduce duplication. Multi-year procurement cycles should be employed for the development and manufacture of complicated items like weapons. Military contractors may feed at the public trough in a shameless manner, but in their behalf it should be said that changing their instructions regularly, as Congress is prone to do, does not make for efficient business. To help longer-cycle budgets work, Congress should devise a "this time we really mean it" clause that could prevent budget decisions from being constantly re-opened for tinkering.

Lobbyists should be denied access to the Capitol. Of course lobbyists are not all sinister; most are simply doing their job. But the number of supplicants gathered round to demand handouts makes it difficult for congressmen to think clearly. Imagine lobbyists for parties in a lawsuit allowed in to see the judge—how credible would his decision be? And having lobbyists crowd outside the chambers of the House and Senate, flashing thumb signs to congressmen like coaches issuing orders to Little Leaguers, is a national disgrace.

There should be a cap on total campaign expenditures for each candidate. The existence of PACs and interest groups is far less corrupting than the need to raise great and ever-greater sums. If House races were limited to, say, $100,000 and Senate races to $500,000, the temptation to pander would be greatly reduced. Also, all campaign funds unspent after a given election should either be returned to donors or be contributed toward retiring the federal debt. If there were a cap on what congressmen could spend and no way for them to hoard what they didn't spend, fundraising would be far less addictive than it is today. Restraining nonconnected and soft-money groups would not be as easy as restraining congressmen. But at least this proposal would get the congressmen out of fund-raising and back to their responsibilities.

What can be done to restrain indirect spending on campaigns when the constitution guarantees freedom of speech? Preserve that freedom by limiting all advertising *to speech*. Whether by candidates or by representatives of soft-money or ideological groups, only *speech*, in which an actual, real, named, identifiable person stands and talks, would be permitted. No electronic graphics; no talking cows; no actors pretending to be men in the street; no sunset walks along the beach. Banning Madison Avenue-style advertising from politics has been advocated by Curtis Gans, the director of the Committtee for the Study of the American Electorate. The Supreme Court ruled in 1976 that money used to buy time on or space in communication media equates to the freedom of speech. This ruling has caused many people to think that the Gans approach would be held unconstitutional. But what do special effects, actors, and graphics have to do with any freedom we hold dear? Their purpose is to evade political debate, not advance it. Let money be used to buy TV spots, but only ones that hold to a standardized format, in which real candidates or real spokesmen for groups stand before the same solid-color background and state their ideas—whatever those ideas might be—with absolute privilege. This would surely satisfy the Founding Fathers, reduce the cost of campaigning, and by the way return the focus of politics to the issues.

The congressional calendar should be fixed, making it harder to put off decisions over and over again. A quarter system might be appropriate. During three quarters of the year congressmen would not be permitted to shuttle home to campaign but would be required to stay in Washington and attend to their work. During the fourth quarter Congress would shut down, and congressmen could return to their districts to find out for themselves what is happening there. During this time they could also hold away-from-Washington hearings—an art that died with television and instant access to publicity—in order to hear testimony from average Americans, not members of the Washington expert set.

None of these reforms would be easy to implement, especially those that involve intrusions upon existing turf and perquisites. But if congressmen cannot govern Congress, how can they hope to govern the country?

In 1984 several governors were begged by national party officials to run for Senate seats; all refused, seeing no reason to surrender jobs where they could accomplish something useful in order to submit themselves to the 535-ring circus that is Congress. A generation ago the idea of politicians who would rather avoid joining the Senate would have been outrageous; now it seems perfectly reasonable. Congress, unique among our government institutions, has control over its own fate—it can't blame another branch of the government for its condition. Before Congress can lead the nation, it must be able to lead itself.

DEBATE FOCUS

Is Congress a Mess or a Responsible Institution?

A LONG-TIME OBSERVER OF CAPITOL HILL ARGUES THAT CONGRESS
HAS EXERCISED POLITICAL LEADERSHIP AND RESPONDED TO POPULAR
DEMANDS

Wall Street Journal Washington correspondent Albert Hunt, well known because of his regular appearances on the PBS program "Washington Week in Review," defends Congress in the following piece. He argues that it has been politically responsible, enacting needed and sometimes innovative legislation. Hunt concludes some changes should be made, but from an overall perspective Congress has served the nation well.

A. R. HUNT

18

In Defense of a Messy Congress

ALBERT R. HUNT

In early 1975 a group of newly elected House Democrats struck up a conversation with Jimmy Burke of Massachusetts. The contrast was stark: the young, ambitious Watergate babies, eager to reform or even replace the political system they so successfully ran against, and Jimmy Burke, the cynical, cigar-chomping old party warhorse.

Jimmy Burke offered some unsolicited advice to the fresh-faced newcomers. There is a simple formula for longevity in the House of Representatives, he explained: "Vote for every tax cut and every spending program and then vote against any increase in the debt ceiling."

One of the freshmen was incredulous, "Why, if everyone did that," he righteously declared, "the whole system would break down."

"What?" replied Jimmy Burke, removing the cigar from his mouth. "You think this place is on the level?"

Jimmy Burke is gone, but his conviction that Congess isn't on the level remains. Editorial writers lament the shortcomings of our national legislature; it is, they tell us, cowardly, chaotic, and crooked. Presidents enjoy railing against Congress, too. With this fall's election approaching, Ronald Reagan, that great communicator, may coin some of the more memorable pejorative phrases. Curiously, he'll have allies on Capitol Hill. Increasingly, members of Congress, who run against the institution to get elected, manage the neat trick of continuing to run against it while serving there.

The failings of Congress even bridge the usual gap between the so-called experts and the man on the street. "Professional critics maintain that it [Congress] is too obese, arthritic, parochial, nonresponsive, over-responsive,"

From The Washingtonian, *September 1982. Reprinted by permission of the author.*

writes Republican Senator William Cohen of Maine in a forthcoming book. "Even the average citizen, who does not possess a doctorate in political science, is frustrated or disappointed in the workings of Congress."

Public-opinion surveys are devastating. On the issue of honesty and ethics, last September's Gallup poll rated the lawmakers below stockbrokers, newspaper reporters, and funeral directors.

The bill of particulars:

- Congress is inept. It took years after the 1973 Arab oil embargo for the House and Senate to enact any energy legislation, and then it pleased almost nobody. Speed isn't Congress's forte. When the legislators a few years ago were given a month to pass an important measure, television commentator David Brinkley observed: "It is widely believed in Washington that it would take Congress 30 days to make instant coffee work."

- Congress is bulky and bureaucratic. Today there are almost 31,000 people working for Congress, about the size of the regular Argentine Navy—and some would say about as competent. Since 1946, the annual appropriations for Congress have soared 2,278 percent, or six times faster than the rate of inflation.

- Congress is avaricious. Almost any powerful special-interest group with lots of campaign cash seems to find a receptive audience in the current Congress, which some call "the best money can buy." Representative David Obey, a Wisconsin Democrat, warns: "We're beginning to look a lot like the state legislatures in the days of the railroads' and mining companies' domination—bought and intimidated." Not to mention the "criminal class" publicized in Abscam.

- Congress is shallow, more preoccupied with publicity than policy. Representative Barber Conable, a New York Republican and one of the more thoughtful members of the House, cringes at the political clichés he frequently hears around the Hill: "Never adopt a political philosophy that won't go on a bumper sticker," or "If you have to explain anything, you're in trouble." Conversely, a lot of attention is paid to image-making. The 535 Senators and representatives churn out about 15,000 press releases a year.

- Congress is craven. In the House, many of the newer, supposedly brighter members are called "bed-wetters" by their more senior colleagues because of their perpetual nervousness over tough issues. "There seems to be a terminal timidity in Congress these days," worries Richard Fenno of Rochester University, one of the knowledgeable political scientists studying Congress.

- Congress has lousy priorities. "We spend more time discussing pay raises than we do nuclear war," laments Senator Patrick Leahy, the Vermont Democrat.

- Congress lacks the legislative giants of yesteryear, some people suggest. Dean Rusk has spoken nostalgically of the congressional "whales" of the past: Sam Rayburn, Robert Taft, Lyndon Johnson, Richard Russell, Wilbur Mills, and Everett Dirksen. These men exercised power and made the system work—in sharp contrast to the little fish of today, it is said.

With all these problems, serious people suggest the need for wide-ranging changes on Capitol Hill. Bold moves, they argue, are necessary if an important institution is to function effectively in this complex world. The underlying premise here is that as the problems have gotten greater, the performance of Congress has gotten worse.

Few are better qualified to assess this premise than Bryce Harlow, who directed congressional relations for Presidents Eisenhower and Nixon and was a close confidant of Sam Rayburn. He also is a very wise man.

"This Congress isn't performing more poorly . . . or much better . . . than most in the past," Bryce Harlow says. "Congress meanders when the American people are indecisive. It dawdles when the American people don't care. It gets nervous and frightened when the people are riled up. And it acts when the people demand action." He concludes: "Congress almost magically mirrors what the American people want."

Congress, or most any legislative body, is reactive by nature; it tends to respond most forcefully when there is strong executive leadership. But with a more complex society and more vocal interest groups, the demands are greater. "We are asking so much more of Congress now," notes Republican Representative Dick Cheney of Wyoming. "That makes comparisons very misleading."

Still, some of the current criticism is tame by historical standards. After Congress enacted its first pay raise in 1816—from $6 per diem to $1,500 a year—voters threw out two thirds of the members of the House in the next election. Fifteen years later, Alexis de Tocqueville, the fabled Frenchman, was anything but awed by the US House of Representatives. The people's body, he charged, has a "vulgar demeanor. . . . The eye frequently does not discover a man of celebrity within its walls."

As for the lack-of-whales theory, Charles Ferris, who as chief aide to Mike Mansfield played a prominent role in the Senate throughout much of the 1960s and '70s, says: "A lot of them looked like giants when they were surrounded by pygmies; overall, there are more talented people around today." Similarly, Robert Peabody, a Johns Hopkins political scientist specializing in congressional leadership, says: "These legends get bigger and bigger with every passing year. My guess is if you look at the current Congress, there are several whales sprouting. In a decade, we'll be talking about the Howard Bakers or the Tip O'Neills or the Bob Doles or the Sam Nunns, among others, as whales. Or at least as extremely big fish."

Before judging how well the old whales ran affairs of state, a few facts are helpful. In the 86th Congress, with almost a two-to-one majority, the vaunted Sam Rayburn still was able to override only two of President Eisenhower's 24 vetoes. It was under the leadership of Everett Dirksen, Richard Russell, and Wilbur Mills that the Vietnam war started and the seeds of economic catastrophe were planted by trying to finance both the war and the Great Society without raising revenues to pay for them.

So are the earlier-mentioned criticisms not valid? They are, though most are exaggerated. The simple fact is that Congress isn't *supposed* to operate neatly, efficiently, or expeditiously. Any system of checks and balances has built-in tensions and rough edges. Bismarck said the two things one never should watch being made are sausage and legislation. And he was talking about a legislative process much tidier than ours.

Yet somehow Congress not only muddles through, but usually responds pretty well to clear-cut crises. Witness the Depression, World War II, the civil-rights battles of the 1960s, Watergate, and perhaps the Reagan economic revolution of the 1980s.

There are ways to improve Congress, to create needed oversight, to reduce the role of money in politics, to curb the deficiencies of staff and a crazy-quilt committee system, and to make the process more thoughtful. These all are and should be discussed and debated. But the greatest threat lies in responding to the particular passions of the moment with sweeping changes that almost surely will produce an inferior institution. . . .

. . . [T]here are some modest changes that might improve Congress. None is a panacea, and the legislative results on most major issues would be unaffected. Still, here are half a dozen improvements that would make the institution better:

1) PUBLICLY FINANCE CONGRESSIONAL CAMPAIGNS AND CURB POLITICAL ACTION COMMITTEES

No single move would do more to improve the perception, and perhaps the performance, of Congress than an overhaul of the campaign-financing system. Sweeping changes are called for only in rare moments. But when the 97th Congress legitimately can be labeled "the best money can buy," one of these moments has arrived. . . .

2) RESTRUCTURE CONGRESSIONAL COMMITTEES

"Congress in its committee rooms is Congress at work," Woodrow Wilson wrote almost 100 years ago. Today, Congress in its committee rooms is also Congress in confusion. The committees and subcommittees—184 in the House, 136 in the Senate—are inefficient and duplicative. In almost every major area—energy, health, transportation, welfare—there are dozens of overlapping jurisdictions crippling efforts to reach consensus legislation. . . .

3) REDUCE CONGRESSIONAL STAFF BY ONE FIFTH

"Senators, I fear, are becoming annoying constitutional impediments to the staff," cracks Senator Patrick Leahy. "Someday, we may just allow the staff to vote and skip the middle man."

Aggressive staff members have dominated much of the legislative process, especially in the Senate, in recent years. Much of the initial growth was justifiable reaction to the Nixon administration's cavalier treatment of Congress in the late 1960s and early '70s. "Congress really was deficient in expertise and too reliant on the executive branch," recalls political scientist Robert Peabody. "But they overcompensated."

Two caveats are in order here. There are hundreds of first-rate staffers on Capitol Hill. . . .

Further, the Senate Republicans deserve credit for actually reducing the size of personal staff by 3 percent and the size of committee staff by more than 14 percent since taking control last year. That's the first time in years that an actual reduction took place. . . .

But it's the nature of staff activity, even more than sheer size, that creates problems. As the American Enterprise Institute's Michael Malbin has convincingly argued, "staff entrepreneurialism" flourishes these days. All the pressures are for staffers to come up with new measures to make the boss (and the staffer) look good. The mushrooming staff, Malbin laments, has turned into a "mechanism for generating more work instead of helping Congress manage its existing work load better." Capitol Hill is full of specialists in narrow fields who devise schemes in absolute isolation from how they fit into the broader picture. Malbin also worries that the reliance on staff prevents members from communicating with one another, a depersonalization of the legislative process. . . .

4) REDUCE THE AMOUNT OF LEGISLATION AND ENCOURAGE MORE OVERSIGHT

Even if staff entrepreneurs are cut, Congress still must find a way to legislate less. Last year 8,719 measures were introduced in the House and Senate, and 921 were passed. Together, the two bodies were in session for 1,732 hours.

At the same time, Congress does a miserable job of checking on the effectiveness of the programs it passes and the agencies it appropriates monies for. The tendency is to go for splash headlines or quick political dividends. "There's no payoff for oversight," notes Representative Conable. "People like to build legislative monuments, they like to have their names on things. But oversight is an exhausting, detailed, thankless requirement." . . .

5) SUNSET ALL ENTITLEMENT AND TAX PROVISIONS

If the legislative veto is a bad idea, sunset laws—under which agencies or programs automatically expire unless positively renewed—are a promising approach if handled properly. Sunset provisions already have been applied to some new departments and agencies approved by Congress. The next step should be to those areas not subject to ordinary review, namely the politically sensitive entitlement and tax provisions. . . .

6) DEVISE A NEW WAY TO SET CONGRESSIONAL PAY

In the relative scheme of inflation, jobs, war, and peace, how much money politicians are paid seems pretty insignificant. But few issues arouse more public passion or cause Congress to make a bigger fool of itself than pay and perquisites. Politically afraid of direct pay boosts, the members turn to surreptitious back-door methods such as last year's secretive move to give members an automatic tax write-off of up to $19,000 a year. The predictable public outcry ensued and this latest outrage was repealed. . . .

[But] there are many legislators who deserve a lot more pay. By any standard, Congress is a very talented group. . . .

In running for President in 1976, Jimmy Carter called for a government "just as good and honest and decent and truthful and fair and competent and idealistic and compassionate and as filled with love as are the American people." We had it then and we have it now. It's called the United States Congress.

CHAPTER TEN
The Bureaucracy

The term "bureaucracy," which has a pejorative connotation in American politics, in government encompasses the various components of the executive branch which are often linked in a hierarchical organization. The president is in many respects, but not all, "chief administrator," directing the bureaucracy with the help of his staff within the Executive Office of the President.

MAKING THE BUREAUCRACY A POLITICAL TARGET

Politicians have periodically made the bureaucracy one of their favorite whipping boys. Presidential candidates in both parties, charging administrative waste and inefficiency, commonly run against the bureaucracy as part of their campaign strategies. Ronald Reagan, attacking the size of government, called for a drastic reduction in programs which would have the effect of substantially reducing the size of the bureaucracy. Jimmy Carter, adopting a populist tone, attacked the Washington political establishment and the bureaucracy that was part of it, and pledged to reduce executive branch agencies from 1900 to 200. He hoped that the size of the bureaucracy would be reduced by normal attrition as civil servants retired without being replaced.

CONSERVATIVE APPROACH TO REFORM

Unlike Carter and most previous presidents who sought to streamline the bureaucracy under presidential control, Reagan's program reductions would eliminate the need for such a vast bureaucracy. His stand echoes past conservative voices which charged that big government, an oversized bureaucracy, and administrative despotism were one and the same thing. Eliminating most of the bureaucracy was the simple solution proposed to solve the persistent problem of administrative inefficiency and lack of democratic accountability.

LIBERAL APPROACH TO THE BUREAUCRACY

Liberal Democrats, on the other hand, advocated administrative reform but viewed the bureaucracy as an essential instrument of positive government. Effective implementation of liberal programs required a large and efficient executive branch. Franklin D. Roosevelt's New Deal created an administrative presidency that presided over a greatly expanded bureaucracy. Lyndon B. Johnson, a Roosevelt protégé and strong New Dealer in his early political career, gave a further impetus to the bureaucracy through his Great Society programs.

NEO-LIBERALS JOIN CONSERVATIVE ATTACK ON BUREAUCRACY

As the Johnson administration was winding down amidst the political turmoil of the 1960s, neo-liberals began to question the democratic effectiveness of a large, unwieldy, and unresponsive executive branch. One of the intellectual leaders of the neo-liberal group was *The Washington Monthly* magazine editor Charles Peters, who has for years criticized bureaucratic red tape. On another front, prominent economists, such as Alfred Kahn of Cornell University, began attacking the need for government regulation of the economy. As their views became more attractive to both Democrats and Republicans, Franklin D. Roosevelt's "alphabet agencies," the independent regulatory commissions, were threatened with extinction. By the early 1980s Congress had deregulated much of the transportation industry, as well as telecommunications. The Civil Aeronautics Board, after a brief ceremony accompanied by the playing of "Taps," formally went out of existence in 1985. Other agencies saw their regulatory responsibilities substantially reduced.

But deregulation did not end the controversy over what, if any, role should be played by the enormous executive branch that remained intact. Neo-liberals and conservatives alike continued their attacks upon the bureaucracy, while politicians kept on finding profit in running against bureaucratic waste and inefficiency.

DEBATE FOCUS

Does the Bureaucracy Subvert the Constitutional System?

TO DEAL WITH THE BUREAUCRACY A NEO-LIBERAL CALLS FOR A NEW
CONSTITUTIONAL BLUEPRINT

The author of the following selection, a *Washington Monthly* editor, Robert M. Kaus, argues that Congress has not conformed to the constitutional blueprint in its creation of many administrative agencies. Congress has delegated law-making authority to agencies, relinquishing its constitutional responsibility to be the primary legislative body. It is primarily in the regulatory sphere that administrators, operating under vague congressional guidelines, make laws independently of Congress. And the president, too, has little power to affect agency decisions. The principal supervisors of the agencies are judges. Judicial review primarily enforces procedural due process upon administrative adjudication and rule making. Even the courts cannot ultimately overturn agency decisions made in conformity with the procedural standards of the law and the Constitution.

The author argues that both the president and Congress must reassert their control over the bureaucracy, and judicial review should be eliminated to make the sprawling fourth branch of the government politically accountable and efficient. To become dominant once again, the president and Congress must work together, requiring fundamental constitutional changes that would change the separation of powers system by giving the president direct authority to choose congressional party leaders, committee chairmen, and the structure of the committee system.

R. M. KAUS

19

Power to the People: Making the Constitution Work Again

ROBERT M. KAUS

Sometime in the next year the 34th state may call for a constitutional convention to balance the budget. It is a prospect that scares many of us—not so much the balanced budget as the idea of the convention itself, and the possibility that it could open up our founding document for a general revision. If the balanced budget drive fails, or even if it succeeds without producing "Con Con II," we will breathe a collective sigh of relief.

We shouldn't. We shouldn't because, to put it simply, we could use a constitutional convention. Our first constitution, and the government it created, aren't working anymore.

At a time when we desperately want our government to act—to meet the energy crisis, to slow inflation, to revitalize the economy—we find that it is paralyzed, unresponding. The two elected wings of the government, though nominally controlled by the same party, spend their efforts in combat with each other. Measures essential to the nation's interest are unable to pass through a legislature choked with the raw demands of locale and lobby. In the throes of a gas shortage, the president proposes a rationing plan; the Congress rejects one version, then amends another to death. It is a familiar pattern: when we demand a program of fair, general sacrifice, our constitutional machine seems programmed to produce only general selfishness.

Reprinted with permission from The Washington Monthly, *October 1979. Copyright by The Washington Monthly Co., 1711 Connecticut Avenue, NW, Washington, DC 20009.*

All the while, a second government, one the Constitution did not create, continues to expand, out of control. This is the government of the agencies. When the president and Congress aren't attacking each other, they seek support by attacking this bureaucracy, seemingly oblivious to the question being begged. So congressmen seek votes by denouncing the regulatory agencies Congress created. The president, having failed to run Washington, runs against it. We are about to witness an extraordinary spectacle: both of the Constitution's democratically-chosen branches campaigning for reelection by opposing the government—neither, apparently, feeling that it might any longer justly be accused of *being* the government.

Something has gone very wrong since the Founding Fathers met in Philadelphia. Perhaps, in a decade or so, we will find that the whole mess has been straightened out—the bureaucracy brought under control, the government freed to act in the national interest—within the framework that was laid down in 1787. But don't count on it. Because the further we trace them, the more the roots of our dissatisfaction with government seem to end at the heart of the Constitution itself—in the inherent parochialism of Congress, the inability of the president to tame it, the built-in antagonism between both institutions. Instead of reforming this constitutional structure, we have tried to escape from it, by creating a new government in the agencies. In the process, we have lost the means of controlling the men and women who rule us—of making them *act*, and act swiftly, to solve our national problems. If we want to regain that ability, we have no choice but to make some fundamental changes in our political system. Not all of these changes require constitutional amendments. But many do. And, together, they represent such a radical departure from our current scheme that it is hard to believe they could be achieved and preserved by anything less than a full campaign for a constitutional overhaul. That is the irony of the balanced budget drive and the fears it raised. Because Con Con II might be the last chance we get to make the government work.

BUILT FOR INACTION

The truth is that our constitution was not designed to allow the government to act quickly on the wishes of the majority. It was designed to frustrate that action. The exaggerated power of "special interests," the debilitating stalemates between the president and Congress, are neither accidental nor necessary features of our politics. As any poli sci major knows, they were intentionally built into our system by men who believed in democracy but were terrified of majority tyranny. So the Federalists set up a legislature, made up of many single-member geographic districts, in order to give every interest and region its champion and prevent the easy coagulation of a majority. They divided the government against itself, into the three branches, the two houses of Congress, the national and local powers. The purpose of these features was, as Madison put it, to make sure any flame would be "unable to spread a general conflagration"—in other words, to protect minority interests by making concerted government action of any sort as difficult as was democratically possible.

The Founding Fathers did their job so well that when, in 1932, we needed a government that could avoid paralysis and take vigorous, sustained action, we abandoned the constitutional plan. In the crisis of the Depression, we wanted officials who could act firmly in the public interest—and we asked the fractious Congress to delegate its lawmaking authority to administrators who were beholden to no particular districts. We needed to overcome the built-in stalemates between the branches of government, so we created agencies, like the Securities and Exchange Commission and the National Labor Relations Board, that purposefully fused all three of the separated powers—executive, legislative and judicial—in a single body. To guide them, these agencies were given little except a few inspirational words of instruction from Congress. The NLRB was to ban "unfair labor practices"; the SEC to ban "manipulative or deceptive devices" where "necessary or appropriate in the public interest or for the protection of investors." But although the rules they turned out in pursuit of these platitudes would never be approved by Congress, those rules would have the force of laws. In the name of action, Congress gave away a substantial chunk of its power.

But the need to act, to escape from the Constitution, was not the only motive behind the creation of the agencies. Mixed in, from the birth of the ICC in 1887 to the creation of the Consumer Product Safety Commission only seven years ago, was a desire to escape from politics itself—a powerful dose of the Progressive dogma that administration should be left to "independent" experts, protected from "partisan" pressures. So Congress, having given away its power to make binding rules, then insulated many of the rulemakers from the only other elected official in government who might have controlled them—the president.

This combination of New Deal activism and agency "independence" has proved a disaster. It was, in a constitutional sense, our original sin. Some of the agencies were in fact staffed with experts. Others weren't. But, freed from the need to please the "partisan" politicians, all these administrators were also freed from the need to please voters. Instead, they were left to satisfy other needs. If they were at the ICC or FCC, those needs were usually the interests of the industry they were supposed to regulate. If they saw business as an adversary—as with newer agencies like EPA and OSHA— they were able to pursue their single mission to the exclusion of all other goals. Regardless of ideology or purpose, they were independent enough to indulge in the natural bureaucratic imperatives of expansion and complication.

Their ability to act swiftly in pursuit of *any* goal was short-lived, however, because they soon fell under the sway of our least democratic branch, the courts. Lawyers instinctively distrusted the bureaucrats—and, indeed, they had a case once the agencies were removed from political control. But to them, the answer was a heavy application of the ritual balm of litigation. So they sued. Soon, agency proceedings began to look more and more like trials, with motions, objections and cross-examination, presided over by officials who looked suspiciously like judges. When these experts finally reached their conclusions, they were then subjected to further "review" by real judges. Even when the only issue was the proper way to list the ingredients of peanut butter, the courts began to pore over the "rulemaking record" to satisfy themselves that the agency had made no procedural missteps, had met its "burden of proof," "considered all the relevant factors," "responded to any especially significant comments." Finally, the courts would ask if, expertise notwithstanding, the agency had committed a "clear error of judgment" or an "abuse of discretion." If the judge disagreed with the agency—or, rather, if his "in-depth review" of the "record" revealed an "abuse of discretion"—it was time for another round.

In most of these proceedings, none of the participants, at any stage, had a compelling reason to act swiftly. The fixed salaries of judges offered no positive incentive for quick deliberation, while the lawyers' fees usually rose in direct proportion to the time they spent on arguments and briefs. Now that this system has been perfected, even a simple action, like setting safety standards for pickup trucks, takes at best a matter of years—while truly complex actions, like the labeling of peanut butter jars, can span decades.

As we created more and more agencies, both the courts and Congress became accustomed to this new role of judges as the roving supervisors of the bureaucracy. Congress—unwilling to take on the messy job itself—began to write even bigger parts for the judiciary into its regulatory scripts. And the judges, who had come to see themselves as the only officials able to bring the agencies to heel, gradually asserted control over even those rulemakers, at HEW or the Department of Interior, who were nominally not "independent," but under the control of the president.

The result of the whole process is that important political decisions—how to stop pollution, how to structure our basic industries, how to conserve energy—are increasingly left, first to the bureaucrats, and then to the arbitrary interplay of judges, interest groups and lawyers. These people have three things in common: they are not chosen by the people whose lives they affect; they have little incentive to act swiftly; and they are not the people whom the authors of the Constitution planned to have make important decisions for the nation.

In our attempt to escape from that constitution, we have come to a dead end. There is a way out. It is, first, to restore the effective control of the government to politicians who can be held accountable by the electorate;

then, to protect their decision from the judicial second-guessing that has crippled the regulatory process; and finally, to remove the obstacles to effective majority rule that the Federalists built into our government's plan, and that led us to abandon the Constitution in the first place.

NOT RESPONSIBLE

In a year we will troop to the polls to judge the performance of Jimmy Carter. Perhaps at that time we may feel that we are evaluating not only Jimmy Carter the man, but Jimmy Carter's *government*, the sum and drift of the federal bureaucracy's decisions during his term in office. It's a nice idea, but it is a delusion. Jimmy Carter cannot be fairly held responsible for many of his administration's actions because he is *not* responsible. He doesn't have enough power.

If this argument seems perverse, it is because over the years we have gotten used to thinking of our chief executive as an imperial, and imperialistic, figure, continually usurping authority from the other parts of the state. But although the president may still be king in foreign affairs, when it comes to domestic policy he has precious few levers to pull in his struggle to control his government. He cannot, thanks to the civil service system, choose the vast majority of those who will work with him. He cannot fire or control the heads of the dozens of "independent agencies," and even the rules made within the executive branch have been shielded by Congress from his influence. How imperial is a president who must plead with the chairman of the Federal Reserve Board—a tenured official who invariably seems to be appointed at a time when the president needs to curry favor with big business—not to pursue monetary policies that sabotage the president's basic economic plans? And, in the wake of Jimmy Carter's show of control over his cabinet, we should remember that he could not have directed any of his cabinet officers to alter a particular "administrative rule" without being taken to court for interfering with the judicially-supervised rulemaking process.

If the president is to have a decent chance to seize control of his own administration, he must first have the constitutional power to direct, and if necessary, fire, the people in the agencies who actually make up the government.

This means, first of all, no more "independent" agencies—no more Federal Reserve Boards, Nuclear Regulatory Commissions, bodies that control government policy on vital national issues but whose heads, once appointed, must be blustered and cajoled by the president into pursuing policies consistent with his own. The Fed, ICC, and NRC might continue to exist or they might not—but if they did they would be under the president's jurisdiction. The only exception we might make to this rule would be for the agencies that do things like decide veterans or workers compensation claims, involving the case-by-case application of settled rules—in other words, agencies whose function is the same as that of the courts. Most "independent agencies," however, whether they make rules, set rates, or license power plants, are doing things the voter should have control over.

But it also means that the president should have the authority to choose enough of the government's staff, up and down the line, in all the agencies, to ensure that the bureaucracy as a whole is committed to the actions he was elected to take. The secretary of HEW can make all the "welfare policy" she wants, but if the file clerk in the regional office misroutes the checks, those policies won't do much good. What virtues the present civil service system possesses—the continuity it guarantees, the protection it affords whistleblowers—could be retained by allowing Congress, if it wishes, the limited constitutional power to scatter a reasonable number of tenured positions around the agencies. Today, the Constitution works in precisely the opposite direction, protecting the file clerk against "political" dismissal, guaranteeing the tenure of all civil servants as "property rights" under the Fifth Amendment.

If these changes can put the president in charge of the domestic bureaucracy, a parallel reform can put Congress back in the business of approving our laws, and standing by the results. The "legislative veto," which would allow the Congress to disapprove the rules proposed by agencies, offers the hope of accomplishing this. The "veto" even has support on Capitol Hill, but in a form that would only *allow* Congress to nullify regulations rather than requiring the House and Senate to actually vote on them. Under this scheme, if Congress simply did nothing, an agency's proposed regulation would become law. The senators and representatives would never have to go on record as supporting it, and the public could go on blaming the agencies and not Congress.

This feature may explain some of the veto's popularity with congressmen, who have grown comfortable with a system in which they can avoid responsibility for agency actions. But it is a defect easily cured—simply by requiring that all regulations be subject to a veto on which there must be a recorded vote. *That* would make the congressmen squirm, which is exactly what we want. If a senator voted against a pollution regulation, he would have to justify it to his constituents. If he voted *for* a set of rules, he would have to be able to stand up and say, "Yes, we need this, this is about the best we can expect to do." His constituents would let him know if he had made the right choice.

The congressmen will object that they simply don't have time to pass upon all the rules the government needs to make. Maybe they will quote Sam Rayburn, who, when he reflected on the regulatory commissions he had bequeathed to the nation, didn't talk about "expertise" or independence," but said simply the agencies "were created to do what we don't have the time to do." And it's fair to say that Congress will never be able to vote on the 8,000 or 9,000 regulations now issued annually. But all this means is that some mechanism would have to be found to separate the important rules, on which Congress would have to vote, from the mass of less significant regulations. Surely it is not impossible to design a system that would require the Congress to approve, for example, the basic fuel economy and emissions standards for cars, while leaving it to the EPA or DOT to come up with the exact prodecures for testing them.

CUT OUT THE COURTS

Together, these changes would move us toward a system in which the president takes responsibility for proposing regulations while the Congress votes them up or down. It is a system that promises to give us better rules, *when* we need them, instead of after years or decades of lawyering.

First, by putting the president in charge of the agencies that propose rules, we would prevent the familiar sight of "independent" agencies with distinct goals taking actions that contradict each other. No longer could the EPA try to encourage higher auto mileage while the National Highway Transportation Safety Administration single-mindedly requires safety features that make cars heavier and less economical. The president would be able to step in and reconcile the two goals. No longer would the government close down factories to improve air quality with one hand while it struggles to shore up those same factory towns with the other. The president, responsible to both environmentalists and labor, would have to make the choice.

Under this system an administrator might think twice before proposing a rule simply to satisfy his agency's constituency, its employees, or a subcommittee chairman—since the rule would have to please the president and a majority of Congress as well. At the least, we could expect a decline in the number of edicts on such essentials as the construction of toilet seats (which OSHA rules once covered) or the burning issue of whether medicines for stomach aches should be labeled "antacids" or should merely reveal that they possess "antiflatulent" properties (recently debated by the FTC). And maybe, once they were responsible for the output of the agencies, the politicians would even be moved to bring some sanity to the government's regulatory structure—eliminating, perhaps, the current situation in which 16 separate agencies and departments (six of them now "independent") take day-to-day actions directly governing the nation's consumption and production of energy.

Finally, once the politicians have chosen their course—be it regulation or deregulation—we might take the truly radical step of protecting them from judicial veto. The rationale is simple: if the people's representatives have spoken, it is no longer relevant that a judge thinks they have "failed to consider all the relevant factors" or have "abused their discretion." That is for the voters to say. In retrospect, we have never really needed the courts to decide things like how to label peanut butter—we drafted them to check up on bureaucrats who were accountable in no other way. Once the agencies are under direct *political* control, we can free the judges for more appropriate, and vital, tasks—like their original job of protecting the Bill of Rights. And, as long as the politicians don't invade those rights, we can free them to take action without having to wait years to read their judicial reviews.

This will take some getting used to. We have been captives in the regulatory trench wars of lawyers for so long that the very thought of the government making a decision of consequence without first asking judicial permission seems—well, it seems unconstitutional. And, without a constitutional amendment, it may actually *be* unconstitutional. There is an elastic clause in the Bill of Rights itself—the "due process" clause—and any even moderately-honed legal mind can come up with a dozen reasons why his client is due no process other than a judge's "probing, in-depth review" of a regulation as a matter of *right*. Several previous attempts by Congress to limit the role of the courts have, in fact, already fallen victim to Justice Brandeis' elegant phrase that "under certain circumstances the constitutional requirement of due process is a requirement of judicial process." Or, as one prominent administrative law expert put it, less elegantly, in a recent article: "Regardless of what the bills say, judicial review will somehow be made available. The only question is whether this fact is recognized now or after numerous appeals and several years of uncertainty."

UNSEPARATE THE POWERS

By giving the president control over the bureaucracy, making the Congress vote on major regulations, and restricting "judicial review," we would restore responsibility for writing all of our laws to the original, elected branches of government. But we would not remove the structural barriers—the separation of powers, the fragmented Congress—that the Framers put in the way of responsible, active government. It was in large part, to avoid these limitations that we created the regulatory bureaucracy, and they will seem all the more ominous if we ask the original constitutional institutions to bear the full load of governing. At its most frightening, there is the possibility that what happened to Jimmy Carter's gas rationing plan would be repeated on a massive scale, with each rule proposed by the executive rejected by the legislature, and the government grinding to a halt. Confronting this problem means asking ourselves whether, in its Madisonian obsession with the tyranny of the majority, our system has produced an equal, maybe greater danger of the tyranny of the minorities.

This is not to say that majorities can't be oppressive. Imagine yourself a midwestern farmer, confronted with a consumerist majority in Congress that cares *only* about low prices, and you will immediately see the basis for the Founding Fathers' fear, and the wisdom in at least one of their solutions—because the farmer's very survival might depend on the ability of his congressman to trade his vote on a number of less pressing issues in exchange for protection of the farmer's essential interest. As a technique for protecting minorities, it is hard to quarrel with the Constitution's choice of a legislature in which the champions of the various regions and interests have a reasonable opportunity to barter their support and reach a consensus.

But, unfortunately, the Framers didn't stop there. Instead, they followed the theory of their day and separated the elected government into the executive and legislative branches. By the simple expedient of maximizing the possibilities for governmental stalemate and breakdown, the threat of the majority was further reduced. Since 1932, the federal government has had a lot more governing to do than in 1787, and the "separation of powers" has served mainly as a blueprint for paralysis among our politicians. The basic pattern is familiar: A president will be elected, claiming a mandate, but he will be unable to get his program through Congress. Congress will manage to pass some laws, but they are vetoed. Each branch blames the other for the impasse and the voters can never be sure whom to believe. Responsibility, as well as the possibility of constructive action, falls through the cracks between the separated powers.

If we are going to ask the president and Congress to resume the full task of governing, we will have to, in the name of majority rule, temper or abandon the Founding Fathers' relentless pursuit of interbranch discord. In particular, we would want to give the president, as the only official elected by a national constituency, a greater chance to accomplish what he was elected to do.

First, we might allow him to structure his party's efforts in Congress. To this end, he could be authorized to name his party's congressional leaders, to determine the committee structure, and, if his party were in the majority, to name the committee chairmen. Where the committees are now set up to meet the internal needs of Congress, they would instead be structured to best serve the president's need for the quickest, most favorable hearing for his legislation. It is not likely, for example, given this power, that a president would subject one of his cabinet departments to the ministrations of 35 different congressional committees and subcommittees, as Congress has done with the Department of Energy. And the effect of committee "patronage" power would strengthen the president's hand by giving chairmen, and would-be chairmen, a vested interest in the fate of their party's leader and his programs.

There is another weapon we could give the president against the inherent selfishness of Congress. This reform would recognize that the power of "special interests" derives from a simple political rule of thumb: a small group with an intense interest frequently can triumph over a majority with a more diffuse, but collectively greater interest. This is a principle that has flourished best in the dark recesses of obscure regulatory agencies—for example, the ICC, where the trucking industry has traditionally defeated the general public's interest in greater competition. But it operates well enough, thank you, in Congress, where the practice of log-rolling enhances the power of narrow, intense minorities. At a time when, on an increasing number of issues, a coalition of these minorities seems able to exploit this natural advantage to thwart the national interest, we need a means of forcing each of them to feel the weight of the majority on the particular issue that concerns them.

There is a way to do this: the plebiscite. The antidote to the special interests might be to allow the president, on occasion, to frame a national referendum on an issue like gun control. This power would bring Congress under some semblance of majoritarian discipline, to balance its built-in centrifugal tendencies. If such a provision had been in effect last spring, for example, we could have had a gas rationing plan in June or July, when we needed it. When Congress rejected the scheme, President Carter could have taken it directly to the voters. The best part about such a power is that it would rarely have to be used. The mere threat of a nationwide vote would have a heartening effect on the willingness of any minority interest group to go to the wall in Congress to block majority action.

All these proposals would violate, intentionally, the theory underlying our Constitution. They would tie the elected branches of government back together, with bonds of political power. But they also might enable our political leaders to do something the Founding Fathers feared—to act.

Today, faced with a political apparatus that seems unable to respond in any direction to our needs, we are in danger of losing our faith in democracy itself. We have taken to sniping at our democratic institutions, while we have grown disturbingly comfortable under our judicial commissars. When we are confronted with the idea of returning regulatory decisions to Congress, we may respond contemptuously, like law professor Abram Chayes, writing in the *Harvard Law Review*: "To retreat to the notion that the legislature itself—Congress!—is in some mystical way adequately representative of all the interests at stake . . . is to impose democratic theory by brute force on observed institutional behavior." Or we may simply say, as Ralph Nader does: "I don't trust a legislature that is for sale. I trust judges who aren't."

The alternative is to realize that if our political institutions aren't responding, we have the power to change them. Then, instead of sneering at the Congress or the presidency, we could be thinking of ways to make them truly responsive and effective. Instead of retreating to the courts, we might accept the challenge of putting the people back in control of their government. Instead of fearing constitutional change, perhaps, we will decide that we will need Con Con II—not to balance the budget, but to make our democracy work again.

Does the Bureaucracy Subvert the Constitutional System?

A STUDENT OF THE BUREAUCRACY VIEWS IT AS A LEGITIMATE FOURTH
BRANCH OF GOVERNMENT

The following selection points out that, although the administrative branch poses constitutional problems, it has deep political roots and performs essential governmental tasks. The bureaucracy is not a conspiracy, but an inevitable consequence of political demands that has led to a vast expansion in the functions of government. In structure, the administrative branch reflects the separation of powers and political pluralism. Modern government requires, from both a political and a practical standpoint, an administrative branch that remains flexible and has a certain amount of discretionary authority.

P. WOLL

20

The Reality of American Bureaucracy

PETER WOLL

The administrative branch today stands at the very center of our governmental process; it is the keystone of the structure. And administrative agencies exercise legislative and judicial as well as executive functions—a fact that is often overlooked. In the selections that follow, classics in the field, we will see the growth of public administration as a discipline, with particular emphasis upon the political role of administration and the way in which the bureaucracy is involved in policy-making. Many proposals are contained in the selections dealing with methods of bringing bureaucracy under control.

How should we view American bureaucracy? Ultimately, the power of government comes to rest in the administrative branch. Agencies are given the responsibility of making concrete decisions carrying out vague policy initiated in Congress or by the President. The agencies can offer expert advice, closely attuned to the most interested pressure groups, and they often not only determine the policies that the legislature and executive recommends in the first place, but also decisively affect the policy-making process. Usually it is felt that the bureaucracy is politically "neutral," completely under the domination of the President, Congress, or the courts. We will see that this is not entirely the case, and that the President and Congress have only sporadic control over the administrative process.

The bureaucracy is a semi-autonomous branch of the government, often dominating Congress, exercising strong influence on the President, and only infrequently subject to review by the courts. If our constitutional democracy is to be fully analyzed, we must focus attention upon the administrative

From Peter Woll, Public Administration and Policy *(New York: Harper & Row, 1966).*

branch. What is the nature of public administration? How are administration and politics intertwined? How are administrative constituencies determined? What is the relationship between agencies and their constituencies? What role should the President assume in relation to the administrative branch? How far should Congress go in controlling agencies which in fact tend to dominate the legislative process? Should judicial review be expanded? What are conditions of judicial review? How do administrative agencies perform judicial functions, and how do these activities affect the ability of courts to oversee their actions? These questions confront us with what is called the problem of administrative responsibility: that is, how can we control the activities of the administrative branch? In order to approach an understanding of this difficult problem it is necessary to appreciate the nature of the administrative process and how it interacts with other branches of the government and with the general public. It is also important to understand the nature of our constitutional system, and the political context within which agencies function.

CONSTITUTIONAL DEMOCRACY AND BUREAUCRATIC POWER

We operate within the framework of a constitutional democracy. This means, first, that the government is to be limited by the separation of powers and Bill of Rights. Another component of the system, federalism, is designed in theory to provide states with a certain amount of authority when it is not implied at the national level. Our separation of powers, the system of checks and balances, and the federal system, help to explain some of the differences between administrative organization here and in other countries. But the Constitution does not explicitly provide for the administrative branch, which has become a new fourth branch of government. This raises the question of how to control the bureaucracy when there are no clear constitutional limits upon it. The second aspect of our system, democracy, is of course implied in the Constitution itself, but has expanded greatly since it was adopted. We are confronted, very broadly speaking, first with the problem of constitutional limitation, and secondly with the problem of democratic participation in the activities of the bureaucracy. The bureaucracy must be accommodated within the framework of our system of constitutional democracy. This is the crux of the problem of administrative responsibility.

Even though the Constitution does not explicitly provide for the bureaucracy, it has had a profound impact upon the structure, functions, and general place that the bureaucracy occupies in government. The administrative process was incorporated into the constitutional system under the heading of "The Executive Branch." But the concept of "administration" at the time of the adoption of the Constitution was a very simple one, involving the "mere execution" of "executive details," to use the phrases of Hamilton in *The Federalist*. The idea, at that time, was simply that the President as Chief Executive would be able to control the executive branch in carrying out the mandate of Congress. In *Federalist 72*, after defining administration in this very narrow way, Hamilton stated:

> . . . The persons, therefore, to whose immediate management the different administrative matters are committed ought to be considered as Assistants or Deputies of the Chief Magistrate, and on this account, they ought to derive their offices from his appointment, at least from his nomination, and ought to be subject to his superintendence.

It was clear that Hamilton felt the President would be responsible for administrative action as long as he was in office. This fact later turned up in what can be called the "presidential supremacy" school of thought, which held and still holds that the President is *constitutionally* responsible for the administrative branch, and that Congress should delegate to him all necessary authority for this purpose. Nevertheless, whatever the framers of the Constitution might have planned if they could have foreseen the nature of bureaucratic development, the fact is that the system they constructed in many ways supported bureaucratic organization and functions independent of the President. The role they assigned to Congress in relation to administration assured this result, as did the general position of Congress in the governmental system as a check or balance to the power of the President. Congress has a great deal of authority over the administrative process.

If we compare the powers of Congress and the President over the bureaucracy it becomes clear that they both have important constitutional responsibility. Congress retains primary control over the organization of the bureaucracy. It alone creates and destroys agencies, and determines whether they are to be located within the executive branch or outside it. This has enabled Congress to create a large number of *independent* agencies beyond presidential control. Congress has the authority to control appropriations and may thus exercise a great deal of power over the administrative arm, although increasingly the Bureau of the Budget and the President have the initial, and more often than not the final say over the budget. Congress also has the authority to define the jurisdiction of agencies. Finally, the Constitution gives to the legislature the power to interfere in presidential appointments, which must be "by and with the advice and consent of the Senate."

Congress may extend the sharing of the appointive power when it sets up new agencies. It may delegate to the President pervasive authority to control the bureaucracy. But one of the most important elements of the separation of powers is the electoral system, which gives to Congress a constituency which is different from and even conflicting with that of the President. This means that Congress often decides to set up agencies beyond presidential purview. Only rarely will it grant the President any kind of final authority to structure the bureaucracy. During World War II, on the basis of the War Powers Act, the President had the authority to reorganize the administrative branch. Today he has the same authority, provided that Congress does not veto presidential proposals within a certain time limit. In refusing to give the President permanent reorganization authority, Congress is jealously guarding one of its important prerogatives.

Turning to the constitutional authority of the President over the bureaucracy, it is somewhat puzzling to see that it gives him a relatively small role. He appoints certain officials by and with the advice and consent of the Senate. He has directive power over agencies that are placed within his jurisdiction by Congress. His control over patronage, once so important, has diminished sharply under the merit system. The President is Comman-der-in-Chief of all military forces, which puts him in a controlling position over the Defense Department and Agencies involved in military matters. In the area of international relations, the President is by constitutional authority the "Chief Diplomat," to use Rossiter's phrase. This means that he appoints Ambassadors (by and with the advice and consent of the Senate), and generally directs national activities in the international arena—a crucially important executive function. But regardless of the apparent intentions of some of the framers of the Constitution as expressed by Hamilton in *The Federalist,* and in spite of the predominance of the Presi-dency in military and foreign affairs, the fact remains that we seek in vain for explicit constitutional authorization for the President to be "Chief Administrator."

This is not to say that the President does not have an important responsibility to act as Chief of the bureaucracy, merely that there is no constitutional mandate for this. As our system evolved, the President was given more and more responsibility until he became, in practice, Chief Administrator. At the same time the constitutional system has often impeded progress in this direction. The President's Committee on Administrative Management in 1937, and later the Hoover Commissions of 1949 and 1955, called upon Congress to initiate a series of reforms increasing presidential authority over the administrative branch. It was felt that this was necessary to make democracy work. The President is the only official elected nationally, and if the administration is to be held democratically accountable, he alone can stand as its representative. But meaningful control from the White House requires that the President have a comprehensive program which encompasses the activities of the bureaucracy. He must be informed as to what they are doing, and be able to control them. He must understand the complex responsibilities of the bureaucracy. Moreover, he must be able to call on sufficient political support to balance the support which the agencies draw from private clientele groups and congressional committees. This has frequently proven a difficult and often impossible task for the President. He may have the *authority* to control the bureaucracy in many areas, but not enough *power*.

On the basis of the Constitution, Congress feels it quite proper that when it delegates legislative authority to administrative agencies it can relatively often place these groups outside the control of the President. For example, in the case of the Interstate Commerce Commission, the subject of an important case study in this book, Congress has delegated final authority to that agency to control railroad mergers and other aspects of the transportation activity, without giving the President the right to veto. The President may feel that a particular merger is undesirable because it is in violation of the antitrust laws, but the Interstate Commerce Commission is likely to feel differently. In such a situation, the President can do nothing because he does not have the *legal authority* to take any action. If he could muster enough political support to exercise influence over the ICC, he would be able to control it, but the absence of legal authority is an important factor in such cases and diminishes presidential power. Moreover, the ICC draws strong support from the railroad industry, which has been able to counterbalance the political support possessed by the President and other groups that have wished to control it. Analogous situations exist with respect to other regulatory agencies.

Besides the problem of congressional and presidential control over the bureaucracy, there is the question of judicial review of administrative decisions. The rule of law is a central element in our Constitution. The rule of law means that decisions judicial in nature should be handled by common law courts, because of their expertise in rendering due process of law. When administrative agencies engage in adjudication their decisions should be subject to judicial review—at least, they should if one supports the idea of the supremacy of law. Judicial decisions are supposed to be rendered on an independent and impartial basis, through the use of tested procedures, in order to arrive at the accurate determination of the truth. Administrative adjudication should not be subject to presidential or congressional control, which would mean political determination of decisions that should be rendered in an objective manner. The idea of the rule of law, derived from the common law and adopted within the framework of our constitutional system, in theory limits legislative and executive control over the bureaucracy.

The nature of our constitutional system poses very serious difficulties to the development of a system of administrative responsibility. The Constitution postulates that the functions of government must be separated into different branches with differing constituencies and separate authority. The idea is that the departments should oppose each other, thereby preventing the arbitrary exercise of political power. Any combination of functions was considered to lead inevitably to arbitrary government. This is a debatable point, but the result of the Constitution is quite clear. The administrative process, on the other hand, often combines various functions of government in the same hands. Attempts are made, of course, to separate those who exercise judicial functions from those in the prosecuting arms of the agencies. But the fact remains that there is a far greater combination of functions in the administrative process than can be accommodated by strict adherence to the Constitution.

It has often been proposed, as a means of alleviating what may be considered the bad effects of combined powers in administrative agencies, to draw a line of control from the original branches of the government to those parts of the bureaucracy exercising similar functions. Congress would control the legislative activities of the agencies, the President the executive aspects, and the courts the judicial functions. This would maintain the symmetry of the constitutional system. But this solution is not feasible, because other parts of the Constitution, giving different authority to these three branches make symmetrical control of this kind almost impossible. The three branches of the government are not willing to give up whatever powers they may have over administrative agencies. For example, Congress is not willing to give the President complete control over all executive functions, nor to give the courts the authority to review all the decisions of the agencies. At present, judicial review takes place only if Congress authorizes it, except in those rare instances where constitutional issues are involved.

Another aspect of the problem of control is reflected in the apparent paradox that the three branches do not always use to the fullest extent their authority to regulate the bureaucracy, even though they wish to retain their power to do so. The courts, for example, have exercised considerable self-restraint in their review of administrative decisions. They are not willing to use all their power over the bureaucracy. Similarly, both Congress and the President will often limit their dealings with the administrative branch for political and practical reasons.

In the final analysis, we are left with a bureaucratic system that has been fragmented by the Constitution, and in which administrative discretion is inevitable. The bureaucracy reflects the general fragmentation of our political system. It is often the battleground for the three branches of government, and for outside pressure groups which seek to control it for their own purposes.

THE RISE OF THE ADMINISTRATIVE PROCESS

What has caused the development of this large administrative branch which exercises all the functions of government, usually within the same agency?

The reasons for the rise of the bureaucracy can be largely explained by observing how the transfer of legislative, executive, and judicial functions has occurred from the primary branches of the government.

Administrative agencies exercise legislative power because Congress and the President are unable and unwilling to cope with all the legislative problems of the nation. The President is "Chief Legislator." Congress is supposed to exercise the primary legislative function. But clearly, given the scope of modern government, it would be impossible for the President and Congress to deal on a continuous basis with the myriad legislative concerns that arise. The President's "program" is necessarily incomplete. It deals with major legislative problems which happen to be of interest to him and of concern to the nation at a particular time. Much of the President's program is formulated by the bureaucracy. In any event, it ultimately has to be carried out by administrative agencies, provided Congress approves.

For the most part Congress is concerned with formulating policy in very broad terms. It has neither the technical information nor the time to cope with the intricate phases of modern legislation. Moreover, it is often unwilling to deal with difficult political questions, for this would necessitate taking sides and alienating various segments of the public. It frequently passes on to the bureaucracy the burden of reconciling group conflict. The bureaucracy receives the unresolved disputes that come both to Congress and to the President, making it one of the most important political arms of the government. The concept of the bureaucracy as neutral is actually contrary to the facts.

Turning to the judicial arena, the development of administrative law has taken place because of the need for a more flexible mechanism for resolving cases and controversies arising under new welfare and regulatory statutes. The idea that the functions of government can be divided into legislative, executive, and judicial categories, and segregated into three separate branches of the government, is outdated because of the growth of a complex and interdependent economy requiring government regulation. Effective regulatory power often requires a combination of legislative and judicial functions.

Examples of the Development of Administrative Agencies

At the beginning of the republic, our bureaucracy was very small. It was quite capable of domination by the President, and at that time the President was the Chief Administrator in fact as well as in theory. No one then could conceive of the growth of a complex bureaucracy such as we know today, and it was only proper to feel that the activities of the executive branch would be, for the most part, politically neutral under the control of the

President and Congress. The fact that the President was supposed to be politically neutral gave the concept of a neutral bureaucracy real meaning.

The original bureaucracy consisted of the War, Navy, State, and Treasury Departments, along with the office of Attorney General (the Department of Justice was created in 1870). These departments were extraordinarily small, and although distance and the difficulty of communications may have created some barriers to presidential domination over an agency such as the State Department, most agencies were easily subject to scrutiny by both Congress and the White House. This was the only time in American history when it was accurate to picture the administrative branch as a hierarchical structure with the President at the apex.

The development of administrative agencies after the Civil War resulted from public pressure which in turn reflected changing economic, social, and political conditions. For the most part agencies were created to deal with specific problems. The growth of the major departments reflected the expansion of government generally. The *laissez faire* ideal of a government remote from the community began to prove inadequate at the end of the nineteenth century. At this time, expanded powers were given to the Justice Department under the Sherman Act of 1890. This was necessary, it was felt, to deal with the rising restraints of trade and the growth of monopolies. In the regulatory area, the Interstate Commerce Commission was created in 1887 as the first national regulatory agency to supervise the railroad industry. The general expansion of the government was reflected in the establishment of the Justice Department in 1870, the Post Office Department in 1882, and the Department of Agriculture in 1889, succeeding the Commissioner of Agriculture, an office established in 1862. Present day bureaucracy has its roots in the latter part of the nineteenth century. But even then the administrative branch was fairly small and relatively powerless.

In examining the characteristics of nineteenth century bureaucracy, it can be seen that although the ideal of *laissez faire* had begin to tarnish, nevertheless it was still powerful and was reflected in the domination of big business interests within the governmental process. Although the frontier had receded significantly, it was still an important factor in absorbing excess energy and alleviating at least some of the grievances caused by economic interdependence. National communications were not highly developed. The integrative force of a strong Presidency was just beginning to be felt. The concept of the welfare state, which led to the vast expansion of the bureaucracy during the New Deal period, was unknown. Both theoretical and practical considerations militated against the creation at that time of a significant and pervasive administrative process. There was, it is true, a great deal of agitation and demand for government action to curb economic abuses. This was quite evident, for example, in the strong agitation of agricultural interests leading to the creation of the ICC. However, these protests were largely ineffective.

The real growth of the administrative process came in the twentieth century, when added powers were given to agencies which were already established, and new agencies were developed to expand government influence.

Expansion of the Bureaucracy in the Twentieth Century

The twentieth century saw the growth of a welfare philosophy of government, an enlargement of the problems created by the interdependence of economic groups, and the development of the country into a national community where the impact of activity in one area was felt in many others. There was increased political pressure for more government action which in turn required an expanded administrative process. Neither Congress, the Presidency, nor the judiciary could cope with the tremendous increase in the workload of government. Nor could they meet all the needs for innovation in the governmental process. Where a new type of adjudication was required to handle an increasing number of complex cases, the common law framework as well as the Constitution prevented the judiciary from embarking upon necessary programs and new procedures. Congress continued to work in modern times much as it had in the past dealing with problems through a rather cumbersome hearing process.

It would be very difficult for Congress radically to change the legislative process because of constitutional as well as political limitations. These create obstacles to unity and continuity in the legislature. The courts too are constrained by the system. To take an example: suppose the judiciary decided to change the "case and controversy" rule, which requires that they adjudicate only cases properly brought before them involving concrete controversies. This would clearly violate Article 3 of the Constitution, and would be very difficult to bring about without a constitutional Amendment. These are the kinds of factors that led increasingly to the growth of bureaucracy. New forms of government were needed, and the administrative branch, which was not hampered by constitutional restrictions to the same degree as the original three branches, was able to fill this need.

Turning to some examples of agencies created in the twentieth century: the Federal Reserve Board, established in 1913 to stand at the head of a Federal Reserve system, was necessitated by changes in the banking industry which had resulted in a need for some kind of national control and standards. The Federal Trade Commission, created in 1914, was designed to expand the control of the national government over restraints of trade and deceptive business practices. The FTC reflects the need for a separate administrative agency with authority distinct from that of the courts and the Justice Department. This need indicated in part the failure of the Sherman Act of 1890 as it had been administered by the Justice Department through an unsympathetic judiciary. By 1920, the Federal Power Commission had been created, and in 1927 initial steps were taken to regulate the communications industry with the establishment of a Federal Radio Commission, which in 1934 was transformed into the Federal Communications Commission.

The proliferation of agencies during the New Deal can be seen in the Securities and Exchange Commission of 1933, the National Labor Relations Board of 1935, the Civil Aeronautics Board and Civil Aeronautics Administration (now the Federal Aviation Agency) created in 1937 and reorganized in 1958. New regulatory bureaus were created in the Department of Agriculture and other executive departments. Many New Deal agencies were created on the basis of presidential support rather than on the demands of private interests. This contrasted with the Interstate Commerce Commission which was created primarily because of strong agrarian demands for government control. The New Deal period was a time when President Roosevelt acted as a focal point for the expansion of the bureaucracy, and it was his ingenuity and power that often provided the balance of political support necessary for this purpose.

Since the New Deal period, there has been a notable expansion of bureaucratic power in the Defense Department, which has been put on a permanent basis since World War II and has strong political support from the armaments industry. Also an agency such as NASA reflects changing technology and subsequent innovations in governmental policy. NASA has now become one of our most important agencies, employing a large number of people and receiving huge appropriations.

CHARACTERISTICS OF ADMINISTRATIVE AGENCIES

Administrative agencies are generally characterized by their size, the complexity of the decisions that they must make, specialization, and the combination of several governmental functions. Another characteristic of primary importance is the fact that no agency can exist without strong political support. All agencies have constituencies to which they are responsible. Their constituencies include congressional committees with which they negotiate appropriations and policy changes; the White House; the courts, which will review certain of their decisions provided the conditions of judicial review are met; and private groups. Administrative agencies operate within a highly charged political environment and this fact immediately distinguishes government bureaucracy from private business. The administrative process in government cannot be considered similar to that in business, except in a very limited range of activities. And insofar as their activities are not political, they are not particularly significant for the study of government.

THE PROBLEM OF ADMINISTRATIVE RESPONSIBILITY

Administrative responsibility requires adherence to the principles of our constitutional democracy by the bureaucracy. Fundamental to the limited government the framers of the Constitution sought is the system of separation of powers and checks and balances. Although the system at times may seem to produce a frustrating deadlock of democracy, it accommodates the political pluralism that is an important part of democracy.

Because it shares powers with all three branches of the government and acts as a check upon each, the bureaucracy, while adding a new dimension to the separation of powers, fits nicely into the constitutional model. Extensive administrative power is a political reality. But each of the three original branches of government controls part of the bureaucracy as it exercises its constitutional responsibilities. An administrative branch completely under the domination of the president, Congress, or the courts would threaten the delicate balance of powers that is so essential to limited government.

The wide-ranging and complex activities of the administrative branch also require supervision by each of the three original branches if democratic accountability and efficiency are to be preserved. The president, Congress, and the courts nicely complement each other in overseeing the bureaucracy. Ultimately the elected branches and the judiciary can rein in politically irresponsible agencies or administrators acting beyond the bounds of their authority. Over the short term administrative waste, inefficiency, and abusive discretion occur, but these attributes are not limited to the bureaucracy.

The fourth branch of government must be recognized as a necessary and legitimate part of our constitutional system. Its fragmented structure and multiple lines of accountability reflect the separation of powers and enable the bureaucracy itself to be part of the checks and balances that the Founding Fathers considered to be so important.

CHAPTER ELEVEN
The Judiciary

The Supreme Court is in many ways a unique American institution, exercising a degree of power over the political branches of government that is unknown in other nations. Even more remarkable is that the Supreme Court's and federal judiciary's power to review the constitutionality of federal and state legislation is not explicitly stated in the Constitution. Yet, from the earliest days of the Republic, the Supreme Court assumed it had the authority to overturn congressional laws it deemed to be unconstitutional. Congress itself gave the High Court the power to review state legislation in the first Judiciary Act of 1789.

It is surprising that the Supreme Court has not been involved in more political controversy over its history, during which it has declared more than 1,000 state legislative and constitutional provisions to be unconstitutional, and struck down federal enactments 127 times.* The Supreme Court's active stance in relation to the states has had the widest and most contentious political impact. But the Court has also raised political disputes at the national level, for example, when it overturned much of Franklin D. Roosevelt's early New Deal legislation. Roosevelt mounted the boldest attack on the Court in its history when he proposed a "court-packing" plan under which he would have been able to nominate six new justices.†

An active or interventionist Supreme Court is always likely to cause political discord. Under the chief justiceship of former governor of California Earl Warren from 1953–1969, the Court made historic decisions curtailing the permissible scope of state power. None was more important than the 1954 desegregation cases requiring 17 southern and border states and the District of Columbia to end their practice that required the separation between blacks and whites in schools. Political discord and threats of defiance followed, and the implementation of desegregation was stalled for more than a decade. In another area of law, the Warren Court's decisions extending the Bill of Rights' protections for those accused of crime to the states also created dissension, particularly among state criminal enforcement officials who argued that the victims, not the perpetrators of crimes, should be shielded.

*Henry J. Abraham, The Judiciary, 6th ed. (Boston: Allyn and Bacon, Inc., 1983), p. 164.

†The plan provided that the president could choose one new justice for each septuagenarian justice on the Court, and at the time there were six justices over the age of 70.

Chief Justice Earl Warren stepped down from the Court in 1969, expressing satisfaction with the interventionist political role his Court had played. Between 1969 and 1971 Richard M. Nixon was able to appoint four members to the Court: Chief Justice Warren Burger, and Justices Harry Blackmun, Lewis Powell, and William H. Rehnquist. With the exception of the moderate Blackmun, the other members were viewed as conservatives who would likely shift the Court to the right and support judicial self-restraint that would grant the states greater law-making authority.

But the Burger Court, by a vote of 7 to 2 with both Blackmun and Powell in the majority, struck down state laws regulating abortion in the highly controversial case of *Roe* v. *Wade* (1973). The decision was the last straw for many conservatives and spurred the Right-to-Life movement that advocates a constitutional amendment to overrule the *Wade* decision. Renewed charges were made that the Court was improperly acting as a superlegislature, taking upon itself the authority to decide matters that should be resolved in the democratically elected bodies of the country. The following selections represent the continuing debate over the role of the Supreme Court and the federal judiciary.

DEBATE FOCUS

Should the Role of the Judiciary Be Curbed?

A CONSERVATIVE CHARGES THAT THE SUPREME COURT HAS BECOME
AN UNDEMOCRATIC SUPERLEGISLATURE

How one views politics, to use an old vernacular expression, depends on whose
ox is being gored. Conservatives applauded the Supreme Court's attempt
during the early phase of the New Deal to prevent what they viewed as
Roosevelt's attempt to shift the country to the left through the expansion of
governmental programs and the regulation of the private sector. At the same
time, liberals charged that the Court was undermining democracy by usurping
legislative power. The following selection presents a 1980s conservative update
on the Supreme Court, now attacking it as an undemocratic political force.

L. A. GRAGLIA

21

Our Regal Judiciary

LINO A. GRAGLIA

The anniversary of our achievement of political independence 208 years ago is an occasion not only for celebration but, more important, for examination of the current condition of our independence. That the ideals of personal liberty, individualism, and self-government with which we began as a nation have been allowed to deteriorate may be illustrated by a relatively minor recent incident that would once have been unthinkable in this country. A few months ago a low-level unelected and unremovable official of the national government—the federal district judge in east Texas—ordered that residents of two 52-unit housing developments in Clarksville, Texas, be evicted from their homes, which some of them had occupied for more than twenty years, because of their race. The Clarksville Housing Authority was ordered to assign them to new quarters so that each of the developments would have a racial balance 50 per cent black and 50 per cent white, give or take 5 per cent. There was of course much unhappiness and complaint from all or nearly all of the people involved, but in the United States of America in the year 1984 the order was carried out; the people were indeed removed from their homes, though not all of them would go where the judge had ordered them assigned.

Now, it is true that these people were poor and that the housing developments were government-subsidized projects—the citizens of Clarksville who could fully pay for their housing, it is reassuring to note, were not required to move and can continue to live in "racially imbalanced" areas, just as those who can pay for private schools can escape court-ordered racial busing—but even so, was there not a time in America when such a government edict would have occasioned protest? What outrages did the

From National Review, *July 18, 1984.* © *National Review, Inc., 150 East 35 Street, New York, N.Y. 10016. Reprinted with permission.*

British perpetrate or threaten that provided better grounds for revolt? We have apparently become so accustomed to the control of our lives by federal judges that we have lost all sense of indignation and all heart for resistance. But if all we did was trade King George III for the federal district judge in east Texas, I doubt it was worth a revolution.

Political liberty requires that government be according to law and with the consent of the governed, not according to the whim of an irresponsible government official. Law is most likely to be good, or at least tolerable, the theory is, if made by those wno must live under it. But where was the law—and who were the people that gave it their consent—that required the eviction of those families from their homes in Clarksville because of their race? Well, the law, the judge told us, was the grandest law of all, the United States Constitution, and surely you do not propose to utter a word against the Constitution. We will not regain our political freedom, my thesis is, unless we fully understand and are prepared to insist that what the judge told us in this case—and what the judges tell us in almost every case in which they invoke the Constitution—is simply not so.

Few people, it seems, have ever actually read the Constitution or have a clear idea of its structure and provisions. This is not surprising, because the Constitution is neither very entertaining nor very informative. Some knowledge of the Constitution has nonetheless become essential in order to understand clearly what it does *not* contain—in order to understand that it does not, for example, in any way limit the power of the states to restrict the availability of abortion or pornography or to permit prayer in the public schools.

Considering the remarkable things our judges have found in it, one could easily imagine that the Constitution is a very long and complex document, perhaps like the Bible or the Talmud or at least the tax code. It may be somewhat surprising, therefore, to be reminded that it is actually very short—easily printed, with all amendments, in a thin booklet of fewer than twenty pages—and apparently quite simple and straightforward. The Constitution was, after all, the result of the very practical and mundane purpose of granting the central government the power to ensure a national common market by removing barriers to interstate commerce.

The original Constitution, adopted in 1789 to replace the Articles of Confederation, is only about ten pages long and consists of seven articles or major sections. The first article, by far the longest, provides for the national legislature, the Congress. It consists mostly of provisions regarding methods of election and operating procedures, some of which are obsolete, having been changed by amendment. Although strengthening the national legislature, the Constitution was careful to leave general policymaking authority—the "general welfare" or "police" power—with the individual states. The national government was limited to specified powers, primarily the powers to tax, regulate foreign and interstate commerce, and provide for the common defense. The possession of wide-ranging and undefined powers by the national judiciary is, of course, totally inconsistent with this basic constitutional scheme.

Article II of the Constitution, on the Presidency, consists largely of a description of the complicated method of selection, much of which is also obsolete. The very short third article, on the judiciary, creates a federal Supreme Court and grants Congress authority to create other federal courts. It explicitly provides for congressional control of the Supreme Court's appellate jurisdiction, a potentially important means of limiting the Court's power. Article III also provides for jury trial in federal criminal cases and narrowly defines the crime of treason. These three articles provide the framework for a complete system of national government, the basic function of the Constitution.

Article IV requires each state to give "full faith and credit" to the official acts and records and court judgments of other states, prohibits discrimination against out-of-staters, provides for the admission of new states, and provides that the United States shall guarantee each state "a republican form of government." Article V provides for the amendment of the Constitution; Article VI provides that the Constitution, and the laws and treaties made pursuant to it, shall be "the supreme law of the land"; and Article VII provides for ratification. That is essentially all there is to the original Constitution.

Apart from the fact that the national government was to be limited to its specified powers, the original Constitution placed very few restrictions on either the federal or the state governments. Some of these restrictions, such as that Congress could not prohibit the slave trade until the year 1808, are obsolete, and others, such as that neither the federal nor the state governments may grant any "title of nobility," have been of little or no importance. The Federal Government is prohibited from suspending the "writ of habeas corpus" except in emergencies, both the federal and the state governments are prohibited from enacting a "bill of attainder" or "ex post facto law," and the states are prohibited from enacting any law "impairing the obligation of contracts." Only the protection of contract rights—a "bulwark" against "socialist fantasy," Sir Henry Maine called it—has been important in giving rise to constitutional litigation.

Surprising as it may seem the Constitution nowhere states that federal judges have the power to invalidate the acts of other officials or institutions of government. The extraordinary nature of this power, and the fact that it was without precedent in English law, should alone be taken as establishing that no such power was granted. Given the very few restrictions in the original Constitution, there was little basis for the exercise of such a power even if it had been granted. It is clear that the Constitution did not—and indeed still does not—contemplate a significant policymaking role for judges.

In 1791, two years after the adoption of the Constitution, ten amendments were adopted, the so-called Bill of Rights. The First Amendment, easily the most celebrated, provides that Congress shall not establish a religion or prohibit the free exercise of religion or abridge the freedom of speech or of the press or the rights of peaceful assembly and to petition government. Its basic purpose was to prohibit the Federal Government from licensing the press and from interfering in any way with state authority in matters of religion. That the religion clauses have become the means by which the Supreme Court *overrides* state authority regarding religion merely illustrates that constitutional law is not only not based on but often directly contrary to the Constitution.

After the First Amendment the Bill of Rights seems to go rapidly downhill. The Second Amendment, creating a right to bear arms in connection with the maintenance of a militia, seems to many people who are otherwise Bill of Rights enthusiasts to be obsolete and irrelevant—at best a nuisance constantly brought up by opponents of gun control. The Third Amendment, having to do with the quartering of soldiers in private houses, seems even more remote from and unrelated to any present-day concern. It is safe to say that few people have heard of it and fewer would miss it if it did not exist.

The remaining substantive provisions of the Bill of Rights have to do mostly with criminal procedure. The Fourth Amendment prohibits "unreasonable searches and seizures" and creates a search-warrant requirement. It creates no "exclusionary rule," which is solely an invention of the Warren Court, the effect of which is to divert the major issue in American criminal trials from the guilt of the accused, which is typically not seriously in doubt, to the procedures by which the evidence of guilt was obtained.

The Fifth Amendment, something of a catchall, requires grand-jury indictments for "capital" and other serious crimes, prohibits putting a person twice in jeopardy of "life or limb" for the same offense, creates a privilege against self-incrimination, provides that no person shall be "deprived of life, liberty, or property without due process of law," and requires just compensation for the taking of private property for public use. The repeated references to capital punishment (referred to still again in the Fourteenth Amendment) are particularly noteworthy in light of the fact that the Supreme Court has come very close to holding (Justices Brennan and Marshall would simply hold) that capital punishment is constitutionally prohibited— another example of constitutional law made in the teeth of rather than in accordance with the Constitution.

The Sixth Amendment creates a right to jury trial in criminal cases, to be informed of the charge, to confront and compel the appearance of witnesses, and to have the assistance of counsel. The Seventh Amendment requires jury trials in civil cases involving more than $20. It is, almost all would agree, simply an embarrassment, an excellent illustration of the desirability of keeping constitutional limitations on self-government to a minimum.

The Eighth Amendment prohibits cruel and unusual punishments and excessive bail. The Ninth provides that the Constitution's enumeration of rights shall not be taken to deny or disparage other rights retained by the people and the Tenth makes explicit that the states and the people retain all powers not delegated to the Federal Government.

It is very important to understand that the various provisions of the Bill of Rights were demanded and ratified by the states as limitations on the Federal Government, not as limitations on themselves, and it was early held by the Supreme Court that they have no application to the states. The next time someone tells you that, for example, a city cannot keep the Ku Klux Klan from parading through the heart of downtown (a recurring issue in Austin, Texas)—or prohibit pornographic bookstores or nude dancing, or permit prayer in public schools—because of the First Amendment, you might point out that that is very surprising considering that the first word of the First Amendment is "Congress" and that it nowhere mentions the states. Of course you might also ask where, in any event, this defender of constitutional rights finds protection of nude dancing in the First Amendment--but be forewarned that the Supreme Court can find it and has found it.

Sixteen more amendments have been adopted since 1791. The Eleventh Amendment was adopted to overturn a Supreme Court decision that allowed states to be sued. The Supreme Court has never liked this amendment, however, and has therefore largely read it out of the Constitution—suing states and cities is today a major industry. Humpty Dumpty and other close students of language would no doubt find it fascinating that the very same act by a state official can be "state action" for the purposes of the Fourteenth Amendment, making the state liable to suit, yet not be state action for the purposes of the Eleventh Amendment, removing the state's immunity from suit.

The Twelfth Amendment changed the procedure for electing the President and Vice President. The Thirteenth, Fourteenth, and Fifteenth Amendments are known as the post-Civil War or Reconstruction Amendments; the Thirteenth abolished slavery, ratifying the Emancipation Proclamation, and the Fifteenth gave blacks the right to vote.

The Fourteenth Amendment was adopted for the very specific and limited purpose of guaranteeing blacks certain basic civil rights, such as to make contracts, own property, sue and be sued, and be subject only to equal punishments. In the hands of the Supreme Court, however, it has become by far the most important provision in the Constitution, in effect a second Constitution that has swallowed the first and transferred all policymaking power not only to the Federal Government but to the unelected branch of the Federal Government, the Court itself. Virtually every constitutional decision involving state law, which is to say the vast majority of all constitutional decisions, purports to be based on a single sentence of the Fourteenth Amendment, and indeed on four words: "due process" and "equal protection." By totally divorcing these words from their historic purposes, the Court has deprived them of meaning and therefore made them capable of meaning anything, magic formulas suitable for the Court's every purpose.

It is therefore essentially misleading to speak of "the Constitution" or "interpretation of the Constitution" in connection with Supreme Court decisions invalidating state law. No more is in fact involved than the Court's purported discovery of new meanings in "due process" and "equal protection." Supposedly on the basis of these two pairs of words the Court has reached such near-incredible decisions as that New York may not refuse to employ Communist Party members as public-school teachers and may not give college scholarship aid to American citizens unless it also gives it to resident aliens, that California may not punish the parading of obscenity through its courthouses, and that Oklahoma may not have a higher legal drinking age for males than for females, even though it is males who present the drunken-driving problem. Except for those four words, these and countless other matters, some of much greater importance, would still be left for decision by elected officials at the state or local level rather than by the majority vote of a committee of nine lawyers, unelected and life-tenured, sitting in Washington, D.C.

To complete our review of the Constitution, the Sixteenth Amendment gave Congress the power to levy an income tax, the Seventeenth provided for the direct election of senators, the Eighteenth gave us Prohibition, the Nineteenth gave women the right to vote, the Twentieth set new dates on which terms of elected federal officials would begin and end, and the Twenty-First repealed the Eighteenth.

The remaining five amendments I think of as modern or contemporary. That is, I can remember when they were adopted. The Twenty-Second Amendment, adopted in 1951, limits the President to two terms—which in my view is, like most limitations on self-government, simply a mistake. The Twenty-Third, adopted in 1961, allows residents of Washington, D.C., to vote for President; the Twenty-Fourth, adopted in 1964, abolishes the poll tax in federal elections. The Supreme Court, however, seeing little value in confining the amendment process to Congress and the states as provided in the Constitution, then decided on its own to abolish the poll tax in state elections as well. The Twenty-Fifth Amendment, adopted in 1967, has to do with presidential succession, and finally the Twenty-Sixth, adopted in 1971, gives 18-year-olds the right to vote.

A proposed Twenty-Seventh Amendment, the Equal Rights Amendment, purported to prohibit all distinctions by government on the basis of sex.

Because its literal interpretation would have been intolerable, its practical effect would have been to leave the difficult policy choices involved to federal judges, authorizing them to do what they now do without authority in the name of the Fourteenth Amendment.

We have lived now under the Constitution for almost two hundred years in unprecedented prosperity and freedom, and sound conservative principle cautions against changing what has proved workable. It may be doubted, however, that our success as a nation has been due to the Constitution, as interpreted by the Supreme Court, rather than in spite of it. We must not forget that but for the Supreme Court's interpretation of the Constitution in the notorious *Dred Scott* case, our greatest national tragedy, the Civil War, costing us more lives than all our other wars combined, might well have been avoided. The Court's decision that the Constitution precluded Congress from dealing with the slavery question made its resolution by war seem inevitable. A better illustration of the dangers of constitutional limitations on self-government would be difficult to imagine. On the basis of this one experience, it is doubtful that the net contribution of the Constitution to our national well-being has been positive, and it is certain that the net contribution of judicial review has been negative.

The *Dred Scott* decision was, however, only one of many injuries inflicted on the nation by the Supreme Court in the name of the Constitution. In the 1883 Civil Rights Cases, its next major constitutional decision invalidating a federal statute, the Court held that Congress could not prohibit compulsory racial segregation in places of public accommodation. The Court thereby gave us such segregation for another eighty years, until Congress again barred it in the 1964 Civil Rights Act. The Court's current contribution in the race area, busing for racial balance in the schools, is solidly in the *Dred Scott* and Civil Rights Cases tradition. Federal courts have recently ruled, for example, that the Atlanta public-school system, having become virtually all black, has finally achieved "unitary" status, after more than twenty years of compliance with court orders, and may therefore terminate its racial-balance efforts. The Boston and Denver public-school systems, however, although they have gone from majority to minority white while obeying busing orders, still have some whites left and must continue to attempt to distribute them evenly among the schools.

Even without judicial review, most constitutional restrictions are just bad ideas, the product of the mistaken and presumptuous notion that the people of one time are better able to deal with future problems than the people of future times will be. In constitution-making the rule should be the less the better, and a major virtue of our Constitution is its brevity. Indeed, except for what the Supreme Court has made of the Fourteenth Amendment, the Constitution would cause few problems today. Even the very brief original Constitution, however, manages to contain several provisions that are at best an inconvenience.

The Constitution provides, for example, that only a "natural born citizen" can be President. A great political leader could arise and become a much-admired senator or governor, but no matter how strongly the people wanted him for their national leader, he could not be elected President, unless he was born an American citizen. Felix Frankfurter and Albert Einstein, for example, were ineligible, as is Henry Kissinger. This was a source of concern some years ago when Governor George Romney of Michigan, who was not born in this country, was seeking the Republican presidential nomination. Surely this is a situation for which there is nothing to be said. Similarly, the Constitution "protects" us from any temptation we might have to elect a 34-year-old President, a 29-year-old senator, or a 24-year-old congressman. We have particular reason to be grateful today that the drafters did not also concern themselves with maximum ages for high federal office.

Still another example of a needless and potentially troublesome constitutional restriction is the provision that a member of Congress cannot be appointed to any federal office during the term for which he was elected if Congress had raised the salary of the office during that term. This caused a serious problem when President Nixon wanted to appoint Senator William Saxbe of Ohio to the office of Attorney General. The Attorney General's salary had recently been increased as part of a general salary increase for all federal employees. The result was that President Nixon wanted Senator Saxbe to be Attorney General, Senator Saxbe wanted to be Attorney General, and no one, apparently, was opposed. Unfortunately, it was unconstitutional, proving that a real constitutional issue can arise, but not necessarily to any good purpose.

Because, as Bishop Hoadly pointed out to the King in 1717, whoever has absolute authority to interpret the law is the true lawgiver, to leave the ultimate interpretation of the Constitution to unelected, lifetime judges is to invite subversion of self-government and tyranny. The prescient Tocqueville warned, long before the Court attained its present power, that though the President, whose power is limited, and Congress, which is subject to the electorate, might err without greatly injuring the nation, "if the Supreme Court is ever composed of imprudent or bad men, the Union may be plunged into anarchy or civil war." *Dred Scott* proved the accuracy of Tocqueville's warning, and the Court seems determined to prove it again.

Purporting merely to enforce the Constitution, the Supreme Court has for some thirty years usurped and exercised legislative powers that its predecessors could not have dreamed of, making itself the most powerful and important institution of government in regard to the nature and quality of life in our society. It has effectively remade America in its own image, according to a doctrinaire ideology based on egalitarianism and the rejection of traditional notions of morality and public order. It has literally decided issues of life and death, removing from the states the power to prevent or significantly restrain the practice of abortion, and, after effectively prohibiting capital punishment for two decades, now imposing such costly and time-consuming restrictions on its use as almost to amount to prohibition.

In the area of morality and religion, the Court has removed from both the federal and state governments nearly all power to prohibit the distribution and sale or exhibition of pornographic materials. It has further weakened traditional sexual restraints, disallowing restrictions on the availability of contraceptives and lessening the stigma of illegitimacy by prohibiting government distinctions on that basis. It has prohibited the states from providing for prayer or Bible-reading in the public schools while also prohibiting virtually all government aid, state or federal, to religious schools.

The Court has created for criminal defendants rights that do not exist under any other system of law—for example, the possibility of almost endless appeals with all costs paid by the state—and which have made the prosecution and conviction of criminals so complex and difficult as to make the attempt frequently seem not worth while. It has severely restricted the power of the states and cities to limit marches and other public demonstrations and otherwise maintain order in the streets and other public places, even though the result may be to require cities to spend thousands of dollars to prevent or control the disturbances the demonstrations may be intended to provoke.

Nothing, however, can better illustrate the extraordinary power the Supreme Court has now achieved than its busing decisions. It would have seemed incredible just a short time ago that the Court would be able to order the exclusion of public-school children from their neighborhood schools and their transportation to more distant schools because of their race. For more than a decade now, however, those orders have been handed down and faithfully complied with across the country despite the fact that they typically operate to increase racial separation not only in the schools but elsewhere and despite their obviously destructive impact on our public-school systems and our cities. Because a requirement of racial integration of the schools—compulsory racial discrimination by government in school assignment—cannot be defended, the Court has always insisted that there is no such requirement and that it orders busing only to enforce the 1954 *Brown* decision's *prohibition* of racial assignment. Difficult as it may be to believe, the only justification ever offered by the Supreme Court for its requirement of racial discrimination by government is that such discrimination is constitutionally prohibited.

Similarly, the Court has boldly asserted that its busing requirement is consistent with the 1964 Civil Rights Act. That act, however, states that "desegregation" means "the assignment of students to public schools . . . without regard to their race" and, redundantly, that it "shall not mean the assignment of students to public schools in order to overcome racial imbalance." The Court's definition of "desegregation" is of course directly to the contrary, requiring the assignment of students to schools on the basis of their race in order to overcome racial imbalance. As Senator Sam Ervin said in justified outrage, the act "says in about as plain words as can be found in English" that assignments are to be nonracial. Congress "could not have found simpler words to express that concept" and was careful to use language "that even a judge ought to be able to understand," he said, but "the Supreme Court nullified this act of Congress" by requiring racial assignment nonetheless in suits brought under the act. Perhaps the Court has obtained a sort of squatter's right to do what it wants with the Constitution, but it can claim no warrant deliberately to pervert a recent, clear, and specific act of Congress. Less egregious abuses of office by other government officials have led to calls for impeachment. But to the Supreme Court truth, logic, and the consequences of its acts impose no insurmountable obstacle. That, one is forced to admit in awe, is real power, power to which no mere elected official could aspire.

Given the Supreme Court's power, the selection of a Supreme Court Justice may well be the most important act a President may have an opportunity to perform. The Justice will decide a much wider range of issues than a President can, and he is likely to remain in office—as in the cases of Justices Douglas and Black, who served for more than a third of a century—long after the President is gone. The power to select Supreme Court Justices has therefore rightly become a major issue in recent presidential campaigns. The system of self-government through elected representatives with which we began as a nation has so deteriorated that we must now choose our highest elected official with care not so much because he will govern us as because he may have an opportunity to choose one or more of the judges who will govern us and whom we will be unable to remove.

Even the election of Presidents who campaign as opponents of judicial power has, however, apparently lost its effectiveness as a means of restraining the Supreme Court. The Court's power is now so firmly established and so widely accepted as to have the status of a force of nature largely impervious to political events. With his very first appointments to the Court, President Franklin D. Roosevelt ended forever the Court's opposition to the New Deal, and never again was a federal statute regulating the national economy or welfare, or a state statute regulating business, held unconstitutional (with one exception, later overruled). President Nixon was exceptionally fortunate to be able to make four appointments to the court during his first term (President Carter, of course, made none, and President Reagan has made only one, and that was due to an unexpected resignation). The Court's power and willingness to govern not only has not been checked as a result of the Nixon appointments, however, but has continued to grow.

Chief Justice Burger, Nixon's first appointment, wrote the opinion in the *Swann* case, in which the Court first ordered busing for racial balance in the schools. Justice Blackmun, Nixon's second appointment, joined Justice Burger's opinion in *Swann* and wrote the opinion for the Court in *Roe v. Wade*, in which the Court for the first time created a constitutional right to have an abortion. Chief Justice Burger and Justice Powell, Nixon's third appointment, concurred in *Roe v. Wade*; of the four Nixon appointees, only Justice Rehnquist dissented. Justice Blackmun also wrote the precedent-shattering opinion in which the court held that a state may not constitutionally prefer American citizens to resident aliens.

Illustrating the utter chanciness of government by the Supreme Court, if the Senate had not rejected President Nixon's first two choices for the seat that finally went to Justice Blackmun, we almost surely would no longer have court-ordered racial busing—the Court's 5 to 4 reaffirmation of busing in 1979, after backing off for some years, required Blackmun's vote—and abortion would probably still be a matter for regulation by the people of each state through the political process. Justice Blackmun has publicly identified the prohibition of such regulation as his greatest contribution to American life. Never in our history has so much turned on the will of a single individual not answerable to the people whose lives he controls.

Justice Stevens, appointed by President Ford to replace Justice Douglas, the most radical Justice in the Court's history, has voted indistinguishably from Douglas on busing, abortion, and most other basic social issues. Justice O'Connor, appointed by President Reagan, wrote the opinion for the Court holding that Mississippi is constitutionally prohibited from maintaining anursing school for women even though it also maintains another nursing school of equal quality that admits men—a result unimaginable just a few years ago. The ERA could be defeated in the political arena, but nothing can prevent the Justices from enacting it anyway, and theirs are the only votes that ultimately count. What Phyllis Schlafly achieved by years of magnificent effort, Justice O'Connor can cancel with a stroke of her pen.

Similarly, despite numerous cases presenting the issue to the Court, the exclusionary rule has still not been rejected. In short, six appointments by Presidents ostensibly opposed to judicial activism have not been sufficient to reverse a single major innovation of the Warren Court and have, instead, produced further innovations.

Proponents of judicial review defend the power of the Supreme Court as necessary to the protection of individual liberties against government officials. The assumption, almost universal among academics, is that the American people are not to be trusted with self-government and are much in need of restraint by their moral and intellectual betters. It is somehow forgotten that Supreme Court Justices are themselves high government officials, and officials who, not being subject to the restraint of the ballot, are more, not less, subject to the corruption of power. It is also hard to understand why the search for moral and intellectual leaders, if that's to be the role of our judges, should be confined to members of the legal profession.

In any event, far from being essential to the preservation of our individual liberties, federal judges have become themselves the greatest source of danger to those liberties. It would be difficult to think of a more serious and widespread violation of liberty than that resulting from the Supreme Court's busing decisions—which also violate equality, in that their immediate impact is primarily on the less well off. By undermining effective enforcement of the criminal law—to say nothing of the Court's invalidation of traditional vagrancy statutes—the Court has diminished our liberty to walk the streets of our cities with a degree of security. The Court has admittedly done wonders for the liberties of street demonstrators, dear to the hearts of academics, but for the poor and elderly, forced to live in fear of the crime the Court's decisions have made more difficult to combat, the Court's contribution to liberty is less clear. Most important, every Court decision removing a policy issue from the political process deprives us of our most basic civil right, the right of self-government.

The issue presented by the Supreme Court's virtually unlimited power is, therefore, not whether we agree or disagree with its exercise in particular cases but whether we acquiesce in its usurpation by the Court. The great Judge Learned Hand protested that he would find it "most irksome to be ruled by a bevy of Platonic Guardians, even if I knew how to choose them, which I assuredly do not." I consider it not merely irksome but shameful to be ruled, not even by Platonic Guardians authorized and supposedly competent to rule, but by a handful of lawyers, elected by no one, holding office for life, and pretending to interpret the Constitution. Whatever may be the best system of government, that surely must be one of the worst. But I would, in any event, rather be misruled by my fellow citizens than saved from misrule by the Supreme Court. Bad government is a risk we must take; government by judges is an insult to our national heritage.

DEBATE FOCUS

Should the Role of the Judiciary Be Curbed?

A FEDERAL JUDGE SUPPORTS JUDICIAL INDEPENDENCE

A federal judge presents his side of the current controversy over the role of the federal judiciary in the following piece. An essential ingredient of constitutional democracy is judicial independence, he argues, and current attempts to undermine the jurisdiction of the courts to prevent them from making "political" decisions run counter to the American political tradition.

I. R. KAUFMAN

22

Congress Versus the Court

IRVING R. KAUFMAN

(For Washington's new conservatives, the power of the Federal courts is an obstacle in the path of social change. Congress currently has before it more than 30 pieces of legislation aimed at taking that power away.)

The first Monday in October, the commencement of the new Supreme Court term, is normally one of the more exciting dates on Washington's calendar. The long summer recess over, the nine Justice[s] don their black robes and enter the marble and oak courtroom where they will ponder questions of truth and justice. This year, however, Oct. 5 will also be a time of no little concern for these esteemed jurists—as it should be for us all. The reason: The role of the High Court as counterbalance to the legislative and executive branches of government—a fundamental pillar of the American system—is under attack. Congress currently has before it more than 30 bills designed to sharply restrict the authority of the Federal judiciary and limit its power to interpret the Constitution.

These bills have been introduced by members of Congress's new conservative coalition, individuals who have been profoundly disturbed by many of the decisions the Supreme Court has made over the last two decades. For example, the Court has forbidden mandatory prayer in public schools, upheld a woman's right to abortion during the first three months of pregnancy, and characterized busing as the only constitutionally adequate remedy in some instances of racial imbalance in public schools. These decisions, all formed on the basis of constitutional principle alone—

From The New York Times Magazine, *September 20, 1981. Copyright © 1981 by the New York Times Company. Reprinted by permission.*

undoubtedly appear as obstacles to the social changes the new legislative coalition intends to make in this country now that the political pendulum is swinging in its direction. The way the coalition proposed to overcome these obstacles threatens not only a number of individual liberties, but also the very independence of the Federal courts, an independence that has safeguarded the rights of American citizens for nearly 200 years.

The current legislative outlook is ominous. A subcommittee of the Senate Judiciary Committee has already approved a bill that would forbid the lower Federal courts to entertain challenges to state antiabortion legislation (even legislation that defined abortion as murder). In the last Congress, the Senate easily passed a proposal to withdraw lower Federal court jurisdiction in school-prayer cases. A discharge petition to move the bill from the House Judiciary Committee to the floor failed by only 32 votes. The bill has been reintroduced and its chances for passage are rated better in this year's Congress. Other bills which would take from the Supreme Court the power to revise state and lower Federal court decisions in school prayer, abortion and busing cases, are now wending their way through the Senate-House Judiciary Committees.

Legal experts from all sections of the political spectrum have begun stepping forward to denounce these proposals. The American Bar Association calls them a danger to the fundamental system of checks and balances. And Prof. Laurence H. Tribe, of the Harvard Law School, has gone so far as to characterize one of the bills as "too palpably unconstitutional to permit reasonable persons to argue the contrary." Still, the possibility that some of these bills may be enacted into law cannot be dismissed. If that should happen, the Supreme Court would either have to accept the Congress's mandate or adjudicate the constitutionality of the laws. If the Supreme Court then decided that the laws were, indeed, unconstitutional, it would be up to Congress either to back down or to permanently reduce the Court's power through constitutional amendment.

Such dilemmas have come close to occurring in the past. Today, it is the conservative wing that is attempting to circumscribe the Court's historical role. At other times in the past, the attack against the Court has been led by liberal reformers—while conservatives stood as sentinels guarding the sanctity of the Constitution. In the early 20th century, the court struck down many pieces of legislation that sought to promote social change, including laws regulating child labor, setting minimum wages and maximum hours, forbidding the use of injunctions in labor disputes, and providing compensation for accident and illness. In response, liberals, and progressives led by Robert M. La Follette, attacked not only the concept of judicial review but the judges themselves. Statutes were introduced in Congress to require the votes of at least six justices to invalidate legislation, and some Congressmen supported constitutional amendments that would have mandated the popular election and recall of Federal judges.

Some years later, after the Supreme Court invalidated much New Deal legislation, President Roosevelt proposed a bill that would have allowed him to increase the Court's membership. Had that bill passed, Roosevelt would have been able to "pack" the Court with political allies, insuring that it would always decide as he saw fit. Fortunately, that plan died in the Senate Judiciary Committee.

Efforts to curb the courts have, if anything, become more frequent in recent years, and they have been proposed by politicians of almost all political stripes. After the Supreme Court's 1954 decision in *Brown* v. *Board of Education*, which declared an end to the purposeful segregation of public schools, a number of bills were introduced in Congress proposing to remove all Federal court jurisdiction in desegregation cases. At about the same time, the call for popular election of Federal judges was renewed. Later, in 1958, at the height of the cold war, serious and widespread support gathered for a bill that would have overturned Supreme Court decisions guaranteeing First Amendment freedoms to political dissidents by removing appellate jurisdiction in cases involving alleged subversive activity. And in 1964, the House of Representatives (but not the Senate) passed a bill that would have deprived the Supreme Court and the lower Federal courts of the power to hear cases regarding enforcement of the Court's new rule of one-man, one-vote for apportionment of state legislatures, a rule that was intended to redress inequities in voting strength caused by racial animus. The reapportionment decisions spurred a furious attack on the Court led by proponents of states' rights, some of whom went so far as to propose that a "Court of the Union," composed of the Chief Justices of all the states, be established to review the decisions of the Supreme Court.

All the bills under consideration this year invoke the concept of jurisdiction, the basic authority of a tribunal to decide a case. Sponsors of the bills cite Article III of the Constitution, which assigns to Congress the power to define and regulate the jurisdiction of all Federal courts including the Supreme Court. Using this power, the Congress has, for example, denied Federal judicial authority in some cases involving lawsuits for less than $10,000. No one questions the legitimacy of that restriction. So why, the sponsors ask, can Congress not also declare, as one bill does, that "the Supreme Court shall not have jurisdiction to review * * * any case arising out of any State statute, ordinance, rule or regulation * * * which relates to abortion?" The answer is not simple. It rest[s] on an understanding of the scope of Congress's authority over the jurisdiction of the Federal courts, which, in turn, depends on an understanding of the Constitution and the role the Constitution mandates that the Federal courts play in the American system.

The framers and early expositors of the Constitution did not fear the power of the courts. With no innate authority either to enforce its own judgments or to control the purse strings, the judiciary was expected to be the weakest of the three branches of government. It was rather the legislative branch that the framers felt a need to restrain. Steeped in English parliamentary history, they know the dangers of legislative tyranny. James Madison, the principal architect of the Constitution, observed: "The legislative department is everywhere extending the sphere of its activity and drawing all power into its impetuous vortex."

The framers set up the Federal court system as one means of checking the Congress. Using the power of judicial review, the courts would invalidate any legislative acts that were inconsistent with the strictures of the Constitution. The theory was, and still is, that Congress should exercise only a delelgated authority, derived from the people. The Constitution, in contrast, was intended to represent the actual embodiment of the people's fundamental and supreme will. Thus, when presented with a case in which a legislative act contravenes the constitutional mandate, it is the duty of the courts to uphold the latter. "To deny this," said Alexander Hamilton, "would be to affirm that the deputy is greater than his principal; that the servant is above his master; that the representatives of the people are superior to the people themselves."

The Supreme Court has therefore struck down laws passed by Congress that conflict with the Constitution ever since the landmark 1803 case of *Marbury* v. *Madison.* For almost as long, the Court has invalidated constitutionally offensive state statutes as well. That duty, scholars insist, is grounded in Article VI of the Constitution, which commands: "This Constitution, and the laws of the United States which shall be made in pursuant thereof . . . shall be the supreme law of the land."

It was inevitable that the judiciary, of the three branches of government, would be charged with the responsibility of assessing the constitutional validity of legislation. To insure the judiciary's ability to perform this sensitive duty faithfully and neutrally, the framers deliberately shielded the judges from political pressures by guaranteeing them, within the Constitution itself, life tenure, and by further providing that their salaries could not be diminished through legislative act. Their independence, to quote Hamilton again, would insure "that inflexible and uniform adherence to the rights of the Constitution, which we perceive to be indispensable in the courts of justice."

This is not to say that the Federal courts' judgment relating to the constitutionality of legislation—including legislation on such issues as abortion, school prayer and busing—cannot be overridden. An unpopular Supreme Court decision on a constitutional issue can be overturned through a constitutionally prescribed means: an amendment to the Constitution. In fact, three times amendments have been proposed and ratified as a way of nullifying controversial Supreme Court decisions. (The 11th Amendment, which forbids a suit in Federal court against a state without its consent, was adopted to overrule a 1793 holding that the Supreme Court had jurisdiction over a case brought by two South Carolinians against the State of Georgia. In 1868, during the Reconstruction period following the Civil War, the 14th Amendment was enacted. This amendment, which proclaims that all persons born in the United States are full citizens of the United States, with all "rights and immunities" of citizens, overruled the infamous Dred Scott decision of 1857, which had declared that black slaves, as no more than pieces of property, lacked the rights of citizens. Finally, in 1913 the 16th Amendment was adopted to overturn a Supreme Court decision holding that the Federal income tax was unconstitutional.)

Constitutional amendments, however, are not a means most critics of the court are eager to employ to bring about the changes they seek. Their passage requires a cumbersome procedure of ratification—as supporters of the proposed equal rights amendment well know. The framers deliberately made the amendment process cumbersome because they did not want expediency to prevail over constitutional rights. They believed that any alteration of the fundamental law of the land should enjoy the overwhelming and sustained support of the citizenry. A simple majority in both Houses of Congress, sufficient to pass the ordinary statute, should not be enough to justify permanent changes in the nation's charter of basic freedoms.

Herein lies the tactical appeal of the withdrawal-of-jurisdiction strategem. Many supporters of the 30 or so divestiture bills now before Congress freely admit that they are attempting to bypass the amendment process. Their rationale is simple: Since the popular support to override Court decisions by amending the Constitution is difficult to garner, why not accomplish the same result with a simple statute restricting the power of the courts to consider the constitutional principles they dislike? In 1964, following the Supreme Court's landmark decision on legislative reapportionment, Senator Everett M. Dirksen introduced a bill to withdraw Federal court jurisdiction in apportionment cases. When asked whether he was attempting to enact a constitutional amendment in the form of a statute, he responded: "[There is] no time in the present [legislative] session to do anything with a constitutional amendment. . . . We are dealing with a condition, not a theory." A candid and revealing response, then as now.

The rationale of our Constitution is not to be lightly ignored. It was designed to protect individual rights by vesting the Federal courts with the final, binding authority to interpret the fundamental law. The only way to override the Constitution as so interpreted is to amend it. The backdoor mechanism of withdrawing the Court's jurisdiction is clearly antithetical to the judiciary's role in the constitutional scheme. If the bills depriving the Court of the authority to hear cases on such topics as abortion, school prayer and busing are considered constitutional, Congress might just as well pass laws depriving the Court of the authority to hear constitutional claims based on such freedoms as speech and religion. The potential consequences are astonishing.

There is another contention being put forward by the proponents of the withdrawal-of-jurisdiction bills that needs to be discussed. These legislators note that the Constitution states that "the Supreme Court shall have appellate jurisdiction, both as to law and fact, with such exceptions, and under such regulations, as the Congress shall make." The "exceptions-and-regulations" clause, they argue, grants Congress wide-ranging authority to restrict the substantive categories of cases that may be appealed from the state and lower Federal courts to the Supreme Court. But to assert that the framers, who clearly intended the Supreme Court to exercise the power of judicial review, also intended to grant Congress plenary authority to nullify that power is to charge the framers with baffling self-contradiction. Indeed, the history of the exceptions-and-regulations clause suggests that it was never intended to carry the heavy constitutional baggage with which the bill's supporters are now loading it.

The clause originated in the fears of some members of the Constitutional Convention that Supreme Court review of factual determinations (appellate review was to be "both as to law and fact") would impair the right-of-jury trial in the states. Hamilton stated: "The propriety of this appellate jurisdiction has scarcely been called in question in regard to matters of law; but the clamors have been loud against it as applied to matters of fact." Since the practices with respect to appellate review of factual determinations varied so widely from state to state, the framers decided to leave to Congress, in the exceptions-and-regulations clause, the authority to regulate the scope of Supreme Court review of facts.

The clause was never meant to confer a broad control over appellate review of substantive legal issues, including issues of Federal constitutional law. Indeed, the Convention considered and rejected proposed constitutional language that "the judicial power shall be exercised in such manner as the legislature shall direct." Far from a mandate to effectively abrogate the vindication of constitutional rights, the clause was intended merely as a way to give Congress the authority to regulate the Supreme Court's docket with reasonable housekeeping measures. Thus, in the Judiciary Act of 1789, Congress restricted the Court's appellate jurisdiction over cases coming from the United States Circuit Courts to those in which the amount in controversy exceeded a prescribed minimum.

On only two or three occasions in its history, has the Supreme Court passed upon the constitutionality of legislation seeking to limit its appellate jurisdiction. Both cases occurred over a century ago and both reveal constitutional defects in the current proposals relating to jurisdiction. In the first case, Ex parte McCardle, decided in 1869, the Court upheld a restriction on its appellate jurisdiction. Although relegated to a small niche in history, this case was enormously important in its day, for it involved a challenge to the post-Civil War Reconstruction program, in which Congress had placed 10 of the former Confederate states under military rule. McCardle had been imprisoned by the military government of Mississippi for the publication of allegedly libelous material. Pursuant to a Federal statute passed in 1867, he applied to a lower Federal court for a writ of habeas corpus ordering his release. He asserted that the Reconstruction Acts were unconstitutional. The court denied his application, and he appealed to the Supreme Court on the basis of that same Federal statute. Before the case was decided by the Court, however, Congress repealed that part of the 1867 statute which authorized appeals to the High Court. "We are not at liberty to inquire into the motives of the legislature," the Court held. "We can only examine into its power under the Constitution; and the power to make exceptions to the appellate jurisdiction of the Court is given by express words."

Despite this pronouncement, the McCardle case is not ordinarily read as authority for a broad Congressional power to restrict the enforcement of constitutional rights in the Supreme Court. Under the Judiciary Act of 1789, McCardle could still apply for an original writ of habeas corpus in the Supreme Court. Therefore, the repealing act actually cut off only one avenue of habeas relief. The Court concluded as much in the 1869 case of Ex parte Yerger, a case that was in many ways strikingly similar to McCardle. Yerger held that the repealing statute did not affect the petitioner's right to apply for an original writ pursuant to the act of 1789. In contrast with the statute under consideration in McCardle, the bills that would forbid any Supreme Court review of busing, school prayer and abortion decisions would totally foreclose the possibility of a Supreme Court hearing on a claim of Federal constitutional right. Surely, McCardle cannot be considered a precedent for that.

This view is confirmed by *United States* v. *Klein* decided in 1872, in which the Court struck down a limitation on its powers of appellate review. Klein administered the estate of a cotton plantation owner whose property was seized and sold by Union agents during the Civil War. Under legislation providing for recovery of seized property of noncombatant rebels upon proof of loyalty, Klein sued and won in the Court of Claims, proferring a Presidential pardon as proof of loyalty. The Court had previously interpreted a Presidential pardon as carrying with it a proof of loyalty. But pending the Government's appeal to the Supreme Court, Congress passed an act which legislated that acceptance of a pardon was, on the contrary, conclusive proof of disloyalty and one which, in addition, required the Supreme Court to dismiss for want of jurisdiction any appeal in which the claim for recovery was based on a pardon.

Invalidating that legislation, the court concluded that Congress had unconstitutionally attempted to interfere with the Court's duty to interpret and give effect to a provision of the Constitution: "The language of the proviso shows plainly that it does not intend to withhold appellate jurisdiction except as a means to an end. Its great and controlling purpose is to deny pardons granted by the President the effect which this Court had adjudged them to have. The proviso declares that pardons shall not be considered by this Court on appeal. We had already decided it was our constitutional duty to consider them and give them effect, in cases like the present, as equivalent proof of loyalty."

In a similar manner, the current withdrawal-of-jurisdiction proposals do "not intend to withhold appellate jurisdiction except as a means to an end." And the end, in this instance, is precisely the same as it was in Klein, the circumvention of the Supreme Court's authoritative interpretation of a constitutional provision. As Klein demonstrates, Congress does not have the power to subvert established constitutional principles under the guise of regulating the Court's appellate jurisdiction.

Those who would read the exceptions-and-regulations clause broadly also argue that state courts, which frequently rely on the Federal Constitution in striking down state legislation, could adequately protect constitutional rights without review in the Supreme Court. The short answer to this contention is that a Federal constitutional right is of dubious value if it means one thing in Mississippi and another in Minnesota. State courts have at times differed profoundly on the meaning of constitutional provisions. To cite but one illustration, in 1965, the Supreme Judicial Court of Massachusetts concluded that the book "Fanny Hill" was unprotected by the First Amendment. At about the same time, the New York Court of Appeals found that it was. Obviously the need for uniformity in matters of Federal constitutional interpretation is essential, and the appellate jurisdiction of the Supreme Court was designed to meet that important need. Chief Justice John Marshall said in *Cohens* v. *Virginia*: "The necessity of uniformity as well as correctness in expounding the Constitution and laws of the United States, would itself suggest the propriety of deciding, in the last resort, all cases in which they are involved. * * * [the framers of the Constitution] declare that, in such cases, the Supreme Court shall exercise appellate jurisdiction."

In connection with this uniformity function, there is an interesting tale concerning one of the most eminent jurists in American history, Judge Learned Hand of the United States Court of Appeals for the Second Circuit. In 1958, at the ripe age of 86, Hand, still nimble of mind and capacious of spirit, was asked by Senator Thomas C. Hennings Jr. of Missouri, chairman of the Senate Judiciary Subcommittee on Constitutional Rights, to comment upon a then-current bill to remove Supreme Court appellate jurisdiction in cases regarding internal security. Hand promptly responded: "It seems to me desirable that the Court should have the last word on questions of the character involved. Of course there is always the chance of abuse of power wherever it is lodged, but at long last the least contentious organ of government generally is the Court. I do not, of course, mean that

I think it is always right, but some final authority is better than unsettled conflict."

It should also be self-evident that the framers saw independent, tenured Federal judges—knowledgeable in Federal law, drawn from all over the country and, as prescribed in the Constitution itself, appointed by the President and confirmed by the Senate—as more appropriate arbiters of conflicts between constitutional and state law than elected state judges, many of whom are popularly elected and who might be partial to state law. The framers realized that only the Federal judges could insure the supremacy of Federal law. As James Madison said: "In controversies relating to the boundary between the two jurisdictions [Federal and state], the tribunal which is ultimately to decide is to be established under the general Government. * * * Some such tribunal is clearly essential to prevent an appeal to the sword and a dissolution of the compact."

The argument for giving Congress the authority to determine the kinds of cases and the types of remedies that the inferior Federal courts may hear is a bit more complicated—if equally unpersuasive. It too is based on Article III of the Constitution, which gives Congress the right to establish "such inferior courts as the Congress may from time to time ordain and establish." Since this provision has been interpreted by many legal experts as giving Congress the right to establish or abolish the lower courts, does it not follow that it also gives Congress the authority to regulate the subject matter of their jurisdiction? The fallacy of this argument is that the framers predicated Congressional discretion on the assumption that litigants would in all cases be able to present their Federal claims or defenses to some Federal court, either in the district court or on appeal. And it was further assumed that, even if no lesser Federal courts were created, the Supreme Court itself would serve as the requisite forum by hearing all constitutional cases appealed from the state courts.

Throughout most of the 19th century, this was possible. The Court's docket was almost empty by today's standards and it could ordinarily hear a constitutional case any time one of the parties so desired. But beginning about 1875, the Supreme Court's case load began to grow enormously, giving rise to a series of acts, culminating in the Judges Bill of 1925, which gave the Court the discretion to decide which cases within certain categories, it would hear. In the process, the Supreme Court was transformed from a general court of appeal into a court which would decide only cases of great constitutional moment of high precedential value.

As the Supreme Court has found itself deciding a progressively smaller percentage of the cases involving Federal, constitutional and statutory law, the role of the lower Federal courts in protecting constitutional rights has expanded to the point of practical and effective primacy. And over the last two decades, a period during which there has been an explosive growth of litigation, the inferior Federal courts have become, in most instances, the only forums in which a litigant could secure a decision on his constitutional claims by a judge life tenured under Article III of the Constitution. If Congress were now to abolish the lower Federal courts, it would effectively cut off almost all opportunity for Federal adjudication of Federal rights. And clearly, the framers did not wish to leave to the states final authority to decide matters of Federal constitutional law. For the reason, the argument that Congress can withdraw jurisdiction over certain classes of Federal cases or rights because it has discretion to abolish the lower courts does not hold up under examination.

Authoritative precedent also strongly suggests that even if Congress had the power to abolish some or all of the lower Federal courts, it may not use its power over lower court jurisdiction to thwart the vindication of constitutional rights. The Court of Appeals for the Second Circuit said in Battaglia v. General Motors Corporation, decided in 1948, that, "while Congress has the undoubted power to give, withhold and restrict the jurisdiction of courts * * * it must not so exercise that power as to deprive any person of life, liberty, or property without due process of law."

The conclusion that can be drawn from all of these arguments is this: Congress does indeed have broad discretion to withdraw jurisdiction from lower Federal courts—where no substantive constitutional rights are at issue. The statutory rights that owe their existence to Congress, as distinguished from constitutional rights, may be taken away either by a repealing statute or by a provision withdrawing Federal Court jurisdiction. Where rights embodied in the Constitution are concerned, however, the discretion of Congress is limited. When Congress deprives a Federal court of the authority to hear a litigant's constitutional claims or defenses, it must provide that litigant with another Federal forum in which to seek an adequate remedy. The distinguished legal scholar Henry Hart once decried the use of statutes withdrawing lower court jurisdiction to undermine constitutional rights: "Why, what monstrous illogic! To build up a mere power to regulate jurisdiction into a power to affect rights having nothing to do with jurisdiction! And into a power to do it in contradiction to all the other terms of the very document which confers the power to regulate jurisdiction!"

Applying these lessons to the divestiture bills now before Congress, there can be no doubt that all of them trench upon established constitutional rights. The Supreme Court has determined that busing may be a constitutionally required remedy in an appropriate case for violations of schoolchildren's equal-protection rights to an education in a desegregated public school. Chief Justice Burger has written for the Court: "Bus transportation has long been an integral part of all public, educational systems, and it is unlikely that a truly effective remedy could be devised without continued reliance upon it." In the landmark case of Roe v. Wade, the Court firmly established a woman's constitutional right to an abortion. And for nearly two decades, the Court has found mandatory prayer in the public schools to violate the constitutional principle of separation of church and state.

One may disagree with these desisions; they may even transgress one's deepest moral convictions. But one cannot doubt that they were based upon informed interpretation of the Constitution—and not on the basis of political or ideological expediency. It is worth recalling the pungent words of Chief Justice Charles Evans Hughes: "We are under a Constitution, but the Constitution is what the judges say it is, and the judiciary is the safeguard of our liberty and of our property under the Constitution." Depriving the Federal courts of the power to adjudicate cases relating to such issues as desegregation, abortion and school prayer effectively precludes Federal protection—the constitutionally envisaged and most reliable form of protection—of our cherished constitutional rights.

The result of the proposed legislation would be to deny citizens the protection of constitutional rights that the Supreme Court has declared they possess. It would be strange indeed if Congress could accomplish through a jurisdictional bill what it clearly may not accomplish directly: a reversal of constitutional principle by an act of Congress. The law is clear, for example, that Congress has no power to declare racial discrimination in Federal Government employment legal. The "logic" of the arguments raised by the proponents of the divestiture bills would, however, permit Congress to remove from the Federal courts all jurisdiction to hear cases involving racial discrimination against Government employees. The motive, discrimination, would be equally patent in either instance.

If one needs to find language in the Constitution as a source for these restrictions on the power of Congress to control the jurisdiction of the lower Federal courts, it is in the due-process clause of the Fifth Amendment. The overarching guarantee of due process is the sacred assurance that the Federal Government will govern fairly, impartially and compassionately. All the powers of Congress—to tax, to make war, to regulate commerce—are constrained by its constitutional inability to deprive us of our rights to life, liberty and property without due process of law. As a power of Congress, the authority to control jurisdiction is therefore restricted by the right of due process. That is the wonder of the American Constitution as it lives and breathes.

Should Congress insist upon restricting the judiciary in ways that the Supreme Court may view as unconstitutional, the Supreme Court might strike down the withdrawal-of-jurisdiction legislation, leaving Congress and the judiciary in conflict. This institutional dissension would continue, until Congress either accepted the Court's determination or passed a constitutional amendment restructuring the basic relationship between the judicial and legislative branches of government.

It is understandable that politically vulnerable legislators would react adversely to judicial nullification of their enactments. Yet those who criticize

the courts for their unresponsiveness to the present national mood tend to
forget that the judicial branch was not designed as just another barometer
of current public opinion. Congress is superbly adequate for that function,
and we ought not to presume that the framers intended the judiciary as
an institutional redundancy. In exercising their power of judicial review,
the courts have represented the long-term, slowly evolving values of the
American people, as enshrined in the Constitution. And when the people
have recognized Congressional court-curbing efforts for what they are—
assaults on the Constitution itself—they have in every instance rejected
them.

It is of no small interest that even some of the supporters of the divestiture
bills have begun to question the constitutionality of these proposals. And,
indeed, there is a glimmer of hope that these doubts will eventually
permeate Congress. The long history of Congressional court-curbing
measures reveals that the legislative branch has in every instance ultimately
yielded to the judiciary's duty to interpret the Constitution and has not (at
least since passing the statute involved in the Klein case more than a century
ago) challenged the courts with a jurisdictional bill that would impinge upon
the fulfillment of that duty. Robert McKay, former dean of the New York
University Law School, wrote of bills to withdraw jurisdiction over
apportionment cases: "Once again, as so often in the past, when the
implications of the proposed legislaton were made clear, the Congress would
not quite cross the threshold of no return."

The political risks attending bills to withdraw Federal jurisdiction create
another check on the legislative goal of certain Congressmen. Groups of
all persuasions have attempted to achieve their political aims through attacks
on the Court's authority to decide constitutional cases. While it is true that
political conservatives are the strongest supporters of the current efforts to
withdraw jurisdiction, liberal reformers have also utilized this strategy in
the past. Employed successfully by today's political majority, it could easily
be manipulated tomorrow by a different majority—and to other ends.

In the final analysis then, while the current divestiture bills should be
a cause for concern about the ability of our constitutional system to
withstand the onslaught of restrictive legislation, there is also room for hope.
In the long history of court-curbing efforts, the majority has always, in the
end, acknowledged the clear intention of the framers. To preserve the rights
of the people, the Federal judiciary must interpret and apply the Constitution
unfettered by unseemly limitations on its jurisdiction. The current Congress
is a body of distinguished and wise legislators who are unlikely to sacrifice
the long-term good of the Republic for speculative and short-term political
gain. As the New England poet James Russell Lowell once said, "Such power
there is in cleareyed self-restraint." As the first Monday in October draws

near, there is reason to believe that Congress will be instructed by the lessons of history and see that the constitutional powers of the highest court in the land—and of other Federal courts—should remain inviolate.